JOSE

FAREWELL TO THE KING

JOSE

FAREWELL TO THE KING

HARRY HARRIS

JOHN BLAKE

Published by John Blake Publishing Ltd,
3 Bramber Court, 2 Bramber Road,
London W14 9PB, England

www.johnblakebooks.com

www.facebook.com/johnblakebooks 🗗
twitter.com/jblakebooks 🗉

First published in hardback, as *Jose Mourinho: Simply the Best*, in 2007. Revised, expanded and updated paperback edition published, as *Jose: Return of the King*, in 2014. This completely revised and updated paperback edition published in 2016.

Paperback: ISBN: 978-1-78606-108-9

ePub: ISBN 978-1-78606-114-0
Mobi: ISBN 978-1-78606-115-7
PDF: ISBN 978-1-78606-116-4

British Library Cataloguing-in-Publication Data:

A catalogue record for this book is available from the British Library.

Design by www.envydesign.co.uk Printed in Great Britain by CPI Group (UK) Ltd

1 3 5 7 9 10 8 6 4 2

Papers used by John Blake Publishing are natural, recyclable products made from wood grown in sustainable forests. The manufacturing processes conform to the environmental regulations of the country of origin.

Every attempt has been made to contact the relevant copyright-holders, but some were unobtainable. We would be grateful if the appropriate people could contact us.

To the Blues in my family (Linda, Ken, Jean, Uncle John),
who love Jose Mourinho's winning ways.

And to all the Chelsea fans in the family who are
still keeping the faith.

ACKNOWLEDGEMENTS

To my publisher, John Blake, whose son, Adam, is such a big Chelsea fan – no wonder he keeps commissioning me for books on Chelsea!

To my various editors at John Blake Publishing, for putting the book together, plus a special mention to my latest editor there, Toby Buchan.

Special thanks to the then FA Cup sponsors E.ON and their PR Tim Collins for the invitation to the FA Cup Final at the new Wembley to record Jose Mourinho winning his full house of domestic prizes.

A wonderful thank you to Mark Mitchinson when he headed up Chelsea sponsors Samsung.

Thanks to Andy Sutherden and Steve Bradley at Hill & Knowlton for their help on the then Carling Cup.

However, this book wouldn't be worthwhile without the charismatic Jose Mourinho and his wonderful way with words. This book is a tribute to the Special One.

The author and publisher are also very grateful to Chris Davies for all his superb editorial work on the original text to produce this new edition.

CONTENTS

INTRODUCTION
FAREWELL TO
A LEGEND

I received a call on my mobile from LBC as I was leaving a matinee performance of *War Horse* at the New London Theatre in Covent Garden, asking if I could do an interview on the demise of Jose Mourinho a little later in the evening.

I would imagine the vast majority of Chelsea fans will recall instantly exactly where they were the moment they discovered their beloved Jose had been fired for a second and, clearly, last time as Chelsea boss. It is one of those defining moments in football fans' lives.

I'm not a Chelsea fan, I hasten to say, but my wife Linda is and she was by my side when I broke the news to her. It came as quite a shock and she rang her family after the show, as they all hail from Chelsea.

My old *Daily Mirror* colleague Nick Ferrari, who is now breakfast presenter at LBC, always likes to rustle me up when there is a major football story breaking and there has been no bigger one for quite some time than the sacking just before Christmas of Jose Mourinho.

More pertinently, I just happen to be Jose Mourinho's 'biographer', having written a series of books for publishers John Blake on this very intriguing and complex character, who never ceases to amaze, confuse and enlighten in equal measure.

Ironically, the latest volume was due to be published in late October/early November but, two months prior to the publication date, on consultation with the publishers, it was decided to put the book on hold 'pending his sacking' from Chelsea. The rationale was that, with the team doing so badly, the celebration of winning the title had already evaporated and a vastly different mood – a black mood – had descended on the Bridge: not a particularly good time to bring out a book to glory in Mourinho's achievements at Chelsea. But I reasoned that a very good time would be a couple of months later as, inevitably, he would be sacked.

I also write a column for a website, Zapsportz.com, of which I share joint ownership with Glenn Hoddle and in which I had been predicting Mourinho's sacking for some time. Then, in aftermath of the defeat at Leicester City, I had confidently predicted that he would get 'the boot' in social-media postings, for a PR project I'd been working on for a new football boot: the Serafino 4th Edge boot.

All fascinating stuff for LBC to get their teeth into when I arrived back at the Millennium Hotel, Mayfair, where there was a clear line for an uninterrupted five-minute slot to discuss the ins and outs of the Mourinho sacking.

Having confidently predicted for several weeks that he

would get the bullet, I was not unduly surprised when the final shot was fired and LBC wanted to know why.

Jose is either loved or hated in equal measure wherever he goes but the outpouring of emotion from Chelsea fans at the decision to kick him out of the door, despite being the most successful manager in the club's history, was something quite special, even by the Special One's standards.

When I was interviewed on LBC, I commented, 'Managers are judged by results; it is a results-based industry – and results have been pathetic. So you sack the manager, irrespective of his former glories. He has taken Chelsea from champions to one point above the drop zone. If it was any other manager, you would have very little sympathy for him.'

Chelsea lost nine of sixteen Premier League matches at the start of what turned out to be a shambolic season and, while the manager was accused of 'losing the dressing room', this, in my view, is a cop-out.

In reality, managers don't even have the dressing room. It's a myth. Players back the manager while he's there and it's only when he's gone that one or two come out of the woodwork to let us know how diabolically they've been treated. The players the manager picks are behind him, their faces fit. They're content, they pick up their bonuses, they love the boss. Those he leaves out stick the knife in at every opportunity as soon as he's gone but wouldn't dare voice publicly their discontent while he can still discipline them. That's the way of the dressing-room world and it doesn't alter, whichever club you manage.

Mourinho, though, did overstep the mark when he claimed he had been 'betrayed' by his players, which he voiced before the game with Leicester City, for, by that point, the Chelsea board had had enough of his latest antics.

He was referring specifically to a failure by flair players to follow instructions to concentrate on their defensive duties. He was also convinced that somehow Porto had learned of his team line-up before their meeting in the Champions League. His relationship with key players had decayed: Diego Costa tossed his training bib at Mourinho after not being brought on as a substitute at Tottenham, while Eden Hazard declined an attempted hug from Mourinho as he left the pitch in that Porto game.

Whether he should have voiced his concerns about the players publicly – and not for the first time in this dramatic season – is another matter. It was a fatal error of judgement. If designed to whip up his players, the consequence was the final straw to determine his fate in the board room. Perhaps he could already see he was on his way out and wanted to make it clear why. Agents like Jorge Mendes, one of the game's most influential middlemen with Mourinho and Ronaldo among his clients, have their ear to the ground and it wouldn't be a surprise if he became aware of the soundings being taken about whether they could bring back Carlo Ancelotti or Guus Hiddink, and with Ancelotti off to replace Pep Guardiola in the summer, it was Hiddink who was more readily available and far more amenable to move straight in as an interim boss, as he had done so successfully before in winning the FA Cup. Pep Guardiola and Diego Simone remained the first choices and Mendes would know the behind-the-scenes secrets better than anyone and would have tipped off Mourinho.

The attitude of the players stank and the fans could smell

it. In fact, the supporters had already let some of the players know what they thought of them, booing them off at half-time or at the end, a condemnation of them more than the manager,

From champions only a few months earlier, their form had been pathetically poor – poor in the extreme – and Mourinho was right to feel let down.

After disastrous below-standard performances, matters reached a head on 3 October 2015, when Chelsea lost 3–1 to Southampton. Under pressure, Mourinho counter-attacked. On Sky, he shocked the live TV audience with his seven-minute rant, during which he said: 'I want to make it clear: one, I don't run away. Two, if the club want to sack me, they have to sack me because I am not running away from my responsibilities, from my team and from my conviction.' As results faltered further, there was an opportunity for his detractors to put the knife in. 'Mourinho is a great coach but, after a year and a half, he ruins his players,' said the former England manager Fabio Capello.

I remarked on the previously mentioned LBC interview that 'a manager is only as good as his players and the attitude of more or less the same group of players has been appalling. For me, it all stems from the end of last season when, having won the league at a canter, they showed a lackadaisical attitude, which has carried on into this season. Mourinho wanted to purchase certain players in the summer to keep the current players on their toes but that didn't happen and that was Chelsea's biggest mistake.'

But, for me, the problems can be traced back to the tail end of the previous season, when Chelsea clinched the title with a less than convincing 1–0 win over Crystal Palace. It was endemic of a long period where Chelsea had gone off the boil, not helped by the injury that deprived Diego Costa of his goalscoring touch, which was so prominent in such a blistering, title-defining start to the season.

With their rivals inept in mounting a challenge, Mourinho's third title with the club was delivered with a far more pragmatic approach to the second half of the season, in contrast to the effusive football that defined the first half. A week after the win over United in the previous season, Chelsea drew 0–0 at Arsenal, to which the home fans chanted, 'Boring, boring Chelsea.' Mourinho responded sarcastically: 'People talk about style and flair but what is that? Sometimes I ask myself about the future and maybe the future of football is a beautiful green-grass carpet without goals, where the team with more ball possession wins the game. The way people analyse style and flair is to take the goals off the pitch.'

Mourinho was proud of winning the title again – and with such a depleted squad – but he must have known that delaying pre-season to give players a long rest was a risk. However, not signing top-class players was an even bigger one.

Mourinho delivered his wish list of players he wanted for the new season but there was a lack of urgency in recruitment; an over-confident attitude of, 'as champions, perhaps we don't need a major overhaul of players.' In reality, they did. They failed to do so, from a mixture of reluctance to pay over-inflated prices, or of the big clubs like Real Madrid to sell the players Mourinho wanted.

As Chelsea suffered the worst opening third to a campaign of any defending champion, it seemed to come as a shock to some of the club's fans when the axe eventually fell but, as I stressed in my LBC assessment, the writing was clearly on the wall if you looked for the signs. And the signs were pretty clear to me. Not in hindsight, I might add, as I had flagged them up consistently in my writings during the season on my internet columns. The signs had been pretty clear to me, particularly the failure to sign key players such as John Stones, and another out-and-out goalscorer rather than a past-his-sell-by-date Falcao, proved costly.

In his post-match press conference, having clinched the title against Crystal Palace, Mourinho had a dig at Pep Guardiola, highlighting his seemingly continued quest to be recognised as the best. 'For me,' Mourinho said, 'I'm not the smartest guy to choose countries and clubs. I could choose another club in another country where to be champion is easier.' He didn't name Guardiola but the inference was that Guardiola had gone to Bayern Munich, where the title is virtually guaranteed. Guardiola's titles, Mourinho was suggesting, meant less than the one he had just won. But the antagonism runs much deeper. In his book *Goal: The Ball Doesn't Go in by Chance*, the then Barcelona CEO Ferran Soriano stated that the decision came down to a straight choice between Mourinho and Guardiola. 'It was clear that Mourinho was a great coach but we thought Guardiola would be even better,' said Soriano. 'Mourinho is a winner, but in order to win he guarantees a level of tension that becomes a problem.'

Mourhino emphasised the point during that telling 'rant' after clinching the title. 'I took a risk. I am so, so happy because I won another Premier League title ten years after [my first] in my second spell at the club. I was champion at every club I coached. I came to Inter [Milan], Real Madrid and Chelsea. Every title is important. To win the title in Spain with a hundred points against the best Barcelona ever was a big achievement that I enjoyed so much. Maybe in the future I have to be smarter and choose another club in another country where everybody is champion. Maybe I will go to a country where a kitman can be coach and win the title. Maybe I need to be smarter but I still enjoy these difficulties. I think I'm at the right place. I'm here until Abramovich tells me to go.'

A few weeks later, Mourinho signed a new four-year deal that ended any insecurity issues – so he thought – which he referenced with 'until Abramovich tells me to go.' He craved security after so many moves and, bizarrely, given his previous form in sacking managers,, so did Abramovich, so a long term deal suited them both.

Who would have thought it would be four months, not four years, before they were parting company again?

Well, the problems began soon after the signing of the new contract. This was only the third time that Mourinho had reached a third season with any club and, on the previous two occasions – at Chelsea the first time round and at Real Madrid – he suffered the third-season syndrome. To avoid it, the solution was to bring in a range of new, dynamic stars to freshen up the team and to keep those who might have thought they were fixtures on their toes. But, rather than sign the players he desired – a youthful John Stones to phase out an aging John Terry, for example, and a recognised young new goalscorer in case Diego Costa faltered again – the club quibbled over the players' valuations, while their rivals paid vastly inflated prices to acquire the players they wanted. Worse still, Mourinho was dead against selling Petr Cech to Arsenal and made it plain that the decision was taken out of his hands by Abramovich.

Earlier in the season, when still a Sky TV pundit and

long before his shock move to manage Seville, Gary Neville slammed Eden Hazard for his poor start to the season, saying he had 'no sympathy'.

Hazard was voted PFA Player of the Year in the previous term when the team romped to the title. The Belgium international personified the poor start and, long before the axe fell on the manager, the Manchester United legend claimed that Hazard needed to knuckle down if was to become truly world class. 'I've got no sympathy for Hazard. I expect more of him,' Neville told Sky Sports. 'The level he got to last season, you started to see a great player. In the Premier League, how many real top, world-class players could you say we have in the league? Aguero, Silva you'd look at. You'd look at Hazard and put him into that level of category. There might be a couple more. I'm not saying we haven't got more but they're the three I can think of off the top of my head.'

Clearly, for those on the outside looking in, it was obvious that the attitude of some key, big-time players was not right. Rather than working even harder to rectify the issues, certain players simply went even deeper into their shells.

This season there was a deluge of new, headline-hugging episodes. Mourinho's handshake row with Arsène Wenger and the row with two members of his medical staff for treating Eden Hazard created havoc and backfired spectacularly. Team doctor Eva Carneiro left the club pursuing hugely embarrassing and humiliating legal proceedings against both Chelsea and Mourinho. As the season unfolded, the rows with the referees continued; he was banished to the stands and faced stadium bans. All Mourinho-esque. He could get away with it while he continued winning, which was his trademark, but the combination of Mourinho's controversial antics while on a losing streak was lethal.

Chelsea beat Aston Villa but then came a defeat at West Ham in which a Chelsea player was sent off just before half-time. Mourinho approached the referee, Jon Moss, in the tunnel and called him 'fucking weak', which led to the manager being banned from attending the next Chelsea match.

Mourinho must have had some inkling of the hierarchy's intentions in the days leading up to his departure; it was pretty obvious the team were underperforming.

Filmed not long before Abramovich finally decided to axe him, Mourinho appeared on BT sport's *The Clare Balding Show*, something that looked, from the outside, routine at the time. But it was, effectively, his last ever TV appearance as Chelsea manager. Introduced as 'the man who's won everything,' he looked unusually uncomfortable; another indicator, perhaps, that he did have an inkling. Asked if he liked the fact that 'everyone here loves you,' he managed only a very self-conscious laugh in reply.

In the interview, filmed on 2 December but not screened until the 17th, just days before he was axed, Mourinho spoke about the players needing to listen once more to his message: 'I think they need to like to work with me. I think they need to understand that I am the best manager they can work with, I think that is very, very important. Like me, don't like me, the person, the man, big friends, that's a supplement but I think it's fundamental that the manager is somebody the players can look at and know that he's good. I always establish the impossible target and I tell them this is the impossible target but the target is to win every match. They know that is impossible and this season is proving that it is really impossible, but I think it's the target, you have to go to every match, it doesn't matter which competition it is, and you want to win and you feel that you can win. I think that's the important thing.

'I give everything I have, sometimes maybe too much, sometimes maybe too emotional but I do that with every club so for me I did that with everyone but the only one where I wear the shirt twice was Chelsea because I was in the club where I was, I left and I came back so I would say Chelsea. But I have also to confess that Inter [Milan] was really special, and Porto was my beginning and I can't forget that. And a giant like Real Madrid is also an honour to manage.'

He went on to speak of a wide range of topics, including whether he would one day manage England, a job he once turned down after having said yes, only to change his mind. On the possibility of coaching the England team, Mourinho said: 'I like to work every day, I like to play three times a week and the national team job is a job where you are on holidays most of the time. Big pressure, big pressure but you don't work specially on the pitch, you don't work every day.'

When asked whether he sends fellow managers Christmas cards, Mourinho revealed that he categorises his colleagues into three different groups. 'One group I just sign. Another one, I send a personalised message and the other one I just don't send,' Mourinho replied. 'To Big Sam, the Christmas card is not big enough as I love to send a message to this guy.'

Clare Balding finished by asking what would bring Christmas cheer to him: 'What are the things that make you smile and give you peace?'

'At this moment? Win a match!' Mourinho responded.

When Mourinho was finally sacked, just days later, as expected, Guardiola announced his departure from Bayern to take effect at the end of the season, with Manchester City his likely destination, but Abramovich was ready to make a third and final attempt to lure him to west London. Speculation was rife in the media that Guardiola remained top of Abramovich's wish list, and it was hard to imagine that he wouldn't be.

In terms of looking back, Mourinho was recognised for past achievements by *Guinness World Records*, for five records picked up during his football managerial career. They are:

Longest football unbeaten home run by a manager (nine years)

Most Champions League titles with different clubs (two)

Youngest manager to reach 100 Champions League matches (49 years, 12 days)

Most points in a Premier League season (95)

Most games unbeaten at home in the Premier League (77)

Yet this is what he had to say about the records on Chelsea's website: 'The fact they gave me the awards in a way that I can put them up in my office is nice. It's something fun and as a kid you could never imagine that one day you would be in the *Guinness Book of Records*. You know me, these awards are for something I did in the past and obviously it's nice, but for me what's more important is what I can do in the future.'

HARRY HARRIS

JOSE MOURINHO

Designer stubble, expensive grey overcoat and scarf, brooding, explosive, animated, flashy, arrogant, young and glamorous. But Jose Mourinho has proved to be more substance than style.

Mourinho was voted the best club coach in the world in 2004 by the International Football Federation of History and Statistics, finishing well ahead of Arsène Wenger and Didier Deschamps of Monaco, and the award came just as he was on the verge of engineering a shift in power within English football away from Highbury and Old Trafford.

It's incredible to realise that Mourinho has performed a meteoric rise – back in the late 1990s he was a glorified interpreter at Sporting Lisbon, Porto and Barcelona.

Some say Mourinho's defining moment was when his Porto team won the Portuguese League Cup for the second year running, and then overwhelmed Monaco to win the European Champions title in May 2004. Perhaps, though, his seminal moment had come in Lisbon four years earlier when, after just nine matches, he walked out on the famous Benfica club. 'It wasn't right,' says Mourinho. 'I could have stayed around, but I knew my work could not prosper there. My ideas could not develop.'

When Roman Abramovich interviewed Mourinho on his yacht in Monte Carlo, the Chelsea owner had had twenty-four hours to read a document sent to him by his prospective coach. It was a stunning appraisal of the situation of the club that had become the richest in the game.

English football writers put to Mourinho some theories about the course of English football, with talk of a renaissance at Arsenal and a rally by Manchester United. Mourinho, in response, frowned. 'Do not tell me about your movie. I am in a movie of my own.'

The choice of metaphor is not accidental. Mourinho loves films. On away trips he carries his laptop with him and, when he describes meeting Abramovich for the first time, it is like a scene from a James Bond flick: the French Riviera, the speedboat, the monumental yacht. And the pressure Mourinho is under? That brings another screen reference. 'Worthy of Don Corleone,' he says.

If Mourinho's life is a movie, its pre-production has been extensive. 'He's an overnight sensation who is twenty years in the making,' UEFA's technical director Andy Roxburgh once said. Roxburgh has been acquainted with Mourinho all that time. It was through Roxburgh that Mourinho acquired his first coaching badge, when he attended a Scottish Football

Association course in Largs, Ayrshire. 'We used small-sided games on that course and it had a profound effect upon him. I know that players appreciate his training methods and attention to detail. He is also very personable and has good communication skills.'

For Roxburgh, Mourinho was a willing, enthusiastic and, above all, interested student. His public image – ice-cool, dispassionate, detached – is misleading, though even his wife, Tami, has said she had to learn to 'decodify him'.

Roxburgh says that, far from public perception, Mourinho does not 'need the limelight'. 'With big-name players you sometimes see that they do,' Roxburgh adds, 'but because of his background that's not the case.'

Mourinho enjoys the good life, but sees it as merely a reflection of success. 'I have a good car, but only one at a time. I like good holidays with my family, I like us to live in a nice place [Eaton Square], but as a football man the most important thing is to be working with the right people and with the right approach to things,' he says.

There is a little secret to his success. He calls it his 'methodology'. Mourinho calls it his ability to 'smell' what to do. 'I have a new way of thinking the game, the players and the practice,' he says. 'I defend the globalisation of the work, the non-separation of the physical, technical, tactical and psychological. The psychological is fundamental.'

Mourinho's ideas are stored on his laptop. He used the machine to make his famous 'Power point' presentation to Abramovich in which he analysed Chelsea's strengths and weaknesses with forensic detail. Also, on the computer is Mourinho's 'bible': an extraordinary document that contains his theories about teamwork (its first line is 'The team is more important than the player'), his philosophies, beliefs and even his definition of what the role of club chairman should be. He never shows it to anyone. It's his secret – as are the notebooks he keeps hidden in his coat, and his private diary.

What strikes all who encounter him is his remarkable belief in himself – a belief that allows him, unusually among managers, to sleep easily. Mourinho's favourite hobby is quad-biking, and he enjoys skiing and snowboarding. He also indulges in more genteel pastimes such as reading and going to the theatre. 'I like to go out for dinner, to go to a show or read a book. My wife suggests books for me to read because she is an insatiable reader. Reading allows me to distract my mind from the rest of my worries.'

In an interview with UEFA's technical director, Andy Roxburgh, the former Scotland manager, the Chelsea coach reveals his international ambitions and also laughs off suggestions that he is arrogant. Mourinho points to the way he was encouraged to develop when assistant manager at Barcelona, first to Bobby Robson and then Louis van Gaal, as a key period in his career.

'Louis gave me the responsibility of taking the team in some friendlies or cup games and he monitored the way I handled things,' he says. 'I was prepared to take charge of a team; I had developed my know-how and confidence. Confident? Yes. Arrogant? No. My friends laugh when they read articles which label me as arrogant – they know it is not true. When I say I think we will win, I am only saying what most coaches think before a match.'

After his time at Barcelona, Mourinho returned to Portugal, ready to become a coach in his own right, and he admits it was not all plain sailing at Porto, with whom he would go on to win the UEFA Cup and Champions League. 'The first six months were difficult because the club and the team were in a very bad situation. I changed players and reorganised the team – it was a crucial period of rebuilding. The next season was fantastic because we won the UEFA Cup and the treble in Portugal. It was a great process, but it did not happen by chance. I have been influenced by some people, although I have never been the type to just accept the truth of others.'

Mourinho is an assiduous note-taker, but only during the first half of games. 'During the half-time team talk I try to control my emotions and be what the team needs me to be – this means I can be cool or I can be emotional because the team needs a certain response. There is always something to tell them at half-time, but after the match not one word, because the players are not ready to be analytical at that moment.' Instead, he analyses the second half at home.

Mourinho took more pleasure from winning the UEFA Cup, when Porto beat Celtic, than he did from the club's triumph in the Champions League. 'The emotion was much greater when winning the UEFA Cup than beating Monaco in the Champions League final because of the game of football. The match against Celtic was dramatic until the last moment. But after the dust has settled, the Champions League title is the greatest prize. The night we won it was difficult because I was full of conflicting emotions, knowing that I would be leaving the team.'

He displays meticulous attention to detail when discussing

what he looks for in a player. 'I have produced profiles for each position in terms of personality, athletic qualities, technical skills, etc. If a player lacks speed he has no chance at the top level.'

His newfound fame has come at a price, but he has few complaints. 'My life has changed. It is part of the job to deal with the demands. However, a principle for me is that I never miss a training session due to other claims on my time. Professional duties always come before external business requests. Football is my job but also my passion.'

Spirit, motivation, togetherness. It used to be the prerogative of 'The Invincibles', as Arsène Wenger's players indulged in on-the- pitch pre-kick off huddles. For Jose Mourinho, the bonding takes places in the privacy and sanctuary of the dressing room. Just before the players go out, they take it in turns to deliver a brief motivational speech.

Frank Lampard explains: 'It's about bonding and it's a way of bringing out people's character. We stand in the dressing room, put our arms around each other and one of us says a few words and finishes by asking, "Who are we?" Everyone shouts, "We are Chelsea." There are a few lads who are a bit quiet, and it's a way of bringing them out of themselves as well as getting everyone motivated.

'John Terry swears an awful lot when he does it. There was a pre- season game against Celtic and he was effing and blinding and I was thinking, 'Hang on, John, it's only a run-out!' Scott Parker did the best one at Newcastle in the Carling Cup. It was the most aggressive speech I've ever heard, about being ready for battle. We already had a good spirit but the manager has taken it a step further.'

There is no room for jokes, a raised voice or any other gimmick in Mourinho's team talks. 'He is simply meticulous,' says Lampard. 'Everything is explained in such detail that the minute he does make a change, we can adjust. We're able to do it because he leaves absolutely nothing to chance; he even tells us how to play if we go a goal up or down. He knows every opponent inside out. Even their subs. He talks to us as a team but also individually. No player likes to be blanked by the manager because even if you're playing well, you still wonder what he's thinking.'

Abramovich made up his mind he wanted Mourinho when he inspected the AC Milan trophy room and was taken aback by all the silverware. He came to the conclusion that Mourinho had won so much in just two years, compared to Claudio Ranieri's record over his entire career, let alone his four trophyless years at the Bridge.

Mourinho immediately stamped his personality on Chelsea, as he was not interested in spending fortunes on stars such as Ronaldinho, Roberto Carlos or David Beckham. Whereas Ranieri recommended only three new players, Mourinho wanted four or five. Ranieri put forward a short list of new players: a striker, a central midfield player and centre-half. Ranieri suggested Gerrard for the midfield berth; Fernando Morientes of Real Madrid, Didier Drogba from Marseille or Samuel Eto'o from Majorca as the new striker; and after his first choice, Walter Samuel, signed for Real, a number of alternatives were suggested for central defence.

Mourinho wanted three of his Porto stars – Paulo Ferreira, midfielder Costinha and playmaker Deco – and wouldn't have said no to Gerrard if he could have been prised from Liverpool.

Ranieri did not want to be too hasty in offloading players such as Jesper Gronkjaer, while Mourinho kicked out a dozen of the Italian's squad. Mourinho shared Peter Kenyon's conviction that Chelsea were vastly over-staffed. Melchiot, Petit, Stanic and Bogarde came to the end of their contracts and they were free to go; Hasselbaink and Desailly, with a year left, could also go on free transfers.

Mourinho arrived with his family at Heathrow on 1 June. His contract was worth 6 million euros (£4.1 million) a year plus 1.5 million euros (£1 million) in bonuses triggered if he repeated the success he enjoyed at Porto in winning the championship and the Champions League. Kenyon negotiated a compensation package for Mourinho and his back-room team of 2.5 million euros (£1.75 million).

Rui Faria is a key part of Team Mourinho. Born in the central Portuguese town of Barcelos, Faria was, like Mourinho, a graduate in physical education who had never played football of any distinction. He met Mourinho at a seminar day at Barcelona's Nou Camp, where Mourinho was working at the time as Louis van Gaal's assistant. Mourinho was impressed and stayed in touch and, when he took the job at Uniao Leiria in April 2001, he appointed Faria fitness coach and video analyst. Uniao Leiria struggled to attract 2,000 fans to their home games. But three years later Mourinho was in charge of a Champions League-winning team. No modern-day coach had achieved it at such a young age, or on such a meagre budget as Porto's.

In his two full seasons in charge of Porto, the team won all but one of the six serious competitions they entered – two Portuguese titles, one UEFA Cup, one European Cup, one

Portuguese Cup – and lost only two matches of consequence: the Portuguese Cup final and the one-off European Super Cup against Milan.

Mourinho enjoys role-reversal games, swapping places with his players and sometimes carrying out their orders while they act as manager. That's what happened to former Manchester United star Karel Poborsky when he told Mourinho – then in charge of Benfica – what position he wanted to play. Mourinho, who saw Poborsky as a winger, called him in and said, 'Right, you're the boss, why do you want to be playmaker?' He listened, let Poborsky pick his own place in the next match and took him off after half an hour. Poborsky says, 'Mourinho then told me, "Right, I'm the manager again. I gave you the chance to prove you were right and you proved nothing. You will play where I tell you from now on, and if you do not want to, you'll play in the reserves."' Porto scout Gil Rui Barros says, 'I have never known a manager prepare his training sessions so thoroughly. Like Zidane with a ball at his feet, Mourinho has this thing that cannot be taught. He is the Zidane of managers.'

Mourinho's special attributes attracted the attention of English clubs even before FC Porto's European Cup victory. He was wooed by Liverpool in the spring but demurred. Sir Bobby Robson asked him to join the staff at Newcastle United with a pledge that within two years he would be head coach. Mourinho declined. Spurs had made inquiries through intermediaries regarding their then vacant manager's job. 'It was in December or January,' said Mourinho. 'There was a contact but not direct. I was not interested at that time; I do not like to leave clubs in the middle of the season, so I thought, at that time, no chance.'

Mourinho, a deeply religious man, was struck by tragedy when his sister died in a diabetic coma during his spell with Barcelona. The experience reinforced his strong bonds with wife Tami, his nine-year-old daughter, Mathilde, and his son Jose, six. It was to see them that he left the scene of Porto's triumph so hurriedly – on the way to Chelsea. Before every kick-off, he kisses a photograph of his two children, and a crucifix.

PART ONE
THE FIRST SEASON

WINTER CHAMPIONS

'LET'S HAVE SOME FUN'

JOSE MOURINHO IN HIS FIRST PROGRAMME NOTES

Jose Mourinho delivers a message of intent at his unveiling at Stamford Bridge. 'We have top players at Chelsea,' he says. 'And, I'm sorry if I sound arrogant, we have a top manager as well. I don't want to be compared with coaches from the past, nor do I want to be viewed as the face of young managers in the game. I have won the Champions League. I'm not one who comes straight out of the bottle. I'm a special one. I am a winner because I'm good at what I do and because I am surrounded by people who think the same.'

The club's chief executive Peter Kenyon admits, 'I don't think we'll need to work on his confidence! He has been charged with being arrogant, but I don't think he is. He's very confident and self-assured and thoughtful about what he does. He's deliberate and has a game plan.'

Mourinho adds, 'I want to win. Over the last two years

I've had the taste. As a manager you want to feel the biggest success you can achieve. I want to keep this taste. I don't want to lose it. I don't want to get to 2010 or 2012 with just the same titles I have now. I want more. The people here have the same ambitions and mentality. We shouldn't be afraid to say, "I want to win."

'I accept that if I don't win this year it will be a failure. If I am sacked, I can always find another job. But I have not come here to give myself nightmares. I have come here to sleep well.'

Mourinho also responds to sniping from the outgoing coach Claudio Ranieri. 'I didn't like what he said about the Portuguese league being an easy one to win. I prefer to use my head and not react to other people's opinions. But what I suggest is that if someone is Mr Ranieri's friend, or has contact with him, you should explain to him that if a team is to win the UEFA Cup or the Champions League, it has to play clubs from other countries. I didn't win the UEFA Cup and the Champions League playing 20 Portuguese teams. I played and beat players and clubs from his country Italy, from England and Spain. Porto beat everyone in Europe. What has Ranieri won in 20 years? The Spanish Cup. I could say things like Ranieri has been in football for 20 years and the only thing he has won is the Spanish Cup. I could say that. I don't like to, but I could.'

Then Mourinho turns his attention to Sir Alex Ferguson, Arsène Wenger and Sven-Goran Eriksson. After Porto had beaten Manchester United in the Champions League in Portugal, Ferguson said the opposition were divers. 'Ferguson had a reaction – something out of nothing,' says Mourinho. 'But I felt my players were big enough to cope with that type of pressure. I had to show them I was not afraid of him and that their boss was ready for a fight. After the second game at Old Trafford he came to the dressing room and congratulated me. And I have respect for such important people. I have not come here specifically to fight. I have come here to win. But at the right moment, if I feel my players, my group and my club are in a situation where they need my help, it's like family. And they will get it.'

Arsenal? 'Their manager is one of the best in the world. As for any weaknesses in his side, how can you identify weakness in an historic team? I need to learn about him and his side. In Portugal I could smell the changes managers would make at half-time. So I now need to look at Wenger and his players and discover their philosophy and playing style. That is why my scouts will watch his stars at Euro 2004 and then again in pre-season friendlies. When you go to war you have to know the opposition's strengths and weaknesses.'

As for Eriksson, Chelsea's first choice to replace Ranieri, Mourinho shrugs his shoulders. 'It is only natural they went for him. Mr Eriksson is a manager with a lot of prestige in the world. He also had a close relationship with Chelsea and, because of that he was their number one choice. I don't mind... because now I'm the man.'

Claudio Ranieri was loved at Stamford Bridge and there was anger at his treatment. But he had won nothing of real consequence in nearly two decades in management; Mourinho won the UEFA Cup, Portugal's league and cup double and the European Cup in two coruscating seasons at Porto. But Mourinho's mentor Sir Bobby Robson is concerned about his move to English football. 'The fact is Jose is coming into an area he doesn't know. He won't find the Premiership anything like the Portuguese league. He is joining the big boys and the big teams, where every game is a potential blip. In Portugal, if you can defeat Benfica and Sporting home and away, you are likely to win the title. What he has done on five or six occasions in European competition over the last two seasons is beat the big teams. He has to do that thirty-eight times in the league.'

Mourinho responds diplomatically, showing his deep affection for Robson: 'I still see Sir Bobby as a father to me. My early times with Bobby were really important, and the way he put faith in me gave me confidence and taught me to be strong in believing myself. Tactically and dealing with players I could not ask for a better teacher, and I could not have learned from anyone better. It was an experience that was invaluable and I still telephone and talk to him now. He is a leader to me and I will go on respecting him as a great manager. He is always close to the players and that is something as a manager you must always be. They are your blood and the most important thing of all. They have to respect you and that is something that I learned from Bobby in the way they respect him and will always play for him. A little something from everything I achieve will always be dedicated to him.'

Mourinho prepared for his new job by sending a code of conduct to each of his stars. Porto's players were handed the same document and they responded. Gone are the days of late-night partying, weekend trips abroad and snubbing the press. Under the new regime all players must stick strictly to the rules or faces heavy fines or even suspension.

Split into seven sections, the rulebook states how players

should behave with each other and the public – and the punishments they face if they break those rules and others that include lifestyle and eating habits, and misconduct on and off the pitch.

Mourinho calls for players not involved in Euro 2004 to attend Stamford Bridge on the first Monday of pre-season training. Hernan Crespo is the one player who does not show up. When Crespo arrives on Wednesday he is told decisively what his options are. Mourinho says publicly, 'We spoke in a very open way about whether he can find the motivation or the happiness for himself and his family to stay. For me, the player's desire is crucial. I told Hernan about the style, the quality of players I want, and the motivation. I was upset that he was not at our breakfast. You have always to be there – if the plane is full from Argentina, you come by bus. You can call. There is always a solution. He gave me excuses – some I could accept.'

Outcome: Crespo is let go on loan to AC Milan; Seba Veron is similarly released on loan back to Italy; and Chelsea successfully pursue Didier Drogba for a record transfer of £24 million. Marcel Desailly also leaves, Jimmy Floyd Hasselbaink departs to Middlesbrough, Mario Melchiot to Birmingham City, and Mario Stanic retires with a knee injury, all in the first week. Boudewijn Zenden, Jesper Gronkjaer, Emmanuel Petit and Winston Bogarde also depart.

Frank Lampard's first meeting with the new boss is etched on his mind. Mourinho stared into his eyes and asked him, 'Are you a winner?' Lampard recalls, 'It was a strange scene, but it felt right and walking out we all thought, "We're going to win something this season."'

So does Mourinho genuinely believe Chelsea can win the Premiership in his first season in charge? 'Yes, I do,' he replies prior to the new season's opening game with Manchester United. 'One hundred per cent. I have no doubts that we can.'

As Mourinho prepares for the first match of the season, the issue that Sir Alex Ferguson refused to shake hands when Porto beat United in last year's Champions League is put to him. Not so, according to Mourinho! It suited the media to suggest bad blood, but he stresses, 'I have no problems with him. He complained about certain things in Porto, but he shook my hand after the match, and at Old Trafford he came to the dressing room to do it. I have respect for every manager when they have respect for me.'

Peter Kenyon, who was chief executive at Old Trafford before being lured to Stamford Bridge, has worked with both Ferguson and Mourinho, and he believes Chelsea's new manager can build dynastic success in the same single-minded way as the Scot has done at Manchester United. Mourinho responds in typical fashion, 'I don't want to be compared with other people. I am what I am, I've done what I've done, and I will try to do well again in the future. But I know that one day, instead of being a champion at the end of the season, I'll get the sack. These things happen in football. I don't think I'm the best in the world when I win, and I don't think I'm the worst when I lose. I'm just me.'

Normally, Ferguson would relish starting a campaign with such a big game. 'Not this season,' he says. 'Not with the injuries we've got. I'd rather have played someone else. You don't want to be three points behind one of your main rivals on the first day of the season.'

SATURDAY, 15 AUGUST
MANCHESTER UNITED 0, CHELSEA 1

Jose Mourinho offers Sir Alex Ferguson a glass of Chelsea's cheapest plonk after sending the Manchester United boss to his first opening-weekend defeat in eight years. Gudjohnsen's first-half strike seals the points. Mourinho and Fergie shake hands and then share a bottle of Argentinean Shiraz in the manager's office. The single goal comes with barely a quarter of an hour gone; yet Chelsea are already aiming to play on the break by then. 'Sometimes you have to play a little different to how you would like,' says Mourinho. 'We did not play better quality football because of our opponents. Sometimes football is beautiful because of competitiveness and organisation. Defensively we played fantastically with unbelievable team spirit. United pushed us back and I had to control the game.'

The goal comes when Geremi beats a sluggish Quinton Fortune to the ball, and Didier Drogba rises high to redirect a diagonal pass into the space behind United's defence, allowing Gudjohnsen to flick the ball home. Eager to protect Gudjohnsen's early goal, Chelsea and their coach re consumed with caution.

So early in the campaign Arsenal's 4–1 rout of Everton bears overtones of the sweeping verve that carried the double to Highbury in 1998 and 2002. Alan Hansen writes in his *Telegraph* column, 'The victory was a clear message that said "Move over Manchester United" and also showed Chelsea that, whatever they spend on new players, Arsenal will continue to pulverise their opponents.'

SATURDAY, 21 AUGUST 2004
BIRMINGHAM CITY 0, CHELSEA 1

Mourinho hails the team spirit that he feels can propel Chelsea to the title. 'It was amazing; I have never known anything like it before. The players who weren't involved were all calling into the dressing room on their mobile phones encouraging and cheering on the players who started the game. Perhaps that is normal for you in England but it is unheard of where I come from and it's a sign that we have a fantastic spirit and determination here.'

This is Joe Cole's day from the moment he is called on just after the hour mark and he delivers with style. Cole's entrance comes after Steve Bruce's five-man midfield has strangled the life out of Chelsea.

Cole is told to play behind Drogba and Kezman. He flits out to the left, takes a pass from the otherwise unimpressive Lampard and makes tracks towards Maik Taylor's goal. His shooting from range isn't normally enough to trouble any keeper, but this time he finds the target with a deflection off Taylor's leg.

Chelsea sit joint top of the Premiership with Arsenal after winning the first two games. But, while the reigning champions have scored nine times in two games, Chelsea have eked out two 1–0 wins based on defensive solidity and organisation. It is a comparison Mourinho believes is unfair. He wants his team to play 'beautiful' football, but first he wants to win – and he reckons teams from this country, including Arsenal and the national side, have not enjoyed international success in recent years simply because they do not defend well enough.

TUESDAY, 24 AUGUST 2004
CRYSTAL PALACE 0, CHELSEA 2

Didier Drogba's first Premiership strike and a thumping clincher from Tiago make it three wins and three clean sheets out of three for Mourinho. The Portuguese takes a leaf out of the *Tinkerman's* book with five changes, including full debuts for Tiago and Kezman. Chelsea are in front after twenty-seven minutes. Kezman threads through for Babayaro to deliver a cross that begs for the powerful downward finish from the Drogba. Seventeen minutes from the end Tiago puts the seal on his impressive personal display as he collects from Drogba and drills a fine shot into the corner.

Mourinho says he plans to turn Lampard into the best midfielder in Europe. He missed UEFA's gala awards ceremony in Monaco to work with Lampard and his team-mates ahead of the home clash against Southampton. At those awards, Porto midfielder Deco was handed the Champions League Player of the Year award. Mourinho arranges for his own award for winning the Champions League to be given to him at Chelsea's home European clash against his old club. He targets the next Player of the Year award for Lampard. 'I want to change Frank Lampard as a player. I want to make him a better one. I want him to win the same trophy that Deco won on Thursday night.'

SUNDAY, 29 AUGUST 2004
CHELSEA 2, SOUTHAMPTON 1

They may not quite have the look of champions in waiting, but Chelsea beat Southampton more convincingly than the score-line suggests, to make their best start to a season in the top flight. Chelsea should be three or four ahead by half-time, despite falling a goal behind to a wonderful strike from James Beattie within twelve seconds of kick-off. After equalising through a Beattie own-goal and then taking the lead with a Lampard penalty, Chelsea fail to kill off a Saints side who rarely threaten. Wayward finishing, outstanding goalkeeping and goal-line clearances keep Chelsea down to a one-goal winning margin for the third weekend running.

SUNDAY, 12 SEPTEMBER 2004
ASTON VILLA 0, CHELSEA 0

Merely ending Chelsea's 100 per cent record is an achievement for Villa. Huth, Duff, Parker, Bridge, Johnson and Geremi are not even required on the bench to emphasise the strength of Chelsea's squad compared to Villa. Chelsea have chances enough to win. In the opening half flowing moves create opportunities for Cole, who miskicks, and Drogba, who hits the bar. Chelsea dominate after the break but Mourinho withdraws Cole and the link between midfield and attack is lost. Four wins and a draw is an excellent start to the season, but it still leaves Chelsea behind Arsenal, who record their fifth straight victory. Later Styles rescinds the yellow card shown to Drogba.

MONDAY, 20 SEPTEMBER 2004
CHELSEA 0, TOTTENHAM HOTSPUR 0

Mourinho feels cheated by an opposition who come solely to achieve a stalemate. Chelsea fail to capitalise on Arsenal's draw against Bolton the day before, and the gap at the top remains two points. Mourinho is furious. Not with his players, who, for the second successive Premiership match, do not score, but with Jacques Santini, his team and their alleged time wasting. 'I think it is frustrating for me, the players, for every Chelsea supporter and for every football supporter. Because people are not paying money to see one team play and for another to keep falling down, kicking balls away, sending for the medical department and spending five minutes to change players. My team played fantastic football. They may as well have put the team bus in front of the goal.'

Chelsea extend their unbeaten run against Spurs to twenty-nine league games, but that matters little in the context of this Premiership season. They need the three points.

SUNDAY, 26 SEPTEMBER 2004
MIDDLESBROUGH 0, CHELSEA 1

Before kick-off, a minute's silence is immaculately observed in memory of local legend Brian Clough, born just a mile from Boro's former home, Ayresome Park. Clough scored a phenomenal 204 goals in 222 league and cup games for the club. Chelsea only have Drogba's eighty-first-minute goal to show for their overwhelming superiority.

Mourinho concedes that the paucity of goals is a cause

for concern: just seven in as many Premiership matches. He complains that 'the knives always go in Chelsea's direction and the flowers in the other direction.' But he adds, 'One day a team will be unlucky: we will score from every situation and win 4–0 or 5–0. We had a lot of chances to score and the only surprise was that we scored so late.'

The goal comes when Lampard pulls a free-kick into the middle for Drogba to crack a right-footed effort from fifteen yards that Mark Schwarzer can only help into the net.

Mourinho's side is taking shape. Lampard, Terry, Makelele and new signings Cech, Ferreira and Drogba have started every game. Gudjohnsen has started seven and come on as a substitute in the other two. With the strikers and back five largely picking themselves, the fiercest competition has been in midfield, with Cole, Duff, Tiago and Smertin sharing the remaining two places alongside Makelele and Lampard. Cole has impressed at the head of the diamond until Duff's return from a shoulder injury reduced his workload, while Tiago and Smertin have started four games each on the right of a deeper midfield three.

William Gallas reveals that Mourinho began his Chelsea tenure by telling his players their standards were not good enough. Mourinho said at the start, "There are a lot of good players at this club, a lot of international players, but you haven't won anything. With this team we must do it." And that is true. This season is our season and everybody feels the same. We know it will be difficult because we know Arsenal are very strong and there's Manchester United, but we want to win all the games. Everybody is fighting on the pitch together and that's important. We play with our hearts.'

Lampard says the studious attention to detail that characterises the new regime means the team expect to win every game they play. 'The most important change is that the mental attitude now is: win, win, win. At times it wasn't like that last season. Now the accent is on winning every game we play – and every competition we're in.'

SUNDAY, 3 OCTOBER 2004
CHELSEA 1, LIVERPOOL 0

Joe Cole scores the winning goal and leaves with a bottle of champagne from Sky as their man of the match, but also with a stinging reproach from his boss. Mourinho accuses Cole of neglecting his defensive duties after the goal and hints that the England international finishes the game playing to the gallery, which includes Sven-Goran Eriksson, rather than for the team.

But Cole catches the eye with the neat finish he applies to Lampard's free-kick and the invention he brings as an auxiliary striker after coming on in the first half for Drogba. Mourinho, though, says Cole's display is 'not good enough' from the moment he finds Liverpool's net. 'Joe Cole scored a goal; that's very important. He gave us good dynamic and played really well in terms of that attacking dynamic. When he scored the goal the game finished for him. After that I need 11 players for my defensive organisation and I had just ten.'

Cole responds by saying, 'The boss has no axe to grind against me. He just wants to make me a better player. I will sit down with him and talk to him and listen to whatever he has to say. He's a fantastic manager.'

Mourinho also hits back at critics who have lambasted his team's four 1–0 wins. 'It is not fair. I think they should criticise the teams playing against us. The midfield is working very well and defensively we are playing great. So Arsenal are playing beautifully and we are playing not so good and not scoring many goals and we are just two points behind them – so in one weekend it can all change.'

In what appears an expertly planned routine Lampard plays a delightful low free-kick for Cole to burst ahead of his marker and clip the ball first time past Kirkland. Cech has to make an important late save from Steve Finnan, while Gudjohnsen and Cole also come close in the final stages. But once again it is 'one-nil to the Chelsea'.

Just eight goals in as many league games does not seem to compare favourably with Arsenal's twenty-six. Chelsea's goalscoring chances are hit by the news that Drogba needs minor surgery on the groin injury that forced him to limp off against Liverpool.

SATURDAY, 16 OCTOBER 2004
MANCHESTER CITY 1, CHELSEA 0

Mourinho's unbeaten record ends in a flurry of frustrated continental-style arm waving at the City of Manchester Stadium. After guiding his men through eight Premiership games without losing, he finally looks hot under the collar as a first-half Nicolas Anelka penalty brings the curtain down on the impressive start.

On a day when Arsenal are the only winners in the title race, Mourinho has to swallow defeat against a revved-up

City side, who deserve their win for a collective effort that leaves Chelsea, for once, unable to conjure a spark of magic.

This first defeat for Mourinho's side sees them drop five points behind Arsène Wenger's spectacular team. And on a day when Jimmy-Floyd Hasselbaink smashes in a hat-trick, the wisdom of selling the Dutchman has to come into question.

Adrian Mutu's situation at the club becomes even more tenuous with the news that he has failed a drugs test. Mutu says he was tempted into taking drugs by the belief it would improve his sex life. The Romanian, who joined Chelsea from Parma in August 2003, has had little impact on the team since falling out of favour with Claudio Ranieri in the second half of last season. Mutu has managed only two brief substitute appearances under Mourinho, for it emerges that he was deliberately targeted by the doping authorities at the request of his manager. Mark Bosnich, also drug-tested at the request of the club, was sacked in 2003. If Chelsea sack Mutu, it would mean writing off the £15.8 million they paid for him a year ago.

Mourinho admits that it was a mistake for Chelsea to have bought Mutu and says he would have burrowed deeper into a player's lifestyle before signing him. 'When you spend big money with a player, you can't bet; you must be sure what you are buying.'

Chelsea decide to sack Mutu but reserve the right to claim compensation if he is not banned by the FA and is given a second chance in the Premiership or at a top club in Europe. Mutu is charged and suspended by the FA. Kenyon defends the club's decision to 'target-test' Mutu and then sack him on grounds of gross misconduct. Gordon Taylor accuses the club of target-testing Mutu 'with a view to getting rid of him'.

Mourinho reveals he confronted Mutu over suspicions the player was using cocaine just days after joining Chelsea. 'When I met him on his first day in the pre-season in July and he was with his two agents Mr Becali and Mr Popescu I told all three, "I have information that you are on cocaine." All three were laughing, denying, saying this was a lot of lies about Adrian. After that I did not speak with them again because they denied the situation. For a long period we saw now and again strange behaviour. Arriving late a few times, not coming in to train other times. A doctor visiting his house and the apparent reason was just headaches. Injured when nobody knows how it happened – for example he was on the bench and did not play against Paris, yet the next day he was injured. We spoke about it. Is he pushing us to let him go in December? Is he doing this to get into a conflict with me [so I] say I don't want this player here? Or is he involved in other things? We began to question and the club doctor, because he has some experience that we do not have, was analysing with different eyes and he arrived at the decision that, maybe, yes. I would never sign him again. Not just because of the drug, but because he called me a liar.'

Peter Kenyon claims the player ignored their efforts to help him with his drug problem and adds that Chelsea would dish out the same treatment to any player who fails a drug test. He claims both Mutu's contract and the FA's guidelines give Chelsea the right to sack their player, even before he has been through the FA disciplinary procedure.

SATURDAY, 23 OCTOBER 2004
CHELSEA 4, BLACKBURN ROVERS 0

Eidur Gudjohnsen produces a sublime hat-trick to hand Abramovich an early thirty-eighth birthday present. Chelsea's league goal tally increases by 50 per cent! This is the response to those who say Chelsea do not possess the attacking power to keep pace with champions Arsenal. After a Paul Dickov penalty appeal is waved away by referee Graham Poll, Chelsea seize their chance with two strikes in a minute. Cole's fantastic touch supplies the first in the 37th minute when he picks up a short Parker ball 35 yards out and chips a pass into Gudjohnsen's run a few yards from goal. With more shin than boot, Gudjohnsen angles the ball past Brad Friedel. Seconds later another long ball – this time from Lampard – has the same timing and precision to give Gudjohnsen the chance to volley in.

Gudjohnsen's commitment pays off in the fiftieth minute when a surging run tempts Craig Short to bring him down just inside the box for a clear penalty. Gudjohnsen gleefully slots away his hat-trick.

Arsenal go down to a contentious and significant 2–0 defeat to Manchester United that reduces their lead to just two points. Everton, who visit Chelsea in two weeks, and who were many experts' tips for potential relegation, are surprisingly just a point further behind. Adrian Mutu is suspended from football for seven months and fined £20,000 following the FA's disciplinary hearing. Mutu's ban is conditional on him successfully completing a period of rehabilitation and is backdated to start on 25 October. That means the suspension concludes on 18 May.

Peter Kenyon criticises the seven-month ban, claiming the FA have been too lenient. Mutu apologises to Chelsea's fans, blaming injury problems and Mutu fires a parting shot at Mourinho. 'I am sure Mourinho didn't notice that I had a busy private life because he simply didn't care about me. My problem with him was to do with the national team. I will always have a problem with a coach who doesn't let me play for my national team. As a coach Mourinho is very good, but as a person I have a big question mark about him.'

SATURDAY, 30 OCTOBER 2004
WEST BROMWICH ALBION 1, CHELSEA 4

Mourinho repeats his claim that Chelsea are statistically the best team in England after their second successive four-goal Premiership win sends them level on points with Arsenal, who are surprisingly held to a draw by Southampton. 'Our first-half display was our worst performance this season,' says Mourinho. 'But it got much better in the second half and the substitutions worked. With the other results it was a fantastic day for Chelsea. That is the beauty of the game in England – if I was five or six points ahead in Portugal, the title would be over. Over 14 matches in all competitions we have a better statistical record than Arsenal because we have won 12 and drawn two, while they have won 10 and four draws – now that gap has widened. I would say they have just been better than us in the Premiership.'

Chelsea break the deadlock late in the first half when Terry dives to guide a looping Lampard delivery across the face of goal. Albion freeze and Gallas volleys home a rare strike. Mourinho is still not happy and hauls off Cole and Bridge. Robben spices up the attack and, within two minutes, sees a shot drift wide. Gudjohnsen makes it 2–0, heading home Duff's fifty-first-minute cross. Albion give themselves hope when Zoltan Gera lashes the ball into the net. But their hopes are short-lived as Lampard runs 70 yards and releases Duff, who clips his shot over Russell Hoult and inside the far post. Lampard then makes it four in the eighty-first minute with a stunning strike. With eight goals in two Premiership games and a five-point deficit on the Gunners wiped out, the table has a different complexion.

Following an impressive 1–0 win in Moscow to romp through to the knockout stages of the Champions League with two games to spare, Chelsea now have the advantage of concentrating on the title, with Arsenal wobbling and United uncharacteristically inconsistent in Europe.

Arsenal's blip raises expectations of the title coming to Stamford Bridge for the first time in fifty years, but Mourinho tells his players to concentrate on themselves. He says, 'We can't think about Arsenal. We have to win our own matches and see what they do. They cannot win every match but will not lose points every weekend.'

SATURDAY, 6 NOVEMBER 2004
CHELSEA 1, EVERTON 0

Robben tells his team-mates in a pep-talk before the game to play so well that Arsenal will 'shit in their pants'. Mourinho likes a player to address the team in the dressing room prior to kick-off and it works. Kezman's appearance from the bench at least galvanises Gudjohnsen and it is his superb turn and floated pass that leads to the breakthrough. Robben dashes clear and not even David Weir's desperate tug can prevent the tricky winger from lifting a delicate lob over Martyn.

Everton boss David Moyes says, 'I thought we could hold out but Robben proved the difference. If I had £12 million, I would buy a player like that. But the fact is if you can't shop at Armani, you have to shop at Marks and Spencer.'

But while he is happy with the team, Mourinho calls on Chelsea fans to be more vocal. He tells Chelsea TV, 'When I can hear 2,000 Everton fans behind me and 35,000 Chelsea fans not being too enthusiastic, I feel we need more.' He also says he wants his long- term future to be at Stamford Bridge. 'I'm so happy with English football, my players and the people that surround me at the club that I want to be here at Chelsea for many, many years.'

John Terry also shows his commitment to the club by signing a new five-year contract just eighteen months after putting pen to paper on his last deal.

Next up for Mourinho's table-toppers are local rivals Fulham at Craven Cottage, while Arsenal face a high-noon showdown at Tottenham. Mourinho taunts Arsenal by insisting Chelsea are so far ahead of the rest that they will win the Premiership two weeks before the end of the season. Mourinho has only been top for seven days but is determined to stay there for the long haul. He says, 'Just ten minutes ago I was driving down the King's Road with one of my assistants and he said that on 14 May it will be crazy because that's the final day of the season. But I said maybe we should do it two weeks earlier and celebrate then.'

SATURDAY, 13 NOVEMBER 2004
FULHAM 1, CHELSEA 4

Arsenal win 5–4 at the Lane in the midday kick-off, but Chelsea respond in style to restore their two-point lead with another Robben- inspired performance. Mourinho chooses a Chelsea side almost unrecognisable from the team that beat Newcastle in the Carling Cup in the week, making seven changes.

Chelsea take a deserved lead through a fantastic Lampard free- kick into the right corner from almost 30 yards. Fulham produce a stunning equaliser on fifty-seven minutes – and it has to be to beat Cech. Terry's headed clearance drops to Diop 30 yards out, and the Senegalese midfielder's vicious volley shoots into Cech's right-hand corner for a memorable first club goal.

But Chelsea regain the lead two minutes later as Robben shows wonderful footwork to elude Zat Knight, Rehman and Mark Pembridge before firing in with his left foot from 15 yards. That proves the catalyst as Gallas seizes on a Diop miskick and heads in from three yards at the far post. Chelsea then seal it with a delightful fourth goal nine minutes from time. Tiago feeds Robben down the left, and the winger's marvellous back-heel gives the Portuguese player time and space to arrow a 16-yard shot into the right corner.

Once again Robben is the difference, with arguably his best performance so far. He takes the match to Fulham, sets up the fourth goal and tops his display with one of the goals of the season. Chelsea's goal difference is closing in on Arsenal's, and Mourinho taunts Arsenal's defence for conceding four times at Spurs.

'I didn't see Arsenal's game, but 5–4 is a joke result. It is not a real football result; it was like a hockey match. For a team to give away four or five goals, the defenders must be a disgrace. I often play three versus three in training and if the score gets to 5–4 then I send the players to the dressing room and stop the game! They are obviously not doing their job properly and it is no point going on with it – and that's just in a three-a-side game. In a true game I cannot believe the defenders are doing their job properly at all and as a manager this would be a nightmare. Some people may go away thinking it was the best game they had ever seen but as a manager how could you be happy?' While the Gunners have conceded four goals in one game, Chelsea have conceded just four Premiership goals all season.

Mourinho adds, 'I do not think I am vain or arrogant but I believe that now we are top of the table Chelsea can go on to win the championship. I don't say this just for the sake of it – I say it because I truly believe we are good enough to win the title. This was a big test for us and we had the answer. We showed we could handle the pressure. I still remain convinced that we can become the champions.'

Mourinho says he is delighted with how quickly the team have gelled. 'It was the big question mark. I'll never forget a word I had with Mario Stanic. He left the club but he was with me on the first day and said something like, "A lot of people have arrived in England and they adapt to the English reality of football. But I know that your methods and your philosophy and your way of thinking are very special. Don't ever change, even if it takes time, don't change." I'll never forget what he said. So it was a question for me whether the players could adapt. I followed an Italian manager, and it cannot be easy when you follow a manager who thinks very differently.

'At the moment I feel we are a very strong team defensively. I don't say we are a defensive team. I say we are a strong team in defensive terms, but at the same time lacking sufficient fluidity in attack, because that will take time to come. But we play very good football at times. The only thing I would like is to have more control of the game in terms of possession.

'We must think more about our football and not play by instinct. When you play another team with the same qualities as you, normally the better one wins. But when you play against other teams who can stop during the game and think collectively, it becomes much more difficult. You see how Spanish, Italians, Portuguese play football? I don't say that they are perfect. English football has a few things to learn from them in the same way they have a lot of things to learn from English football. I have a lot to learn from English football and am completely open to good influences. But I also have things to give. The lines of communication between me and my players are wide open and the intention is to improve the whole team by each one of us giving our best. I believe it can make us a strong team. I cannot say we will win the Champions League or the Premiership, but I know that we can do it. Real Madrid have a group of stars and they have a group of young boys who are not ready to cope with that pressure and that quality. What is missing is what I call low-profile players. For example, in my team I love to have Geremi on the bench because he's a low-profile player who is ready to help, to fight for the team, to do the job I want him to do. If I need him to play right-back, he can play right-back. If I need him to play right-winger, he can play right-winger. If I need him to pick up a man and mark him out of the game, he does it.'

SATURDAY, 20 NOVEMBER 2004
CHELSEA 2, BOLTON WANDERERS 2

Never before in his managerial career can Mourinho recall losing a two-goal lead. 'No, no, no, never. Never, never, never,' he insists. A club record ninth successive victory in all competitions is snatched away by the set-piece specialists, who earn a draw from two free-kicks, the second three minutes from the end.

The noisiest roar of the afternoon greets the news that Arsenal have mysteriously failed to see off West Bromwich Albion at Highbury, but that is eventually followed by 40,000 groans at Bolton's equaliser.

Duff makes a blistering start after kick-off is delayed by transport problems, scoring after thirty-six seconds. A goal right at the start of the second half by Tiago seems to have extended Chelsea's advantage at the head of the table to four points, but Kevin Davies and then Rahdi Jaidi do Arsenal a huge favour.

Mourinho is dignified in his disappointment. 'I don't think many people like the way Bolton play, but they're effective and dangerous. It was a bad result because we want to win every game. Yet we have to be fair. It is very difficult to play against them. Bolton can beat everybody because they create danger from nothing. It is a style I don't like – but we have to give them credit. I'm happy we only have to play them once more.'

Despite Cech flapping for Bolton's first goal, Mourinho insists, 'I have no criticism of my players. We're top of the league. My confidence doesn't change; my happiness with the players doesn't change. I never speak about my players when they make big mistakes. I never consider one player individually guilty for a defeat; if anyone is guilty, it's the manager. Petr will face Charlton with my confidence.'

SATURDAY, 27 NOVEMBER 2004
CHARLTON ATHLETIC 0, CHELSEA 4

John Terry and Frank Lampard are once again the driving force behind another Chelsea victory. Terry's second-half goals, separated by just three minutes, are a testament to his determination to get forward, as well as marshal the meanest defence in the top flight. While Lampard gives a performance that is a fitting tribute to his grandfather, who passed away the day before.

Another lightning start sees Duff on the scoresheet after 229 seconds. Gudjohnsen gets the ball deep and flicks it hard and low into Duff's path. The Irishman sweeps past Paul Konchesky and arrogantly pokes the ball into the far corner of Dean Kiely's goal.

Charlton's hopes go into decline within five minutes of the second half restart as Terry stages his scoring spree. First he bustles in with a header from Duff's looping corner. Then he taps in after another Duff corner is headed back across goal and Radostin Kishishev can only clear the ball to the Chelsea captain. Just before being replaced by Drogba, Gudjohnsen holds himself onside just long enough to score the fourth after a stunning low pass from Lampard leaves him the simple task of tapping past Kiely.

A year ago Alan Curbishley's side gave Ranieri's title pretenders a harsh lesson as they beat the Blues 4–2 on Boxing Day. But Mourinho's Chelsea are a different class and the efficiency of their victory echoes around the dressing rooms of Highbury and Old Trafford.

Arsenal lose 2–1 at Anfield, leaving them five points behind Chelsea in a remarkable turnaround at the top of the table. Their hopes of retaining the title are dealt a further blow when Vieira is ruled out of the crucial showdown with Chelsea at Highbury after receiving his fifth caution of the season.

But first up for Chelsea are Newcastle under new manager Graeme Souness. The Scot believes fans will look back in future years and acclaim Mourinho's Chelsea for their starring role in a golden era in the game's history. As a player, Souness was a hugely influential figure during Liverpool's golden era. 'People often talk to me about the good old days, but in 20 years' time what we are doing today will be considered the good old days. In my opinion these are the glory days and as a manager it's a privilege to be involved. In years to come I think they'll be saying, "D'you remember the great Chelsea and Arsenal teams at the start of the century?"

'It's easy to be dismissive of Chelsea's success and say they've achieved this and that simply because of the money they have,' adds Souness. 'But the manager still has to do the job. He has to sign the right players, pick the right team and get them to win consistently. He's done all that in my opinion with some style. You also have to say that he has an outstanding pedigree. You don't win the Champions League and the UEFA Cup without talent and without making the right decisions.'

SATURDAY, 4 DECEMBER 2004
CHELSEA 4, NEWCASTLE UNITED 0

Chelsea consolidate their position at the top with four second-half goals. Drogba stands in front of the adoring Chelsea faithful bellowing 'I'm back!' in celebration of his superb strike. The curse that normally comes with both the Player and Manager of the Month awards is lifted as both Mourinho and Robben receive their accolades before kick-off and again make their own special contributions. The deepest joy, though, is reserved for Mateja Kezman's first league goal: an absolutely delightful chip from the spot.

Lampard breaks Newcastle's resistance with the opener in the sixty-third minute, and substitute Drogba adds the vital second five minutes later before Robben and Kezman wrap up the points with two goals in the final minutes. It is the fifth time in seven Premiership games that Chelsea have scored four times. Newcastle, like Blackburn, West Brom, Fulham and Charlton before them, are simply blown apart. Chelsea are now 33–1 for a clean sweep of the Premiership, the FA Cup, the Carling Cup and the Champions League.

Both Arsenal and Manchester United win 3–0 at home later in the afternoon and Sir Alex Ferguson says he expects

Chelsea to slip up in the title race. 'Chelsea will have a blip. They will lose games. It's then a case of how their players react which will be important. Arsenal and ourselves have got that experience. We have seen title challenges be over by March. Chelsea don't have the experience of winning when it really matters.'

Chelsea warm up for the title showdown at Arsenal with a Champions League defeat at Porto. Claudio Ranieri will be in the stands against Arsenal to watch his old side for the first time since being sacked.

Having led Chelsea to second place in the Premiership and the Champions League semi-finals last season, Ranieri is convinced they can go one better this time around. 'Chelsea must be one of the favourites for the Champions League because Mourinho has won it before and my players had a good experience last year. It's possible for them to win the Champions League and the Premiership. Why not? Chelsea are very strong. We did a very good job last year putting the foundations in place and they're continuing to progress.'

Arsène Wenger sends his stars to the bowling alley to ease the pressure ahead of the game. While Mourinho was pushing his stars through a gruelling training session, Arsenal's first-team squad enjoyed skittles for three hours. The Arsenal manager insists his side are back to top form after crucial wins over Birmingham and Rosenborg – and will prove it with a victory at Highbury, even without the suspended Vieira.

But Mourinho sees things differently. 'At the end of the game Chelsea will be top of the league. So it's not a question of whether this game can decide a change of positions. It's not a case that because of this game Arsenal could go top and Chelsea go second. The only question left is: two points difference, five points difference or eight points difference? And I tell you eight points difference is a lot. If we win, it is significant. If we draw, it's five points; if we lose, it's two points. But our next two matches are at home against Norwich and Aston Villa. So it's significant if we win.'

Wenger is sure the neutrals are behind Arsenal because Chelsea are backed by Abramovich. He says, 'I am surprised that more people are not behind us because we have less money than Manchester United and Chelsea, with whom we are [in] direct competition. We have 30-times less investment capacity.'

But Mourinho ridicules that notion: 'When Thierry Henry signed for Arsenal was that for free? Did Juventus give him to Arsenal? When Vieira came here was that on loan? Did they rent him for £100,000? Was Reyes free from Sevilla? That surprises me, the fact that Sevilla made Reyes a Christmas gift. Ha! How much have I spent at Chelsea? Sometimes you confuse things by saying how much Chelsea have spent. We don't spend too much – maybe Man United spend more than me.'

Mourinho has splashed £70 million of Abramovich's money on five players in his short time in charge, and, even though Wenger has laid out £95 million, his net expenditure is just £9 million in eight years. Mourinho says that Vieira's suspension will be a big blow to Arsenal, but he points to the fact that Arsenal's magnificent, free- scoring run at the start of the season came without the Frenchman, who was recovering from injury. He says, 'They will miss him. The same way that I would miss John Terry if he was not involved in the game.'

Mourinho also points out that he has not lost a big game in his entire career. In two and a half seasons with Porto, Mourinho was unbeaten in games against major rivals Benfica and Sporting Lisbon. So far this season Chelsea have already beaten Liverpool and Manchester United. 'In 12 or 13 big games with Porto, classics as we call them in Portugal, we never lost. I've got a very good record in important matches and have every confidence in my team.'

SUNDAY, 12 DECEMBER 2004
ARSENAL 2, CHELSEA 2

A global television audience of 600 million watches events that underline the growing interest in Chelsea's attempt to oust their London rivals as Premiership champions.

One of only four Englishmen in the starting line-ups, Terry's leadership is as important as the contributions from more glamorous names. But Mourinho is angry that Thierry Henry's quickly taken twenty-ninth-minute free-kick is allowed to stand, even though referee Graham Poll has not blown his whistle and Cech is still busy lining up his defensive wall. Mourinho is grateful for a late let-off as Henry misses a glorious seventy-seventh-minute chance to wrap up victory for the Gunners, who are still left trailing leaders Chelsea by five points.

Henry sets the tone for a pulsating contest when he scores within seventy-five seconds. Cesc Fabregas picks out Henry with a great ball forward, and his nod-off allows Jose Antonio Reyes time to find the striker once again with Chelsea unaccountably standing off. Henry controls with his right foot

42

before spinning to arrow home with his left. Manuel Almunia, given the nod ahead of Jens Lehmann once more, shows his quality with a flying leap to turn aside Lampard's rocket. Yet when Robben swings in the resulting corner, Sol Campbell is inadvertently blocked by Henry to allow Terry a free header.

On the half-hour Robert Pires earns a free-kick after tangling with Terry and Makelele. Poll stands over the ball with Henry, and Gudjohnsen refuses to retreat. But Poll gives the nod and Henry beats the unprepared Cech with a deflection off Tiago's shoulder. Chelsea are furious but the goal is legitimate.

Mourinho's interval switch, with Drogba and Bridge coming on, leaves Arsenal trying to work out their marking duties. Within thirty-five seconds of the restart, Lampard delivers a free-kick from the left, Gallas outjumps Ashley Cole and nods down into the six-yard box for Gudjohnsen to loop the ball in with a stooping header.

The hugs between Terry and Henry at the end are proof of mutual respect. Henry, though, has shown why Abramovich waved a £50 million cheque in front of Arsenal vice-chairman David Dein for his services a year earlier. Even without Henry, Chelsea remain favourites to lift the league crown. With him, it would be no contest. Arsenal are left in third place behind Everton, but the Merseysiders are punching well above their weight.

To twice come from behind against the champions at Highbury says something about Chelsea's character. 'I thought my players were fantastic after Arsenal's second goal,' says Mourinho. 'They kept cool, remained in control and gave proof of their strong mental state. When a strange thing has happened, players can lose control. But after Arsenal's second goal – if you can call it a goal – my players were fantastic. We cannot promise anything yet as we don't know. Maybe we'll finish second or third, but maybe we will finish first.'

Sir Alex Ferguson switches his psychological attack to Chelsea. He says, 'Chelsea? They will find it difficult coming north to get points. Without doubt, Chelsea are the new force. Yet their form is not much different from last season. If you look at the last few seasons, Chelsea have always been up there at this time. It is when they come up north you will see. They have got to go to Liverpool and Everton. It's different after New Year – different pressures, you see. I always think the league starts on New Year's Day.'

Mourinho must make at least one change for the next game against Norwich, with Bridge replacing Carvalho. The Portuguese centre-back will be out for two to three weeks with a broken toe and, with Robert Huth still injured, Gallas moves to partner Terry at the heart of the defence.

SATURDAY, 18 DECEMBER 2004
CHELSEA 4, NORWICH CITY 0

Chelsea ensure they will be top at Christmas, with a performance of speed and finesse that swamps the visitors and has the game safe by half-time.

Mourinho pays Norwich the dubious compliment of fielding what has come to be regarded as his strongest team. Thomas Helveg and Gary Doherty hand Chelsea a comfortable two-goal lead. The first blunder comes in the tenth minute when Helveg's attempt at a back-pass goes straight to Duff. The Irishman storms forward and curls a low shot into the net.

Chelsea do not have to wait long for a second goal and it is Doherty who obliges in the thirty-fourth minute. The former Spurs defender crazily flicks the ball out of his area to Robben, and the Dutchman's square pass sets up Lampard to power a stunning shot into the top left-hand corner. A minute from the break, Robben drifts in from the right flank and finds Lampard in the box, who flicks the ball to Tiago. The Portuguese player's back-heel falls to Robben, who completes the sorcery with a ferocious smack that gives Rob Green no chance.

Asked what could stop Chelsea winning the league, Mourinho shrugs and says, 'A better team than us. At the moment nobody is better than us, but you never know. If we keep our present mental and tactical strength, I think nobody can stop us. We have to lose matches in the second half of the season but at this moment no one is better than us. In the future, I don't know. Maybe Arsenal or Manchester United can jump to a different level or maybe we can slide into a lower level. We could have injuries and players could lose form, but at this moment my confidence of winning the league is big.'

Sol Campbell's stunning late strike at Portsmouth lifts Arsenal back within five points, and Arsène Wenger warns Mourinho that Chelsea are not unstoppable. 'We are back in the race,' says Wenger. 'We are very hungry and we have talent and the ingredients to make the race interesting.'

Mourinho responds to Sir Alex Ferguson's suggestion that Chelsea will drop points when they have to play up north by saying, 'I know that Manchester United will lose points in the south – because they already have done. They lost three points at Stamford Bridge, three points at Portsmouth and two at Fulham. For sure, they have a problem in the south. We will have to wait and see whether we have a problem up north.'

After a session at the club's new training ground in the Surrey countryside, Mourinho says the chequebook will not be coming out more than once, and only then because of the injury to Scott Parker. But with four matches in the next ten days, starting at home to Aston Villa, and with Carvalho, Huth and Babayaro all on the injury list, Mourinho knows he needs his whole squad to be ready. But David O'Leary's troubles put Mourinho's situation in perspective. He is struggling to fill his side's bench, as his squad is decimated by injuries and he is unable to field Carlton Cole because of his loan deal with Chelsea.

SUNDAY, 26 DECEMBER 2004
CHELSEA 1, ASTON VILLA 0

Damien Duff's goal is enough to beat Villa and Mourinho insists he is more than happy to grind out 1–0 wins for the rest of the season if it means winning the Premiership. 'It is not our target to be winter champions,' he says. 'The aim is for us to be champions at the end of the season. At the moment we have a five-point advantage and this result was important to keep that distance.'

For the sixth time in his last nine games Duff opens the scoring to set his team on the road to victory. On the half-hour a Villa attack breaks down just inside the Chelsea penalty area and Lampard's pass immediately feeds Robben for a run from inside his own half. Villa's defence backs off the advancing Dutchman and, as Gareth Barry comes inside to cover, Robben slips the ball out to Duff, who cuts inside Liam Ridgewell and beats Thomas Sorensen with a low shot inside his near post. It is a goal that has been coming for some time.

Thierry Henry hits his 20th goal of the season in Arsenal's 2–0 win over Fulham at Highbury, lifting him up to joint second alongside Ian Wright in the all-time list of Arsenal's league scorers with 128.

Mourinho is named as coach of a 2004 fantasy team by French sports daily *L'Equipe*. He ends a magical year with his Chelsea side on top of the Premiership after winning the Champions League and the Portuguese title with former club Porto. Two Chelsea players – central defenders John Terry and Ricardo Carvalho – are also named in the team.

Mourinho's first taste of the English festive football calendar is not to his liking. 'I understand Boxing Day is an important day for your football culture and I accept that we have to play on 26 December,' he says. 'But it makes no sense to play again on the 28th. And if some important players get injuries during these matches then we really have to think about this programme. The fact is we have just 24 hours after the Villa game to train and travel to Portsmouth for our next match. I know it is the same for every other team and we must all play under the same circumstances. But to have just one day's rest makes the circumstances so difficult.'

He already faces a defensive headache as William Gallas has picked up a hamstring strain during the Villa victory. With

Huth crocked and Carvalho not 100 per cent, Mourinho has few options.

TUESDAY, 28 DECEMBER 2004
PORTSMOUTH 0, CHELSEA 2

Mourinho is full of praise for the way Chelsea hold off a pumped-up Pompey, who give them the runaround for forty-five minutes. 'I told my players at half-time this was not a day to dribble or play wonderful possession football. But it was a day to show how to be champions – which we did. Only top players can fight like we did today. From a mental point of view we have overcome a great obstacle by winning at Christmas. Six points out of six shows we do not have a jinx. There are still some hard tests ahead but my players have shown they have the desire to win the title and they know they have the ability.'

Robben celebrates the opener by whipping off his shirt and is booked and substituted all within two minutes. He laughs all the way to the dugout, pausing only to shake hands with referee Alan Wiley. An added-time goal from substitute Joe Cole confirms an eight-point lead at the top of the Premiership. The Chelsea celebrations are tinged with relief, as they hardly look potential champions for the first forty-five minutes. Pompey come at them with the sort of passion and non-stop aggression that has seen them beat Manchester United and almost hold Arsenal at Fratton Park.

Since their lone league reverse at Manchester City, the team have dropped just four points out of thirty-three, with Cech and his backline amassing fourteen clean sheets in twenty

Premiership outings. Although Mourinho admits it will be impossible to have a more 'perfect' year personally than 2004, his new club still have every target in front of them. Mourinho says, 'It was a good year for the club – but they didn't win anything and in 2005 we have to start bringing titles to the club. Unless we go and win trophies, what we've done so far will mean nothing. We have to be top still in May to win the trophy and the Premiership is the trophy we really want.'

Portsmouth coach Joe Jordan says, 'It was terrible to lose to Chelsea after playing so well, but at the end of the game you had to acknowledge you had been up against something special, something you don't encounter so often these days. Chelsea have great talent and resources, but you have to admit they have something else, something put there by Jose Mourinho.'

Manchester United make it seven wins and a draw from eight games with victory at Villa, but still can't close their nine-point deficit on Chelsea. Arsenal also maintain their challenge with Patrick Vieira's 20-metre volley enough to give them a 1–0 win at Newcastle.

Mourinho describes John Terry as 'the best central defender in the world'. 'Since the first minute I arrived here he's played at the same level. Not up and down, no mistakes. Not more committed against Man United and less concentration against West Bromwich. It's not like he prefers to play against tall and strong strikers and has it difficult against fast ones. For him every game is the same, every opponent is the same, the level of his performance is the same. He leads the team. He is an important voice on the pitch, where I'm not. He's absolutely amazing.'

Mourinho adds, 'In some clubs the captain is the captain of the manager. In other clubs he's the captain of the players. In another club he's the captain of the club because he's been at the club for ten years. John Terry is everything here.'

Mourinho is also clear in his admiration for Lampard. 'Frank is improving every day. Like Steven Gerrard he is one of the best in the world. It's difficult to say who is the best because some midfield players are more defensive, some more offensive. I would say Frank Lampard and Steven Gerrard can both do things. They are great players.' Gerrard remains top of Mourinho's wanted list while Chelsea are fifteen points clear of sixth-placed Liverpool going into their New Year's Day match at Anfield.

HALF A CENTURY –
WELL WORTH
THE WAIT

SATURDAY, 1 JANUARY 2005
LIVERPOOL 0, CHELSEA 1

Chelsea's victory is steeped in good fortune as Liverpool dominate and the referee misses a certain penalty. And, like at Portsmouth, the breakthrough comes from a deflected shot. Chelsea have to get back to attacking in a fluent fashion. Gudjohnsen is off colour, while Drogba has still to regain his confidence and power after returning from injury.

Mourinho takes pride in his side's resilience in the north, which Sir Alex Ferguson had put into question. 'I am proud of my players,' says Mourinho. 'We needed some luck, but luck has a habit of turning up for the champions at the right times and at the right places. We have proved to Manchester United and Arsenal that they will have to really fight for this title, but I think it will now be very difficult for them to catch us.'

Cole follows up his goal at Portsmouth on Boxing Day by crashing home a late winner. Chelsea struggle to impose themselves at Anfield but, with seventy-six minutes gone, Mourinho sends on Cole for Duff and is rewarded almost instantly. Robben's corner is headed towards the edge of the box by Johnson, and Cole fires home a low shot that heightens an already rampant sense of injustice fuelled by referee Mike Riley's decision to reject two justified penalty appeals from Liverpool. Undaunted, Chelsea hold out to the end.

But this is a day for defenders as the Blues complete their first league double over Liverpool for eighty-five years. Arsenal and Manchester United both win later in the day to keep up their challenges, but Chelsea are on course to beat United's ninety-one-point Premier League record.

TUESDAY, 4 JANUARY 2005
CHELSEA 2, MIDDLESBROUGH 0

Didier Drogba's double sends Chelsea seven points clear as title rivals Arsenal and Manchester United both slip up at home. Drogba signals his return to sharpness with blistering strikes in the fourteenth and seventeenth minutes.

Already favourites, the leaders are installed as champions-elect by Sir Alex Ferguson. 'Chelsea can only throw it away,' the Manchester United manager says after his team's 0–0 draw at home to Tottenham Hotspur. At Highbury, after a 1–1 draw against Manchester City, Wenger is a little more defiant. 'To give up and say they have won the title would be criminal and totally unprofessional.'

From the moment Drogba latches on to Lampard's pass to

slip the ball past Mark Schwarzer, there is only ever going to be one outcome. Drogba then uses his head to connect with Lampard's free- kick and beat Schwarzer again.

Mourinho has used Geremi as an example of a faithful squad player, but now the Cameroon international wants to leave to find first-team football. Geremi says, 'I'm not satisfied at Chelsea because I am not playing. Mourinho is not giving me opportunities and I do not like being on the bench.' Geremi is the first player to demand a move and says he preferred life under Claudio Ranieri. 'Mourinho is a good coach but makes few changes,' he says. 'Ranieri made more rotations than Mourinho. This way the players were more satisfied. I am good enough to play in the Premier League and I have demonstrated it in the last two seasons – but in this one I cannot. I don't regret coming to England because in my time here I have learned a lot. But I want to play.'

Steve Clarke says none of Mourinho's squad will be leaving, and that includes the unhappy Geremi and defender Robert Huth, who is interesting Bayern Munich. Chelsea agree a £10 million fee with Feyenoord for their nineteen-year-old striker Salomon Kalou, who will not move to Stamford Bridge until the summer.

Adrian Mutu signs a five-year contract with Juventus and could even play for Italy's Serie A giants in the Champions League final against his former club as his seven-month ban ends a week before it on 18 May. Juventus announce Mutu's signature as a free transfer as he is technically a free agent, but Chelsea demand a transfer fee to offset the loss of an asset valued at £13.7 million. The club still hold the player's registration and it will not be released until after his claim for wrongful dismissal is heard by the Premier League. If they fail to extract a transfer fee from Juventus, Chelsea could pursue compensation through the courts.

SATURDAY, 15 JANUARY 2005
TOTTENHAM HOTSPUR 0, CHELSEA 2

Thanks to a double from Frank Lampard, Chelsea become the first Premiership side to keep six consecutive clean sheets while winning every game. Lampard snaps back at a spectator dishing out abuse as he walks off for half-time. His crime is to have converted a disputed first-half penalty. Alexei Smertin goes down over Ledley King's outstretched leg, prompting vehement Spurs protests. But Lampard coolly smacks home the spot-kick.

The fourth official signals four injury-time minutes, before Lampard finally ends Spurs' stubborn resistance and gives the score-line a gloss that is harsh on hard-working Tottenham. But this is Chelsea's 14th match unbeaten and it is 601 minutes since Cech conceded – a statistic that is testimony not only to the Czech's prowess but to the defensive qualities of the entire squad. Even Joe Cole has shed his reputation for failing to track back. As a second-half substitute, he makes three important tackles, each visibly applauded from the bench by Mourinho.

Clarke's message to Chelsea's rivals is the bleakest of all. 'Other people talk about us having a blip. Well, maybe we have had our poor run already when we drew either side of our defeat to Manchester City. Maybe we've had our blip already.'

In the evening, Arsenal lose 1–0 at Bolton to extend Chelsea's lead to a formidable ten points plus a vastly superior goal difference. United lie a further point behind after winning at Anfield. The Gunners overcame a nine-point deficit to beat Manchester United to the title in 1998 but, just as in April 2003 when Arsenal blew a two-goal lead to draw 2–2, the Reebok Stadium has become the graveyard of their title aspirations.

Mourinho says he is so relaxed that he no longer watches Arsenal and Manchester United and is amused by the escalating war of words between Sir Alex Ferguson and Arsène Wenger. 'They can say what they want,' he says. 'It doesn't interfere with what I think. There is no pressure at the top. The pressure's being second or third. When you lead you can forget about the other teams. I don't see Arsenal and Manchester United's matches on television; I'm not listening to the radio waiting for their results. If we win, then our job for that week is done.'

With one eye on the upcoming Carling Cup semi-final second leg, Sir Alex Ferguson heaps unprecedented praise on Mourinho. 'Jose has done great since coming here,' he says. 'He has a confidence about him that has seeped into his team. He has got an assuredness and determination about them. He has been good for the Premiership. He has a wit and a humour about him. He comes across well and I get on OK with him. We had a spat last year but...'

SATURDAY, 22 JANUARY 2005
CHELSEA 3, PORTSMOUTH 0

Didier Drogba's brace takes him to eleven for the season, overtaking Gudjohnsen as top scorer. But it is Robben who inspires this victory in the opening thirty-nine minutes. Having resisted the temptation to go down after being fouled, Robben crosses for Drogba to score the first before hitting the target himself shortly afterwards, again staying on his feet as he stumbles past the keeper. Robben takes the opportunity to once more refute diving insinuations. Drogba scores his second, converting a free-kick won by Robben. The Dutchman is deservedly given a standing ovation when he is substituted late on.

The second half is something of a procession, with Mourinho removing Drogba, Duff and Robben, but showing his strength in depth as Gudjohnsen, Kezman and Tiago come on.

Mourinho is voted the best club coach in the world in 2004 by the International Football Federation of History and Statistics, finishing well ahead of Arsène Wenger and Didier Deschamps. He now plans to finish well ahead of Wenger and Sir Alex Ferguson in English football.

Meanwhile, Mourinho responds to comments from Wenger claiming that Chelsea are merely an 'effective' team who lack the flair of Arsenal. 'In the beginning we were called boring Chelsea,' says Mourinho. 'After that we couldn't score goals. After that we were top but would not be for long. After that, when Christmas arrives, we will lose matches. After that it is Boxing Day and Chelsea never win on Boxing Day. After that they said we cannot win in the North. After that they said if we lost the Carling Cup semi-final, the blip would start. If they really believed we are not strong enough to win this competition, they would not speak about us. They speak about us because they know we can win.'

Chelsea's season continues serenely as they complete a Carling Cup semi-final victory over Manchester United and then beat Birmingham to reach the fifth round of the FA Cup. Next up is a league game with Blackburn but, before that, Mourinho knows that one of Chelsea's closest challengers in the league will suffer a further setback with Arsenal set to take on United at Highbury. 'It's a good game for us,' says Mourinho.

In the end it is United who take the points as they win another tasty encounter between the two 4–2, with Wenger conceding the title after the final whistle.

WEDNESDAY, 2 FEBRUARY 2005
BLACKBURN ROVERS 0, CHELSEA 1

After completing their hard-fought victory, Chelsea's players take a few seconds to comprehend Mourinho's tugging at his trademark grey overcoat; then they pull off their shirts and vests and hurl them to their travelling fans. 'This was not a football match,' Mourinho says afterwards. 'It was a fight.' So much for Sir Alex Ferguson's jibe that Chelsea would struggle in the North.

Robben scores the only goal after five minutes before Cech brilliantly saves Paul Dickov's penalty to help Chelsea open up an eleven-point lead at the top. Cech sets a new Premiership record for not conceding a goal; it is now 781 minutes since he has been beaten, surpassing Peter Schmeichel's 1997 mark.

But it is not all good news for Chelsea as Robben is forced off with an injury after just twelve minutes and sits on the bench with crutches beside him and a hospital appointment for X-rays and a scan the next morning on an injured foot. Only five minutes have gone when Chelsea burst into the lead. Lampard spreads a long ball for Gudjohnsen to flick on to Robben, who turns Lucas Neill and unleashes an angled drive that dips under Brad Friedel. Then Robben tries to win possession to launch another attack, but Mokoena catches him late and the Dutchman limps off to be replaced by Cole.

Dickov hits the penalty low to Cech's left but the giant goalkeeper flings himself across his goal to parry. Cech then hurls himself at the loose ball and takes a hefty kick in the ribs from Dickov, provoking one of many ugly scenes. Mourinho is furious and his mood is hardly improved when Dominic Matteo cuts Cole down right in front of the Chelsea bench.

Despite getting his chance to impress as a replacement for Robben, Cole spends the match being chastised by Mourinho for drifting out of position, and the substitute is substituted with eleven minutes to go. It is so clearly a punishment that Cole does not bother to wait on the bench to watch the closing stages.

Mourinho accuses Blackburn of trying to kick his side off the pitch. 'I think they felt they couldn't beat us at football so they tried to beat us with a different kind of football,' he says. 'I'm not saying they tried to get players injured, but they were nasty, and they tried to intimidate our players. We gave a big answer here tonight; we showed we can deal with that tactic. We fought fantastically well, everyone battling for the same cause. The blond boy in the middle, yes, Robbie Savage, made 20 faults and no yellow card. It's difficult to control emotions. They were direct for every ball. They were aggressive, hard and nasty.'

The tapping-up row over Ashley Cole rumbles on relentlessly. Arsenal vice-chairman David Dein says, 'We will see what the quality of the evidence is and take it from there. Ashley Cole is committed to Arsenal and under contract until 2007.'

Ironically, Mourinho describes Cole as 'the best English defender' in an article in the Portuguese newspaper *A Bola*.

Talking of his future transfer targets, Mourinho says, 'We'll buy two – one left-sided defender, because I only have one – and another player. The defender has to be good to join our squad. About the other, it has to be a great player. We are already scouting half a dozen of them, who are the best in the world, because only they have the ability to join a super, balanced squad like ours.'

However, Wenger maintains Cole will still sign a new contract at Highbury. Chelsea have major concerns about Robben after scans of his damaged foot are inconclusive due to the amount of swelling and bruising. Meanwhile, Blackburn and Chelsea are charged by the FA with failing to ensure their players conduct themselves in an orderly fashion.

Mourinho, whose contract is worth more than £4 million a year over four years, says he hopes to stay at Chelsea for a long time. 'I signed an extraterrestrial contract and the intention is here to sign a new one and ideally it would be from four to eight years. Improving the four-year one makes no sense, because I knew what I signed and I know that I'll abide by it. I'm happy with my conditions and I'm completely committed to the growth of the club [on] many different levels. I like English football a lot; I like to live in England a lot. Therefore I can't see myself anywhere else. I mentioned, it's true, that I'd like to coach in Italy and also the national squad, but I see this day as very far away.'

Next up for Chelsea are Manchester City, the only team to have beaten them in the league all season. City manager Kevin Keegan is fulsome in his praise for Mourinho. 'He was very gracious when we beat them at our place earlier in the season,' he says. 'What I find most remarkable is within weeks he turned a set of talented individuals into an exceptional team.'

But Chelsea will have to face City without Robben, who

fears he has broken his foot again and could be out for the rest of the season.

SUNDAY, 6 FEBRUARY 2005
CHELSEA 0, MANCHESTER CITY 0

Manchester City frustrate Chelsea again, with David James somehow keeping out Lampard's close-range volley in the last minute. Mourinho is in a prickly mood after seeing his side's lead at the top of the table cut to nine points. 'I prefer to say my players in finishing situations weren't lucky and they had in David James a goalkeeper who made incredible saves to get them the point,' he says. 'Only one team had chances to score goals, but we couldn't score and they fought a lot, defended a lot and had a good goalkeeper. They were lucky.'

Before the match the Premier League announced they had received a formal complaint from Arsenal and would convene a commission into the Cole tapping-up allegations. Mourinho reacts with contempt for the Premier League's decision. 'I know nothing about it, I don't know and I don't want to know,' he says. 'I'm not a lawyer; I'm a football manager. What matters to me is to train to get the best results. When I win I am happy and when I don't I am not.'

Chelsea's hopes of landing an unprecedented quadruple are dealt the biggest possible blow with confirmation that Robben has broken his foot. Once the initial swelling around the injury had subsided, scans revealed a double break that could keep the Blues star sidelined for up to two months. Robben will miss the Carling Cup final and the first leg of the Champions League last-sixteen clash against Barcelona.

Mourinho stands to earn a £4.2 million bonus if Chelsea win the quadruple. Winning the Premier League title will earn him a £1 million bonus – double what Ranieri would have received – with more than £2 million extra if he then wins the Champions League. Again that is double the bonus that would have been paid to Ranieri. In all, the bonuses effectively add up to an extra year's salary for Mourinho, who will then be by far the highest-paid football manager in the world.

Abramovich has been paying the players an extra £4,000 for every Premiership game they win, and £1,500 for a draw, on top of their lucrative salaries. Abramovich has also been handing over 50 per cent of all prize money from the Champions League to the players. Last season that meant the squad shared £3 million – £200,000 each if they were in every squad. The players negotiated their deal when Abramovich bought Chelsea, but the system of payments per game has been dismantled by Mourinho, who does not agree with appearance money and has rolled it into lump-sum bonuses to be paid to the squad at the end of the season, depending on what they win.

SATURDAY, 12 FEBRUARY 2005
EVERTON 0, CHELSEA 1

James Beattie helps make a difficult trip much easier with a senseless red card after just eight minutes as Chelsea record their ninth 1–0 win in the Premiership.

Beattie's moment of madness costs Everton dear when he chases a long ball down the left with Gallas obstructing his run. First the striker pushes the Chelsea defender and then, moments later, he butts the back of his head. Everton's ten men put up a long, brave fight until a second-half Gudjohnsen tap-in breaks the deadlock. Chelsea return to their 4-3-3 formation, with Cole on the right and Duff on the left, and they dominate the early possession. Everton barely have a decent touch of the ball before they are reduced to ten men.

The home side's work-rate underlines their approach to the whole season, but they tire in the face of Chelsea's persistent attacks and eventually concede after sixty-nine minutes. Ferreira's low cross fizzes into the box, Gallas hits the bar from close range and Gudjohnsen has a simple tap-in.

Gudjohnsen hails the win as 'massive'. Manchester United beat Manchester City 2–0 for their thirteenth win in fifteen league outings, but such form is immaterial with Chelsea's consistency. The quest for the Premiership is on hold for three weeks, but the squad face three cup ties in eight days. First Mourinho's men go to Newcastle in the FA Cup, from where they will fly direct to Barcelona for the Champions League last-sixteen clash three days later. Four days after that, Chelsea face Liverpool in the Carling Cup final at the Millennium Stadium.

Chelsea pull off a clean sweep of the Barclays awards for January. Mourinho is named Manager of the Month for four straight wins, Terry is Player of the Month, and there is a special merit award for Cech keeping ten clean sheets in a row. Chelsea's Premiership break starts badly, with back-to-back defeats in the FA Cup and away to Barcelona in the Champions League. A goalscorer tops Chelsea's list, with everyone from Michael Owen to European Footballer of the Year Andriy Shevchenko being linked with a move to Stamford

Bridge. But the AC Milan and Ukraine striker stresses that he is not prepared to join Mourinho's foreign legion, even though he holds both coach and Abramovich in high regard.

Liverpool skipper Steven Gerrard or Lyon's highly rated Michael Essien are contenders for the midfield slot, while Mourinho dismisses the idea of signing Ronaldinho. With Chelsea preparing for the Carling Cup final, Manchester United scrap through against Portsmouth to close the gap at the top to six points. But Arsenal's pursuit is dealt a blow when they are held 1–1 at Southampton. Chelsea end their testing week by getting back to winning ways and claiming their first bit of silverware in the Carling Cup final. Mourinho escapes any FA sanctions after being ordered out of the dugout during the match. It has been a feisty week of cup football before a return to the Premiership.

Manchester United blow their chance to close the gap at the top to three points. Playing ahead of Chelsea, United are held to a 0–0 draw by ten-man Crystal Palace. So Chelsea's lead stays at a healthy five points, with Norwich away the first of two matches in hand to come.

SATURDAY, 5 MARCH 2005
NORWICH CITY 1, CHELSEA 3

Chelsea require two goals in seven second-half minutes from Kezman and Carvalho to silence relegation-haunted Norwich after Leon McKenzie dares to threaten an upset.

Mourinho deliberately chooses not to tell his players about United's earlier draw at Palace. 'We don't think about them – they think about us,' Mourinho says. 'I always like my players to be under pressure. Because Manchester United dropped points, it could influence my players in a negative way – so I did not want them to know.'

Cole does everything possible in his man-of-the-match display against Norwich to prove Chelsea can survive without the injured Robben. Cole's performance – only the second time he has completed ninety Premiership minutes for Mourinho – is not just about his splendid goal. There is also excellent movement and a growing awareness of when to perform the tricks and when to keep it simple.

Early on Makelele plays a through-pass to Cole, who is caught in possession and seems to have lost the ball as he crashes to the ground. But Cole jumps to his feet and is first to the loose ball. He strides on two paces and unleashes a left-foot shot that simply flies past Green.

But when McKenzie gets in front of Ferreira to head in a Huckerby cross – Norwich's first genuine chance of the match – it looks as though Chelsea have squandered two points. Cech's record run without conceding a goal finally ends at 1,025 Premiership minutes. Mourinho immediately springs into action, introducing Kezman and Gudjohnsen. He is instantly rewarded, with both substitutes involved in what proves to be the vital second. A Cole cross is deflected into Gudjohnsen's path, and he picks out Lampard with a half-volleyed forward pass. Lampard touches it past the keeper but it needs Kezman to guide it into the gaping net.

Carvalho grabs his first goal for the club, a header from a Lampard corner in the seventy-ninth minute, to end the contest. If anything sums up Chelsea's iron grip on the Premiership it is the almost total lack of celebrations. Brief hugs and grasped hands sum up a team already focusing on the next task with mighty Barcelona. As Mourinho predicted, the Carling Cup triumph makes his men more relaxed and able to play with conviction.

Mourinho comments, 'I try to show the players every day, every match, my experience and my confidence, just by saying to them, "How can we be under pressure when we have a six-point advantage with a game in hand?" I try to motivate them by saying one weekend that we need eight victories, the next that we need seven. Now we need six.'

Mourinho reveals that the players dedicated their win at Norwich to Wayne Bridge, who will be out for ten months, missing much of the start of the next season, after breaking his ankle in the FA Cup loss at Newcastle. Already linked with one left back, Mourinho will need two.

Mourinho is fined £5,000 and warned about his future conduct by an FA disciplinary commission for accusing Manchester United players of diving following the Carling Cup semi-final first-leg tie against Manchester United.

In a meeting with the Premier League's lawyers, Peter Kenyon states that a meeting has taken place with himself, Ashley Cole, Cole's agent Jonathan Barnett, Jose Mourinho and Pini Zahavi. However, Chelsea refute Arsenal's claims that they approached the England international, while also rebutting reports that they have opened provisional negotiations with Cole. Chelsea's testimony is that the player and his agent contacted Zahavi to request a meeting.

The Cole camp admit they asked to meet Zahavi as part of their strategy after contract talks with Arsenal turned sour. But Barnett declares, 'I am happy to confirm on the record that the accusations levelled at Ashley are entirely false. For it to be suggested that I cynically set up a meeting with Chelsea and dragged them to it almost against their will is ludicrous.' Cole is dropped to the bench by Arsène Wenger for Arsenal's FA Cup win at Bolton.

Mourinho gives evidence to the Premiership lawyers on the same day Cole turns up to present his side of the story. Mourinho backs up Kenyon's claim that Chelsea did not make an illegal approach. The Blues manager, like Kenyon, argues that they merely attended out of curiosity, listened to what Cole and his agent had to say and then left. Mourinho insists Cole was not enticed to quit the Gunners and that no offers were made. In his evidence, Cole is adamant he never had any intention of discussing anything with Kenyon and Mourinho. He tells the inquiry he was having a meeting with Barnett in his office when Zahavi called and told them he wanted to talk at the nearby Royal Park Hotel.

Mourinho is reported to have said, 'I never dreamt I could consider signing you. You are already the best left-back in the world but I want to see it in your face that you want to play for us. Join us and you can win everything – the Champions League, the Premier League … everything.' There was some speculation that Cole would be teaming up with Gerrard next season. Liverpool make it clear they are not lodging a complaint.

TUESDAY, 15 MARCH 2005
CHELSEA 1, WEST BROMWICH ALBION 0

Mourinho collects an award from the League Managers Association but, facing charges from the FA over the Ashley Cole affair and UEFA following comments after the Champions League clash with Barcelona, he has the worried look of a man at the centre of several storms. When Drogba scores, he rushes over to his manager, insisting he joins in the celebrations.

It is hardly the flourish of the spectacular against Barcelona but Drogba's first-half clincher sends them eleven points clear with just nine games to go. Steve Clarke says, 'Jose is only worried about winning trophies. We have one trophy already with the Carling Cup, we are through to the last eight of the Champions League and 11 points clear in the Premiership. We aim to add those two as well, so what more can we do? It's not won yet, but it's another big step on the way, with another three points. That's what we wanted before the game and that's what we got.'

Mourinho chooses to concentrate on the next assignment against Palace rather than worry about drawing Bayern Munich in the Champions League quarter-finals. He says, 'This is a time to remember we have not won the league. Chelsea have not won it for 50 years and this Chelsea side hasn't won it yet in 2005. We want to win the league and we want to win it properly. It is over a year since Chelsea have lost at home and that includes all the time I have been here. Our home record is good but it can still be even better. There's five more home league games and we're aiming at two more Champions League home games, so we can go as high as 24 home wins in one season. I believe we can achieve this.'

SATURDAY, 19 MARCH 2005
CHELSEA 4, CRYSTAL PALACE 1

Spring is in the air, Robben is back, and on a scorching afternoon Mourinho sports a scarf! Joe Cole responds to the long-awaited return of Robben by inspiring Chelsea to a convincing victory as Mourinho's side take another major step towards the title. Palace commit the cardinal sin of allowing Lampard far too much space outside the penalty box. Still 25 yards out from goal, he takes aim with 28 minutes gone and powers a superb drive into the corner of the net. Palace make Chelsea pay for an uncharacteristic defensive lapse just before the break. Chelsea fail to deal with a weak, low corner from Wayne Routledge, with Lampard missing his kick at the near post. The ball speeds across the turf to Aki Riihilahti, whose shot from just six yards out deflects slightly off Carvalho and into the net.

Cole has profited from Robben's injury-induced absence and his vital fifty-fourth-minute strike is proof of his renaissance. The midfielder scampers downfield as Chelsea counter-attack and, despite initially tripping over, he hauls himself to his feet and times his run perfectly to race onto Gudjohnsen's pass. Cole briefly weighs up his options before striking his shot into the far corner, leaving Kiraly helplessly rooted to the spot.

Mourinho initially turns to Tiago to shore up his midfield when Drogba comes off, but Robben is finally brought on with seventeen minutes left. Significantly, it is Duff – not Cole – who makes way. The Dutchman is immediately involved in the third goal, although there is little obvious danger until Kiraly's blunder allows Kezman's shot to slip through his grasp.

Robben almost scores himself in the closing stages before Kezman rounds off the scoring from close range in the last minute after a scramble in the Palace penalty area.

The board of the FA Premier League charges Chelsea, Jose Mourinho and Ashley Cole with breaches of their rules over the tapping-up affair. World Cup qualifiers mean another Premiership break but little rest for Chelsea's squad of international players.

But the internationals bring bad news for Chelsea when Arjen Robben limps out of Holland's 2–0 win in Romania after setting up the opening goal for Phillip Cocu. Mourinho spends part of the international break in Tel Aviv, invited by former Israeli Prime Minister Shimon Peres. 'Coming here makes you realise that football is not the most important thing. My world of football is very different to theirs. Football has a magical power in social terms. I am happy to be able to use that power to help this cause. Professional football does not always set the best example. I admit and accept that. When I have finished with football there are many things in the world that will make me feel happy. This is one of them. From now on, if there is anything I can do to help, I will. If they want my support they can count on me.

He adds that he plans to retire from football management at the age of fifty-five after spending another ten years with Chelsea and three years in charge of his native Portugal. Chelsea are dealt another major injury blow as Paulo Ferreira suffers a suspected fracture to his right foot during Portugal's World Cup qualifier against Slovakia. He is expected to miss the remainder of the season.

Reports in Portugal claim Mourinho may consider walking out on Chelsea at the end of the season. Chelsea immediately dismiss the story – which started on the privately owned Portuguese SIC television station – as nothing more than an April Fool. But the station has a close relationship with the Chelsea manager, who is due to start presenting his own chat show on the channel in May. Mourinho had been handed a two-match touchline ban by UEFA for comments about the referee in Chelsea's Champions League tie with Barcelona.

Mourinho, the reports claim, took his own legal advice – contacting lawyer Jean-Louis Dupont, who handled the Jean-Marc Bosman case. Mourinho felt an appeal was more than justified.

SATURDAY, 2 APRIL 2005
SOUTHAMPTON 1, CHELSEA 3

On the surface it is business as normal for Mourinho as Chelsea outclass Southampton on their home turf, where they have not lost since September. But with the dust still settling on his UEFA ban, Mourinho dodges the post-match media conference and beats a hasty retreat to the team bus.

Chelsea appear to be saving themselves for the Champions League clash with Bayern Munich as they play well within themselves. A dubious free-kick goes Chelsea's way and Lampard's thumping effort takes an outrageous deflection off Rory Delap on the end of the wall to confound Antti Niemi.

In the thirty-ninth minute Johnson's penetrating run past a series of half-hearted challenges ends with a subtle pull-back for Gudjohnsen to drill past Niemi for 2–0. Kevin Phillips gives the Saints hope just three minutes after coming on when he fires a left-foot shot from Delap's cross past Cech after a lapse from Gudjohnsen. But with eight minutes left, Chelsea unfurl the kind of smooth passing move that is the hallmark of a great team. It culminates with a slick pass from substitute Drogba to Gudjohnsen, who turns the final pass into the corner.

The strike, which confirms that Chelsea's lead at the top

will stretch to thirteen points after Manchester United's home draw with Blackburn earlier in the afternoon, is his fourteenth of the season, taking him past Drogba as the club's leading scorer.

SATURDAY, 9 APRIL 2005
CHELSEA 1, BIRMINGHAM CITY 1

Chelsea find it difficult to get to grips with a tenacious City side that deny their midfield time and space to weave its usual brand of free- flowing magic. In the end, Chelsea need a late strike from Drogba just to rescue a point, and Arsenal's victory at Middlesbrough cuts the lead to eleven points. Mourinho says he is content with a 'positive point', but admits, 'It was a bad performance in the first half. It looked like a friendly in August. Not enough ambition to win the game.'

It is Mourinho's first words in public for two weeks, which, for a man who can pack a lifetime's worth of controversy into a single press conference, is a stupendously long time. Mourinho adds that the rumours suggesting he is unhappy at the club are wide of the mark. 'We are fantastic,' he says. 'We could not be better. We have a trophy, we are top of the league by eleven points and we are in the quarter-finals of the Champions League and won the first game. We could not be better. I am happy. The only reason I am not happy is that we did not get the three points against Birmingham.

'Maybe this season has been better than everybody could dream, including me. I always thought we could win the league but to have an eleven-point lead with a month to go is better than I thought we could do. For me, being champions

71

today, next week or two weeks' time, away or at home, doesn't matter. I just want to be champions.'

Steve Bruce spends five minutes eulogising on the merits of Mourinho, conceding he can hardly find a fault. 'I think I speak for all managers when I say we've got huge respect for Mourinho,' he says. 'He has been a breath of fresh air for us all. We were getting a bit sick of Wenger v Fergie all the time. There's another one on the block now.'

A rare moment of dissatisfaction in the Chelsea camp occurs when William Gallas reveals he is fed up playing out of position at left- back. However, Chelsea dominate the nominations for the PFA Players' Player of the Year award with Terry, Lampard and Cech all on the shortlist, along with Thierry Henry – winner in 2004 – Crystal Palace's Andy Johnson and Steven Gerrard.

Next up for Chelsea is the showdown with Arsenal, and the good news is that Thierry Henry is out injured. Arsenal were the last team to beat the Blues at Stamford Bridge – thirty-five games and fourteen months ago. Arsène Wenger admits Chelsea have had an exceptional season. 'After 32 games there is no coincidence. You have to respect what Chelsea have done on the pitch. They are 11 points better so that means there was a gap this year. But it is not over yet, we have a chance to close the gap and then there are five games to go.'

WEDNESDAY, 20 APRIL 2005
CHELSEA 0, ARSENAL 0

Wenger shakes hands with Mourinho at the end and finally says, 'Of course Chelsea will win the title now. I always felt that if they didn't lose this game they would be champions – unless someone puts a bomb here! But they are worthy champions because they have been remarkably consistent and that is most difficult in top sport. I can only say congratulations for what they have achieved.'

Cheeky Blues fans make Ashley Cole feel at home by holding a placard saying 'Welcome Home'. But Cole doesn't have much to say to Mourinho, who even more cheekily gives him a high-five as the Arsenal defender leaves the field – just as he shook Steven Gerrard's hand after the Carling Cup final! However, neither side can make the breakthrough in a tense affair as the game ends goalless.

With the title now in touching distance, Lampard already has his sights on sustained success. 'The title is almost there but the hard thing now is to back it up,' he says. 'It's well documented that the second title is harder to win than the first and next season we'll start all over again. Arsenal haven't backed it up but have been a dominant force for the past few years. This year we're the best team. We have to make sure that we're not just the best team this year but the best for future seasons. We're all hungry and are not going to settle for one title. We want to win everything we're involved in and we will play with the same attitude next year.'

Mourinho admits he has made errors during the season but says what matters is the final outcome. 'My life in football is about being popular and loved by my team's supporters – and being hated by the opponents' supporters. That's the way I want to carry on because it means we're winning things. Of course I've made mistakes. I can analyse a situation and have the wrong point of view. Of course there will be fights. I can't say I don't like a fight because that's my nature. But sometimes maybe I must be in control of a situation and not react. I always try to do the best for my team. What matters is my club and my players. When we have the cups in our hands we will forget everything.

'I think it is great for English football that a club who has not been champions for 50 years becomes the champion. It is good to run away with this. I can tell you that in Portugal we have been looking for something like this for a long time.'

SATURDAY, 23 APRIL 2005
CHELSEA 3, FULHAM 1

It is fifty years to the day since Chelsea last lifted the title and the captain of that side, Roy Bentley, now eighty-one, returns to mark the occasion. Robben destroyed Fulham in the game at Craven Cottage and Chelsea are labouring until he replaces Cole. Robben's match-winning display moves Chelsea within two points of just the second title in their history.

Cole gives Chelsea the ideal platform when he swivels onto Drogba's pass and sends a scorching shot past Edwin van der Sar with seventeen minutes gone. Just before half-time Carvalho is guilty of an uncharacteristic error in allowing Collins John to latch onto Luis Boa Morte's pass before finishing. Robben comes on at the interval and changes the game instantly. He speeds past Moritz Volz and expertly picks out Lampard to score before Gudjohnsen makes certain of victory with just four minutes left as he is put clear by substitute Tiago and notches his hundredth goal in English football.

Mourinho assesses the season so far and says, 'It's not about the treble. The Carling Cup is not such a big thing, but at that time for Chelsea to win a trophy was very important, be it a small or a big competition. But to win the championship after fifty years is very big. Fifty years ago and the fans have not forgotten – this year they will not forget either. Whether it is the players, the staff, the managers... whoever. Roy Bentley is rightly remembered as the captain of that team and so too will John Terry be of this one. Nobody forgets their names.'

John Terry's remarkable season is recognised as he receives the PFA Player of the Year award from Alan Shearer. Terry clutches his precious silverware and refuses to put it down as he discusses Mourinho. 'Jose has been fantastic; I can't speak highly enough of him for what he's done for me personally. He has given me a lot of confidence, gave me the armband at the start of the season and made me believe I'm up there with the best players in the Premiership.'

Meanwhile, Arsenal make Chelsea wait to clinch the title by beating local rivals Spurs at Highbury. Mourinho wants to keep his men fresh for the semi-final decider at Liverpool, but also wants to finish off the job of winning the title at Bolton. Bolton are still chasing a Champions League qualifying spot, four points behind Everton in fourth. Ahead of the match, Allardyce taunts Mourinho by claiming Wenger should be known as the 'Special One'. He says, 'Wenger has been the best foreign manager in this country. He is one of the most successful managers there have been here and he showed the way forward in this country with the players he has brought in. Some of the foreign coaches who have come over here have been a disaster. Jacques Santini at Tottenham this season, for instance, lasted no more than two minutes.' But Allardyce adds, 'Mourinho has done brilliantly because he has grasped it in one year. He has swanned into London and Chelsea and said from the start he was going to be successful. He hung his neck on the line and it looks like he is going to achieve. Chelsea should not only win the championship but there is a big possibility they could win the European Cup.

The morning papers are full of headlines of cracks in the camp, based on Robben's reluctance to start the tie with Liverpool and Kezman's frustrations as a squad player. Suggestions that Robben refused to play when Duff failed a fitness test are wide of the mark, and the winger came off the bench for the last thirty minutes.

Chelsea issue a statement insisting the relationship between Robben and Mourinho is 'excellent' and maintain he is 'working hard to get back to full fitness'. Chelsea fans will toast former vice-chairman Matthew Harding if the team clinches the Premiership title at Bolton. The millionaire businessman was killed in a helicopter crash returning from a League Cup tie at Bolton in October 1996. Harding had big ambitions for the club he had supported all his life and had invested in Chelsea. His widow Ruth says, 'It's a fantastic idea and lovely that the fans still remember him. I don't know what the fans are planning for Bolton but it is a lovely gesture and one which is greatly appreciated by all the family.'

When Chelsea last won the title, the rest of the country was debating how Britain would cope with the arrival of more immigrants from the Caribbean; the Government promised women working in the Civil Service would have equal pay with men by 1961; Sir Winston Churchill resigned as Prime Minister and Anthony Eden, his successor, quickly called a general election that increased the Tory majority; Princess

Margaret announced that she was calling off her wedding to Group Captain Peter Townsend; James Dean was killed when his Porsche plunged off the road in California; in Britain, motorists were being a little more careful, especially when the price of a gallon of petrol rose to 4s 6d.

SATURDAY, 30 APRIL 2005
BOLTON WANDERERS 0, CHELSEA 2

Mourinho takes his place in history as the first foreign coach to win the championship in his first season in English football, and it vindicates the confidence he has had since the day he arrived. Lampard has been immense with goals and performances, and his match-winning brace seals his own contribution to the title as the team's top scorer from midfield. Quite an achievement.

Mourinho's managerial genius, combined with hunger, desire and ferocity of spirit, are the cornerstones of the title triumph. He immediately expresses his affinity to the club. 'Am I the "Special One"?' he asks. 'No, the whole group at Chelsea is special and no one can say we didn't deserve this title. The players have been fantastic. I am proud of every single one of them and they are worthy champions. But Roman Abramovich, the big boss, also deserves it, and so does Peter Kenyon and his group. This group is really special – that's why I want to stay with them for the maximum time, maybe for longer than the contract I have.'

As his players celebrate in front of the travelling supporters, Mourinho sits in the dugout with his mobile phone. 'I was speaking to my wife and children,' he says. 'They went to

Portugal for the weekend but they saw it live and they are happy of course – like me. Football is crazy sometimes. We knew a few months ago we had a lead of some distance but anything is possible – so only now is the moment we really feel we are champions. It's not easy the way we are champions and it was the same story this weekend. This game was the perfect game to be champions because Bolton have a difficult style of play and we had to adapt – and we did. We fought like lions. This squad is incredible. When we play, we play together. When we fight, we fight together. When we suffer, we suffer together. And no one who has any sense of fairness can deny that we deserve the title."

Terry reveals how Mourinho – who dashed away from the celebrations to allow his players to take the glory – lost his temper after a goalless first half. 'Bolton probably out-battled us in the first half which didn't please the manager. At half-time he gave us a bit of a bollocking, but we came out and responded well in the second half. The gaffer was fuming. He had a go at everybody, telling us we were 45 minutes from the Premiership and that we had to liven up, that we'd have been better putting him out there than us. And he was right, too. Everybody was under-performing.'

Mourinho has to start the match without his two wingers, Duff and Robben, while Joe Cole is left on the bench. There is also a scare in the first minute when Lampard shoots from distance and pulls up, temporarily lame. To the considerable relief of Mourinho and his men, the England midfielder is able to run off the problem.

Terry plays on despite having a black eye that restricts his vision in one eye following a clash with Davies just before half-time. Tempers start to fray, especially when Geremi goes down easily under a tackle from El-Hadji Diouf, which earns the Senegal international a booking. Bolton are livid when, from the ensuing free-kick, Chelsea seize the lead against the run of play. Lampard shows great composure in cutting back inside Vincent Candela as he seizes on Drogba's headed knockdown, before picking his spot past Jussi Jaaskelainen.

Mourinho is concerned with protecting his side's advantage, with the towering figure of Huth soon replacing Drogba. That leaves Gudjohnsen up front on his own, while Chelsea form a five-man defence. Bolton rally once again, but they are caught on the break with fourteen minutes left as Lampard races clear. The midfielder has Carvalho bursting his lungs to provide an option to his right, but instead he uses the defender as a decoy before dipping his shoulder and skipping past Jaaskelainen. His finish is assured and sparks delirium on the touchline, with Mourinho dancing for joy and Drogba even seizing an inflatable Premiership trophy from the crowd in expected triumph.

He has to wait just fifteen minutes longer to repeat the feat, this time for real, as Chelsea's path to the title is complete. Roman Abramovich parades arm in arm with Terry and Lampard on the pitch as the Chelsea pair join the fans singing the owner's name.

Terry is still inside the ground performing his media rounds, gripping a little transparent plastic bag tightly to his side: inside is his shirt from the game – a memento he will treasure forever. Some of his team-mates threw theirs into the crowd after the final whistle. Others changed into T-shirts with 'Champions' written on them. Like Lampard, Terry played in every game of Chelsea's march to the title.

Mourinho only gives one interview, to Sky TV, sending a

message to journalists that he has no problem with the press but wants the players to bask in the glory. Mourinho's first season has never been dull. Chelsea faced twelve separate disciplinary charges. Two months into the season the club was charged by the FA, along with West Ham, with failing to ensure the proper behaviour of fans during their Carling Cup tie. After the first leg of the Carling Cup semi-final against Manchester United, he described the second half as 'whistle after whistle, fault after fault, cheat after cheat'. Guilty of improper conduct, he was fined £5,000 and warned about his conduct. February was a bad month. Chelsea were fined £15,000 after a brawl in their Premiership match against Blackburn. After the match against Barcelona in the Nou Camp, UEFA charged Chelsea, Mourinho, Clarke and Miles, the club's security officer, with making false declarations about an alleged half-time chat between Anders Frisk, the Swedish referee, and Frank Rijkaard, the Barcelona coach. A £33,000 fine for Chelsea and £9,000 for Mourinho resulted. Mourinho collected another warning for his 'silence' gesture to Liverpool fans during the Carling Cup final, and the affair of an alleged illegal approach to Ashley Cole, rumbles on.

Kenyon hails Mourinho as 'undoubtedly' the best manager in the Premiership and predicts that the forty-two-year-old will remain in charge at Stamford Bridge for at least another nine years. Chelsea expect to secure his long-term future by finalising the terms of a five-year deal within days.

'In order to be a top team, you have to win things more than once and do it over a sustained period of time. That's what attracted Jose to Chelsea. He is a manager that can get us there and I know that is what he wants to do. He wants not to tell everyone that he's the best manager in the world, but to prove that he is.'

Gary Lineker gives his verdict on Chelsea's season. 'People will accuse them of buying the title. But although Mourinho has had a massive budget, you still have to get the right players in and put a team together. If you want proof that money does not give you the right to dominate everything, just look at Real Madrid, who have spent more than anyone and now look certain to finish a second successive season without a trophy. Chelsea have spent big, but they haven't gone out and bought Madrid-style *galacticos*.

'For all his buys, Mourinho has achieved something that untold millions cannot bring into a club: a sense of camaraderie and fierce collective spirit. And although there has been something of a siege mentality inside the club, after all the shenanigans surrounding the Barcelona game and referee Anders Frisk, that consistency and team spirit has been obvious from the early weeks of the season. Of course, when you start well and build up a winning habit, everything is rosy in the garden. But Mourinho had to construct that positive mentality in a dressing room full of new signings and huge egos. That he managed to do so in such a short space of time is remarkable, especially when he was new to the club himself. In fact, managing to adjust so swiftly to the Premiership and all the differing demands compared to other European leagues is perhaps his greatest achievement. Maybe he really is the "Special One".'

Despite his 'special' talents, even Mourinho cannot prevent Chelsea crashing out of the Champions League at Anfield. His immediate reaction is to give the players two days off while he returns to the Bridge to agree a new five-year contract and plan for next season with the vow that his side will come back even better. Mourinho says, 'I am delighted to be signing this new contract. My heart is with Chelsea and the fantastic group of players I have. They have done a great job this season. But the vision of the owner and the board for the future of Chelsea is also one I want to be part of. I'm totally behind this project and their support in achieving it means Chelsea is the place where I will be happiest in my work. I cannot imagine another club or situation where I would be happier.'

Chelsea insert a hands-off clause worth more than £5 million into his new contract. His new deal is worth £5.2 million a year, but the real value could be as much as double that with more success. Mourinho's contract contains a clause stipulating that his next employers must pay Chelsea the value of his contract for a year should he leave within the next five years. Mourinho and Abramovich would like European Footballer of the Year Andriy Shevchenko, but the Ukrainian star wants to stay in Italy. Earmarked to leave the club are Crespo, on loan at AC, and Veron, on loan at Inter, plus Geremi, Smertin, Parker, Cudicini, Johnson, and Kezman. However, top target Steven Gerrard hints he might stay at Anfield. If Gerrard commits to Liverpool, Lyon's highly rated midfielder Michael Essien remains the favoured alternative.

Frank Lampard beats off the challenge of John Terry to land the Football Writers' Association vote as Footballer of the Year, becoming only the second Englishman since Alan Shearer in 1994 to win football's oldest and most prestigious individual award. Teddy Sheringham was the other in 2001.

Mourinho insists that winning the Premiership and not the Champions League was always their top priority. 'I always say, since I arrived here, that the best team always wins the league championship,' he says. 'What I can also say is that there are not many times when the best team wins the Champions League. In the Premiership things can happen, you can make a mistake one day, you will have players missing another day, you will have bad luck or good luck in other days but at the end, when the battle is over, the best team always wins the title. That is why the Premiership was our top target. We wanted to prove we are the best. So to win the Premiership and prove we are the best makes me very happy because we are a young group who has worked together just this season. To win two out of four trophies was very good and just what we want at the beginning of a wonderful Chelsea period.'

'My contract is for five years from now. It means the club very much wants me to stay and I also want very much to stay. We are committed. We want to work together for the future of this club. This season was not the end, just the start. To win the championship after 50 years was a fantastic achievement. We must look forward now to win more silverware, not after another half a century but year after year.'

'We will be back for pre-season training on 6 July and I expect to have all the new signings in place by then. Last year I did not arrive at Chelsea until the end of May and I had just one month to make a lot of changes to the playing and coaching staff. This time I only need to make a couple of changes and I have two months to do it. So it will be much easier. It will be difficult for me to sign any English players because to improve the squad I need the very top players. But the best Englishmen are already with the top Premiership clubs. In Italy it's easy because AC Milan are not afraid to sell to Inter or Juventus. But here Chelsea and Manchester United will not swap players because we're scared they will perform well for our rivals.'

SATURDAY, 7 MAY 2005
CHELSEA 1, CHARLTON ATHLETIC 0

It's a day of celebration as John Terry lifts the Premiership trophy, 50 years after Chelsea's last league triumph. The players are still on the pitch nearly two hours after the final whistle as Mourinho quietly leaves the stadium with wife Tami and kids Matilde and Jose. 'I am happy, I am tired and I need a holiday,' Jose declares. 'But now we look ahead. Enjoy today because tomorrow we start planning for next season. It's not in my nature to be happy with what I have got now ... I want more.'

Chelsea's unbeaten league run stretches to twenty-seven games. Carlo Cudicini, appearing in his first league game of the campaign, has the satisfaction of keeping the clean sheet that takes Chelsea past the Premiership record of twenty-four in a season. In his programme notes he simply lists the 102 members of his staff – from captain to cook – and declares, 'These are my champions.'

Compared to the celebrations, the match is merely a side-show. Chelsea wait until the final minute before Lampard is brought down on the edge of the box. The foul looks to have been outside the area and contact is, at best, minimal, but the penalty is still given. The ball is handed to Makelele, whose first effort is saved, but he nets the rebound with a mishit to score his first goal for the club in his ninety-fourth appearance.

Mourinho insists his players disobeyed his strict orders. 'I said if there's a penalty – Frank Lampard. If there's a penalty in minute 90 with us leading 2–0, then Makelele.'

The Premiership trophy awaits and Stamford Bridge's celebrations can finally begin in earnest. There is an elongated presentation ceremony as all the backroom staff are individually introduced and paraded before the fans and make their way to the winners' podium before the players. Mourinho explains, 'On the pitch I got my entire staff together and said to them, "Enjoy the day because tomorrow we must think about the future."'

Before the 2005 team lift the trophy, thirteen members of the 1955 side are brought out with the old Football League trophy. Terry and Lampard hand over the trophy to them that was never publicly presented fifty years ago. It is a wonderful addition to the occasion. Then it is on to the main event. 'Are you watching, Arsenal?' and 'Chelsea are back!' are sung with gusto as staff and players are brought out of the tunnel one by one. Roy Bentley and Stan Willemse, legends from 1955, carry out the Premiership trophy and Terry lifts it to the accompaniment of explosions and streamers.

Finally, the team reluctantly troop off down the tunnel, Lampard, Terry, Gudjohnsen and the trophy the last to leave. One banner reads 'What blip? Chelsea FC Champions 2005', while another simply states 'Jose Mourinho for Prime Minister'.

TUESDAY, 10 MAY 2005
MANCHESTER UNITED 1, CHELSEA 3

For the first time in 103 league matches, United are beaten after taking the lead. Goals from Tiago, Gudjohnsen and Cole not only inflict United's only home league defeat of the season, but also allow Mourinho's men to rewrite the record books. Victory means Chelsea break United's Premiership records for points and wins in a season. After going behind to Ruud van Nistelrooy's goal, Chelsea take total control. Those United fans who remain to the end clap Chelsea off the pitch. Sir Alex Ferguson now knows just how far his team are behind Chelsea.

Ferguson lauds Mourinho's 'formidable achievement' in his programme notes and promises 'no cheap Portuguese plonk in the manager's office tonight, but fine wine deserving of a champion.'

'For a manager new to the country and the English game, breaking entirely new ground, it is a formidable achievement. We know Chelsea have raised the financial stakes but money isn't the total reason for success. There's still a team to be built, balance to be created, tactics to be applied and spirit generated. All this Jose has done. To come into the Premiership and leave us all standing is brilliant and everyone at Manchester United offers sincere congratulations.' Ferguson makes his players form a guard of honour for Mourinho's title-winners – a sporting gesture, although possibly done to remind his charges that their standards have slipped. United are ahead, with Keane and particularly Wayne Rooney playing their parts in Van Nistelrooy's eighth-minute poacher's goal.

Chelsea respond stylishly to the rare indignity of falling behind in a Premiership game and, within ten minutes, the new champions are level. Tiago collects possession 35 yards out and spots the United players are dropping off him expecting a pass, so he lets fly. His beautiful arcing shot rises and dips, leaving Roy Carroll completely bemused in the United goal.

After the break it is not long before Chelsea are in front

as Lampard feeds Tiago, whose driven low pass is controlled by Gudjohnsen. The Icelander waits for Carroll to commit himself and coolly dinks the ball over the on-rushing keeper. Gaps begin to appear in the United defence and, sure enough, inside the last ten minutes, Wes Brown's clearance is cut out by Lampard, who darts into the area and cuts the ball back for Cole. There are clear suspicions of offside as he turns the ball home, but the travelling Chelsea faithful are not bothered.

Mourinho describes beating United's record points total as 'perfect'. 'The record was our motivation,' says Mourinho. 'We wanted to beat it and this is a special moment. It is the perfect way to do it – at a great stadium against a team who in Sir Alex Ferguson have a manager who leads by example in success and fair play.'

There is only ever going to be one winner of the Barclays Manager of the Year award. Mourinho's landslide victory in the championship race earns him the required majority in the voting panel's ballot.

SUNDAY, 15 MAY 2005
NEWCASTLE 1, CHELSEA 1

Mourinho concedes that he will struggle to surpass this record-breaking season as Chelsea move on to an unprecedented Premiership haul of ninety-five points and set yet another record for the fewest goals conceded in a season – a mere fifteen.

Newcastle are gifted with the lead when Geremi inadvertently diverts the ball in after Alan Shearer rises to head on Charles N'Zogbia's thirty-second-minute corner.

The home side's advantage is short-lived. Celestine Babayaro misjudges Lampard's through-ball and resorts to fouling Gudjohnsen inside the penalty box. Lampard steps up to beat Given, driving the ball straight down the middle, despite losing his footing as he strikes the ball, for his nineteenth goal of a memorable campaign. Chelsea's record on the road is fifteen wins, three draws and one defeat. Their total of ninety-five points – meaning they finish twelve points ahead of Arsenal – will take some matching. So will the record twenty-five clean sheets.

'It is an unbelievable record,' says Mourinho with all the modesty he can muster. 'Ninety-five points is a lot of points. The clean sheets gave us a big push to be champions. At the beginning of the season, when we were not so fluent, clean sheets gave us a lot of points. People said Chelsea were boring, but Chelsea were building.'

And Mourinho has not finished building just yet. 'We started thinking about the next campaign a few months ago,' he says. 'It's easy to prepare for next season as we have a group of champions and want to keep them. We want to make two or three adjustments but we have the base.'

CHAMPIONS LEAGUE TRIBULATIONS

Chelsea's Champions League campaign couldn't start with a more controversial and intriguing draw in Monte Carlo. Jose Mourinho will begin the defence of the Champions League he won with Porto in a group that includes CSKA Moscow: a team sponsored by Roman Abramovich. The other teams in Group H are Paris Saint-Germain and Porto.

After carrying out a week-long investigation, UEFA declare them- selves satisfied that Chelsea owner Abramovich, who has ploughed £40 million into a sponsorship deal with CSKA, does not have a controlling interest in CSKA Moscow.

Meanwhile anyone who thinks Mourinho cares only for big-money signings should see him on the morning before the Champions League draw. He is watching Chelsea Under-13s from behind one of the goals. 'That's the second time he's been down here in two weeks,' says Chelsea's academy director Neil Bath.

Striker Didier Drogba expects a hostile reception from Chelsea's opening Champions League tie in Paris crowd because of his Marseille associations. So far this season PSG have failed to win a single league game and are fourteenth in the table.

TUESDAY, 14 SEPTEMBER 2004
PARIS SAINT-GERMAIN 0, CHELSEA 3

Jeered by PSG fans from the moment his name is announced, striker Didier Drogba has cause to laugh after his two goals secure an away victory that already makes Chelsea's progression to the second round look a safe bet.

Joe Cole's clever turn brings the corner that results in the opener. Frank Lampard floats in a cross from the left, goalkeeper Lionel Letizi flaps at the ball and John Terry can hardly believe his good fortune as he nods in. Mateja Kezman is brought down for a free-kick fifteen minutes from time and Drogba picks his spot over the wall, leaving the keeper without a prayer.

The game is settled in added time when Tiago wins the ball and Cole instantly releases Kezman through on the left. The Serb, on for Gudjohnsen, shoots straight at Letizi, but Drogba is perfectly placed to strike home the rebound.

Mischief in the fixture calendar brings FC Porto to Stamford Bridge four months after Mourinho led Porto to victory in the European Cup. Abramovich paid £33 million to Porto for defenders Paulo Ferreira and Ricardo Carvalho. Porto also sold Deco to Barcelona and Pedro Mendes to Tottenham.

Despite their newfound wealth, Porto are struggling. Going into the weekend, they have drawn all three of their domestic Superliga matches and, in their opening Champions League contest, they could do no better than manage a goalless draw at home to CSKA Moscow.

With six wins and two draws in his first eight matches, the only thing upsetting Mourinho is what he perceives to be persistent and unfair criticism of his tactics.

WEDNESDAY, 29 SEPTEMBER 2004
CHELSEA 3, PORTO 1

The match begins with an unsavoury incident as Jose Mourinho goes over to shake the hands of Porto fans before kick-off and a yob pushes forward and spits on his shirt. Disgusted at what has happened, Mourinho takes a step back and security guards manhandle the idiot out of the ground.

After seven minutes, Chelsea score their first goal when Damien Duff flicks the ball over the head of a defender for Eidur Gudjohnsen to hook a first-time cross into the middle, where the unmarked Alexei Smertin drives a shot deep into the far corner for his first goal for the club. It brings the former Porto boss to his feet in celebration – not far from the Portuguese fans – which, in turn, produces a warning from the fourth official for Mourinho to cool it. With Chelsea coasting on the back of Smertin's opener, Drogba strikes with a header from a Duff free-kick in the fiftieth minute to reignite the game.

Benni McCarthy then gives Porto a lifeline by netting a sixty-eighth-minute rebound after Petr Cech fails to hold a stinging shot from Carlos Alberto, which skims John Terry's head, but the Chelsea skipper takes just two minutes to respond, diving full length to head home Frank Lampard's free-kick.

After the game, a jubilant Mourinho lavishes praise on a group of players he clearly believes is good enough to bring the Champions League trophy to Stamford Bridge. 'It's great. We've beaten the European champions, have six points and are in a fantastic position to go through to the next stage. Chelsea have now ended a run of four successive Champions League draws at Stamford Bridge. It also marks the end of a record-breaking run of twelve Champions League games without defeat for Porto and continues a sorry run in which they have been beaten seven times in eight trips to England. Chelsea face CSKA Moscow in a week.

Mourinho's main worry is the form of Vagner Love, the Brazilian whose goals have taken CSKA to the top of the Russian league, which they lead by one point with four games to play.

WEDNESDAY, 20 OCTOBER 2004
CHELSEA 2, CSKA MOSCOW 0

Before the match, Jose Mourinho is presented with the European Club Manager of the Year award by Sir Bobby Robson.

In the ninth minute, Chelsea make the Russians pay when they expose their defensive frailties as John Terry stoops to head home Lampard's corner from close range. It is his third goal of the season and maintains his record of scoring in every Champions League game this campaign.

CSKA's aerial weakness at the back undoes them again in first- half injury-time when Duff swings over a free-kick from the right-hand side of the area and Gudjohnsen runs unchallenged between two defenders and leaps to power his header past Igor Akinfeev. A win in Moscow will guarantee Chelsea top spot and would render the visit of PSG largely academic.

Mourinho's side need just a point in Moscow to claim their place in the last sixteen of the European Cup and they trail Premiership leaders Arsenal only on goal difference. But he plays down growing expectations of a double by claiming that clubs from Europe's biggest leagues cannot conquer the continent as well as their own country. 'I know Manchester United won the title and the Champions League in 1999 but it's really difficult. It happens once in a lifetime. For me it's happened twice in the last two years [with Porto]. I don't think this will be the third consecutive year.'

Mourinho insists this is just another game for Abramovich, which is hard to believe. The Russian is on home soil and, as well as his sponsorship of CSKA, he is also a close friend of the club's president, Evgeny Giner.

Victory will allow Chelsea to turn their attention to the Premiership. Indeed, they face Arsenal just five days after their final Champions League group game, away to Porto, which may be meaningless by then. A result here could make the twin challenge less of an impossible task.

TUESDAY, 2 NOVEMBER 2004
CSKA MOSCOW 0, CHELSEA 1

Mourinho hails Arjen Robben as his 'extra dimension' after the Dutchman's first goal enables Chelsea to become the first team to qualify for the last sixteen, with two games to spare. Robben's sweetly stroked first-half finish is enough to complete Chelsea's perfect passage through Group H. The build-up to the twenty-third-minute goal is elegant as Robben slips through to find Damien Duff's diagonal run before racing into the box to receive the Irishman's back-heel.

The finish is sublime, as Robben allows the ball to run beyond the lunge of Sergei Semak before looking up and passing it left-footed into the bottom corner. Chelsea have conceded only four times in sixteen matches this season and their performances will have been noted in Madrid, Barcelona, Milan and Turin, as well as Highbury and Old Trafford.

Having now won the group, Chelsea are free to focus on the Premiership until the knockout stages begin at the end of February, though there will be no let-up from Mourinho. He says, 'We will face the next stage against the second-placed team but I promise CSKA that we will play exactly the same way against PSG and Porto. Anyone who thinks we will take it easy is making a big mistake.'

The French club are third in the Group H table with four points and desperately need good results to progress. When Mourinho left the pitch in the Lokomotiv Stadium after victory over CSKA Moscow, he assured CSKA coach Valeri Gazzayev that, even though they were through to the last sixteen, his team would not be relaxing in their final fixtures against Paris Saint-Germain and FC Porto.

WEDNESDAY, 24 NOVEMBER 2004
CHELSEA 0, PARIS SAINT-GERMAIN 0

PSG have failed to win an away game in Europe for seven years. But the French club have plenty to play for with qualification between them, Porto and CSKA Moscow still in the balance but the match never catches fire. Jose Mourinho rests nearly £80 million' worth of talent in Petr Cech, John Terry, Eidur Gudjohnsen, Damien Duff, Claude Makelele and Tiago. Didier Drogba returns from injury to sit on the bench but Chelsea still lose their 100 per cent record in Group H. Having already reached the second phase before the game starts, Chelsea do not create a real chance until the eighty-first minute, when Drogba fires straight at keeper Lionel Letizi.

Mourinho makes no excuses for sending out a much-changed side. 'The fact that I rested a lot of players was good. My attitude will be the same against Porto in the sense that we will try to win. We did not give the match to PSG – they had to fight.' Reflecting on the end of Chelsea's perfect record in the Champions League, Mourinho says, 'It's nice to have a 100 per cent record. But the first objective in this competition is to go through.'

Ahead of his first return to face Porto since his summer departure, Mourinho relates how his greatest triumph – managing the European champions in 2004 – nearly turned into a nightmare. The evening before Porto beat Monaco 3–0 in Gelsenkirchen, Mourinho took a call. It was from a well-known figure in Porto's underworld. 'The person on the other end told me, "You think you're the best, you bastard. We won't do anything now because you have a final tomorrow. But as soon as it's over, consider yourself a dead man because we'll get you. As soon as you get back to Porto, your fate is sealed. You don't have a chance." I replied, "You must be mad, I don't know what you're talking about."'

Porto president Pinta da Costa adds to the controversy by claiming that Mourinho deserves the threats because of his 'bizarre' behaviour and insists he left the club in a mess by quitting with two years left on his contract.

In these circumstances, Chelsea change their travel plans, bring in private security guards and take police advice on whether Mourinho will be breaking UEFA rules by ducking public appearances. The team will not train on the Porto pitch before the game and Mourinho will skip UEFA's compulsory pre-match press conference.

Chelsea receive a police escort from the airport to their hotel and Steve Clarke admits, 'We are expecting a hostile atmosphere but that is the case in all European away matches. I don't know how Porto's fans will react to Jose. All I know is that, if he won the European Cup for Chelsea and then came back to Stamford Bridge with another club, Jose would get a fantastic reception.'

Da Costa makes it clear he will not be shaking the hand of Mourinho, but the Chelsea coach will find at least one friendly face in the Porto ranks. Defender Pedro Emanuel insists, 'Meeting Mourinho again is going to be very special. He was the person who brought me to Porto and who took a chance on me. I had an excellent relationship with him because of all the good work he did during his time at this club.'

TUESDAY, 7 DECEMBER 2004
FC PORTO 2, CHELSEA 1

Ruthless Mourinho shatters any hopes that he will make things easy for his old side when he fields a powerful-looking team. However, Porto are desperate to avoid becoming the first defending champions to crash out of the competition at the group stages and they are also motivated to prevent their ex-coach Mourinho from being the man who knocks them out. They also cling to the fact that, in seven matches on their home turf, they have never been beaten by English opposition.

This, however, is no ordinary English opposition. Damien Duff strikes on thirty-three minutes. A solo run is capped by a powerful strike, which Nuno E Santo lets slip through his fingers to prove exactly why he is normally on the bench when Victor Baia is fit.

Diego responds with a stunning goal on the hour. Petr Cech is left rooted to the spot as the Brazilian playmaker sends a 25-yard volley scorching past him with such ferocity that it nearly leaves a hole in the net. Benni McCarthy then strikes with a header to inflict the first defeat on Chelsea in the Champions League and only the second reverse of the season. Before this setback, Mourinho has lost just once in his twenty-four games in charge.

The possible opponents for Chelsea in the Champions League draw in Nyon are Real Madrid, Barcelona, Bayern Munich, PSV Eindhoven and Werder Bremen.

Mourinho is specific about who he wants Chelsea to face: he wants the Catalan giants. After all, he learned his trade at the Nou Camp under Bobby Robson. 'For emotional reasons, I'd like to play Barca. First of all I love the club and the city; I spent four incredible years there. And the second reason is because everyone says they're Europe's best, who play beautiful football. I'd like to play them.

'Everyone is tipping them to win the competition. They play great football and it would be two incredible matches. The Spanish leaders against the English leaders would be a fantastic game – the most powerful tie of the draw.'

As group winners, Arsenal and Chelsea get to play their first-leg games away. When the draw is made, Chelsea are matched against the sixteen-time Spanish title-winners Barcelona, just as Mourinho predicted. Barcelona have met Chelsea once before in the Champions League, at the quarter-final stage in April 2000. The Catalans overturned a 3–1 first-leg defeat at Stamford Bridge to go through 6–4 on aggregate after a 5–1 extra-time victory at the Nou Camp.

Mourinho shrugs off the dangers of facing the runaway La Liga leaders by claiming his number-one priority is to see Chelsea crowned as English champions for the first time in fifty years. 'I've never won the Premiership and I like to win new things. The Premiership is the ultimate test. It takes a great team to win the Champions League – but the great teams still need luck. There are almost 40 games in England and only the best team wins.'

Mourinho reckons he learned the skills that have made him Europe's hottest boss working under Bobby Robson and Dutchman Louis van Gaal at Barcelona. He left four years ago after helping break Chelsea hearts in that epic 6–4 Champions League quarter- final double bill. He says, 'I go back to Barcelona as European Champion and Chelsea manager. I have a friend in every corner, so it will be a very emotional time for me. But I am keen to play against them because they want to win and play football the pure way. Barcelona is more than a football club; it represents a country. Catalonia is for them a country and Barcelona is its face around the world.

'My son, Jose, was born in Barcelona and has a Spanish passport; he is a little Catalan, so my blood is speaking here. But he will be supporting Chelsea.

Mourinho continues, 'My dream final would be Chelsea v Arsenal. English football hasn't won enough in Europe; that's not right. It's time to put an end to that injustice.'

Barcelona boss Frank Rijkaard is a meticulous manager and has spent time analysing the way Chelsea play. 'I've seen some matches on the telly, they are a great team. Very functional…'

That subtle put-down highlights Barcelona's contrasting reputation for playing football rich in finesse and skill. The personal battle of the coaches will be as fascinating as the on-field struggle. Though there are obvious similarities, both being sophisticated, forty-two-year-old multi-linguists oozing self-worth, there is a plain distinction. If Mourinho's searing ambition is motivated by his failures as a player who never came close to the first rank, Rijkaard will always form one point of a sublime triangle of Dutch talent alongside Ruud Gullit and Marco van Basten. Rijkaard has won the European Cup three times – twice with Milan and once with Ajax – and could become one of the few men to lift the trophy as both a player and manager.

Acknowledging Rijkaard's 'fantastic' playing legacy, Mourinho remarks that, as a manager, his counterpart 'has zero trophies and I have a lot of them.'

'I haven't met him yet,' Rijkaard replies. 'All I know is what we see on TV or read in the papers. Our papers are very interested in him because he worked here once.' Rijkaard is surprised by the possibility of verbal sparring. 'You call them mind games? How do they work?' After hearing a few examples of Mourinho's more cunning jibes, Rijkaard laughs loudly. 'Thank you! Thank you! I look forward to this kind of game.'

Rijkaard will find it hard to avoid talking about Mourinho. 'I can't say yet if I will like him. How can you really judge a man until you come face to face? Maybe I'll find out what he's really like over these next few weeks. I know he's very successful but we'll learn a little more about both him and his team. He can say the same for me. So, sure, when we finally meet, it could be quite a moment.'

Mourinho prepares Chelsea for his biggest game since arriving in English football. 'I have to defend what is mine. The Champions League is mine at the moment. I am the last winner as manager of the Champions League – so it is my competition. I have to try and fight for Chelsea and I have to try and fight for myself by defending my cup until the last moment. Maybe winning the Champions League enabled me to come to a big football country like this. The competition means a lot to me. At 42, I am very young as a manager. I have 15 more years to work in football. I hope to get that taste of winning the Champions League again. But it is so difficult to win. You can perform well, have a good team and have big ambition. But make one mistake and you are out of the competition – even if you don't deserve to be.' Mourinho has already formulated a plan he believes will neutralise Eto'o and Ronaldinho, and his self-belief is illustrated by his suggestion that his first six months at Chelsea have already begun to transform the face of English football.

Chelsea's preferred 4-3-3 formation has been adopted by Manchester United, other Premiership sides and was tried – unsuccessfully – by Sven Goran Eriksson in the draw with Holland. 'The long-ball tactics still exist, but the traditional 4-4-2 is changing,' he says. 'In two years it will all be very different.'

After being dumped out of the FA Cup 1–0 at Newcastle, Chelsea fly direct from Newcastle to Barcelona on Sunday night and hold light training the next day at the city's Olympic stadium. Mourinho insists three injured players travel to Spain in a last-minute attempt to get them fit. The problem with Duff's knee and Gallas's groin does not deter Mourinho from bringing them to Barcelona in the belief they can recover in time.

There is also private optimism about Drogba's chances of recovering from a thigh strain in time. Mourinho recalls what he sees as the most significant moment from the last twelve months. 'My players are crazy to win something important. When we were in the USA last summer we were together 24 hours a day and talked a lot and exchanged feelings. The message that came over clear from that is that, while it is a club full of stars and rich players who have earned a lot of money, only Claude Makelele and the ones I brought from Porto have won titles. The others: zero. When I said that to them, they said, "You are right, it's true." So I said, "If I'm right, why didn't YOU win anything? And if I'm right, why don't you try to follow my concepts and projects?" That is what we have done. I now have a very ambitious squad.'

Meanwhile, Barca's quest for a first La Liga title since Mourinho was assistant to Louis van Gaal in 1999 comes closer as they open up a seven-point gap over Real Madrid. The mood in the Catalan capital could hardly be better ahead of the visit of Chelsea.

Mourinho proudly boasts that he has *never* lost two games in a row as a manager. 'We are confident,' Mourinho says, before illustrating the point in a barbed answer to a journalist's question. 'In the eight or nine years since I was here I have progressed in life, I've evolved. You haven't.' In typically mischievous style, Mourinho attempts to plant an element of uncertainty in Rijkaard's mind by naming his team early. Duff, he says, will not be fit. Yet Duff trains and has not given up hope of making a surprise appearance.

WEDNESDAY, 23 FEBRUARY 2005
BARCELONA 2, CHELSEA 1

When the same two teams met in the Nou Camp four years ago, referee Anders Frisk dismissed full-back Celestine Babayaro and awarded Barcelona two penalties as the Spanish side romped to a 5–1 victory in extra-time. Blond-streaked Frisk is widely regarded as one of the top officials in world football, and games he is involved in rarely pass without the forty-two-year-old Swede leaving a lasting impression. So it proves this time.

Chelsea start off solidly in defence as Barcelona make good use of the flanks. Mourinho springs a major surprise by including Damien Duff – a day after insisting it was 'almost impossible' for the winger to recover from a knee injury. And it is Duff who speeds on to Lampard's pinpoint 40-yard pass to collect with precision control and then flick a cross towards the unmarked Joe Cole, which right-back Juliano Belletti slides into his own net at the near post in the thirty-third minute.

The game erupts in the fifty-fifth minute when Swedish referee Frisk dismisses Drogba after an attempt to reach a back-header in a challenge with Valdes. A series of rash challenges by Drogba leads up to his second-half dismissal – and his reluctance to leave the pitch may prompt a UEFA punishment. Both players go down, but Drogba picks up his second booking, having earned a first-half yellow card for a foul on Rafael Marquez. It leaves the Blues with ten men for the second game in a row.

Not long afterwards, Maxi Lopez squirms clear of William Gallas in a crowded area, after a move involving Ronaldinho and Samuel Eto'o, before finding a glimmer of space to angle a right-footer into the far corner. Worse follows in the seventy-third minute, when Lopez's mishit cross-shot from the right is left by Carvalho as Eto'o emerges from between two Blues defenders to slam home an eight-yard winner. Mourinho has now suffered two losses in a row for the first time as a manager, but it is the manner of the defeat, the harsh dismissal of Drogba, and a fracas at the interval that push the manager into hyper drive.

The London club plan an official complaint about Rijkaard's conversation with the referee at half-time. Mourinho is upset at what he sees as fraternisation between the Swedish referee and Barcelona's manager, plus the fact that Chelsea went down to ten men so soon after the interval. Mourinho is so angry that he refuses to take part in any post- match interview: a violation of UEFA regulations that is likely to result in a fine.

Later, Frank Rijkaard confirms that he did chat to Anders Frisk but insists, 'I was not the cause of the incident. I said, "Hello, pleased to meet you," to the referee. I said something about the game in a very polite and informal way. So the reaction of the Chelsea side was a little bit exaggerated. It is not true that the referee went into our dressing room and I am glad this rumour has come out because now it all seems even more ridiculous to me. Maybe they want to start something and make it worse than it is.'

Jose Mourinho's philosophy, which he restates, is that 'when the game is finished, the next one has already started.' The return at Stamford Bridge will be a true test of his managerial mettle.

The Dutch contingent are ganging up on Mourinho. Johan Cruyff backs up the 'boring' attack by Barca, while Tottenham head coach Martin Jol maintains there is nothing wrong with speaking to officials – it is a common occurrence in European football. Cruyff says, 'I'm sure Mourinho is going to be the best coach in the world but I don't support his type of football. It bores me to sleep. I recognise that Chelsea defend very well but it's not what I want to see. Chelsea are a copy of Porto, a max-mix of English and Portuguese football but playing only on defence.'

Mourinho finally gives part of his version of the row with

Rijkaard and Frisk in his media press conference ahead of the Carling Cup final. Mourinho maintains that his Barcelona counterpart and the referee talked 'in a private place', rather than the tunnel. 'Sometimes you can talk to the referee, but usually in a common space. It is different in a tunnel with 20 people around. You can't say you can't communicate or there should be a wall. But it is another thing to talk to a referee in a private place.'

In his weekly column for Portuguese sports supplement *Record Dez*, Mourinho calls for Italian Pierluigi Collina to take charge of the second leg.

'In Barcelona, the referee was inefficient. It was an adulterated result. When Deco produced a ridiculous dive in the area, the referee didn't show him a yellow card. When I saw Rijkaard enter the referee's changing room at half-time, I couldn't believe it. When Drogba was sent off, I wasn't surprised. When the game finished I breathed a sigh of relief. Drogba wasn't unlucky. Unlucky is when you waste a shot in front of Valdes. The red card was not unlucky. It is a fact. It is wrong.

'In Barcelona the team that played best won. However, they only did that against ten; I think the game would never have been lost if it had been 11 against 11.'

Fulfilling the prediction made by Mourinho, Pierluigi Collina is named as the man in the middle for the Barcelona game. As the verbal war intensifies ahead of the second leg, Mourinho changes the time of his pre-match press conference so he can have the last word. Originally, Mourinho was going to speak at 4.30pm. Now he plans to give his sermon at 7pm, half an hour after Frank Rijkaard's.

In Barcelona it was Mourinho who spoke first before the match and took the unusual step of naming his own side, as well as predicting Barcelona's team. This time Mourinho wants the benefit of hearing Rijkaard's address to the media before he offers his own thoughts. He believes the psychological warfare can have a significant impact on the result. The Dutch coach is bemused by the change of times for the press conferences but feels to complain would be to play into Mourinho's hands.

Chelsea can go through with a 1–0 win.

TUESDAY, 8 MARCH 2005
CHELSEA 4, BARCELONA 2
(CHELSEA WIN 5–4 ON AGGREGATE)

Chelsea earn a place in the folklore of the European game with this magnificent victory in a spectacle of explosive drama and swaying fortunes. Having been accused of negative tactics in the Nou Camp, Mourinho bravely fields Mateja Kezman just ahead of Eidur Gudjohnsen. Kezman makes an immediate impact, surging down the right flank after Frank Lampard wins possession before producing an inviting cross for his strike partner. Gudjohnsen's first touch takes him past Gerard, before he lunges forward to power his shot past Victor Valdes with just eight minutes gone.

When Joe Cole's shot is deflected, Valdes can only parry the ball and Lampard is on to it in a flash to finish. 'Boring, boring Chelsea' rings out ironically around Stamford Bridge. Then Cole produces more midfield inspiration, driving a through-ball for Duff to scamper onto and roll underneath the body of the stranded Valdes. That should be game over. Instead, Barca surge back. Paulo Ferreira, with his back to the ball, handles unnecessarily, and Ronaldinho converts the ensuing penalty, even though Cech guesses right and gets a hand to the ball. Barcelona only need one goal to go through and, even though Cech again performs acrobatics to deny Deco, Ronaldinho conjures one of the greatest goals ever in this tournament – an all-time classic!

Swivelling his foot and his hips with Ricardo Carvalho in front of him, and with minimal back-lift, he crafts a shot that curls into the far corner, leaving Cech motionless. Pushing forward, Chelsea leave themselves open to the counter-attack and, when Cech tips Andres Iniesta's shot onto the post, Eto'o fails to punish Johnson's hesitation and blazes over. That is the let-off Chelsea need. When Terry heads home Duff's corner, Barcelona's pleas for a foul on Valdes are ignored.

Mourinho immediately introduces Tiago for Gudjohnsen and then Huth soon follows amid a frantic final spell as Deco flashes an injury-time free-kick just wide. When the final whistle blows and Terry's seventy-sixth-minute header has sent the Blues roaring into the last eight after a nail-biting tussle, Mourinho dances along the touchline and flings himself into an ecstatic sea of players – later, he insists Chelsea's amazing win is sweeter than his Champions League triumph at Porto.

Mourinho says, 'I'm so happy to beat the side supposed to be the best in the world. Even after I won the Champions League final with Porto, I did not celebrate like I did tonight. Tonight the game was changing every five minutes and the result was in doubt right up to the whistle. Over 180 minutes the best team goes through. But the point of the night is not beating Barcelona. The point is getting to the quarter-finals.'

The club's astonishing victory is marred by ugly scenes and Eto'o claims he was called a monkey by a steward. 'Chelsea going through is a disaster for football,' he tells the Barcelona-based newspaper *El Mundo Deportivo*. 'And if this team wins the Champions League, it would make you want to retire. With so much money and so many players, what they do is not football.'

With Real Madrid crashing out at Juventus, there are no Spanish teams in the European Cup quarter-finals for the first time in twelve years. But some of the great names of European football still stand between Chelsea and a place in the last four. The quarter-finalists are made up of six former European champions, with the other two places going to Chelsea and Lyon. Clubs from the same countries are no longer kept apart in the draw, so it is possible that Chelsea and Liverpool could meet in the next round in what would be a repeat of the Carling Cup final.

David Beckham is tipping Chelsea. 'Mourinho has been there and done it and will have that experience for his players and his team. Seeing the way Chelsea beat Barcelona and the way they've been performing all season, they have to be major contenders to win the Champions League this season.'

Meanwhile, referee Anders Frisk announces that worries over his own and his family's safety have prompted him to quit refereeing. Frisk, ironically a big Chelsea fan, says he has received death threats since the match. Mourinho is blamed by Volker Roth, chairman of UEFA's Referees Committee, for the incidents that led to Frisk's retirement. Roth says, 'People like Mourinho are the enemy of football. It's the coaches who whip up the masses and make them threaten people to death.

We can't accept that one of our best referees is forced to quit because of this.' Swiss referee Urs Meier, who suffered a hate campaign by England fans after disallowing a Sol Campbell 'goal' against Portugal at Euro 2004, says, 'It's not OK for a coach to put this much pressure on a referee. He [Mourinho] has to be punished.'

But Mourinho insists he is not to blame. 'Mr Roth, he has only two ways out – he apologises or he will be sued. I regret that Frisk has decided to leave football. If as some people say his decision is associated with the criticism of his exhibition in the match against Barcelona, I find it odd. Every day, everywhere, there are criticisms like these from coaches, directors and players. It is a normal situation. A referee with the experience of Mr Frisk would not take such a drastic decision because of criticism of his performance at Barcelona. If there are other motives I do not know them and I would like them to be known. If it has something to do with the threats – which should obviously be condemned – then it is a police case.'

Mourinho faces a ban from the touchline and the dressing room for the quarter-finals if he continues his war of words with UEFA. Gaillard, UEFA's director of communications, confirms that Mourinho's latest outburst has been 'added to the file'. Mourinho's conduct in Barcelona will be considered by UEFA's disciplinary body. Mourinho maintains he is still anxious to avoid the Italian sides in the draw.

Bayern chairman Karl-Heinz Rummenigge wants to avoid Chelsea, describing them as 'one of the strongest teams in the Champions League.' In the event, the draw is intriguing, pairing Chelsea with Bayern, AC Milan with Inter Milan and outsiders Olympique Lyon and PSV Eindhoven together. Liverpool play Juventus for the first time since the Heysel Stadium disaster at the 1985 European Cup final, in which thirty-nine fans died.

So it is sod's law for Rummenigge, as Bayern get the draw he did not want. It will be the first time the pair have met in European competition. The winners will be matched against the winners of Juventus versus Liverpool in the semi-final. Bayern Munich boss Felix Magath confidently claims, 'Three months ago we would have had no chance against Chelsea. But the winter break we had in Germany will make a big difference and now is the ideal time to strike against Chelsea.'

The first leg at Stamford Bridge will be Chelsea's forty-ninth game – six more than Bayern, who had a six-week break over the Christmas and New Year period. Chelsea have never lost a tie to a German team. Swedish referee Anders Frisk says he will not go back on his decision, despite efforts by UEFA and the game's worldwide body FIFA to persuade him to change his mind. In an interview with the *Sunday Times*, Frisk describes the period after the game in Barcelona as 'the worst 16 days of my life.' Without naming Mourinho directly, Frisk is quoted as saying, 'He violated my integrity. When you attack something that is so important to refereeing and so important to my culture, as well as to this fantastic hobby I have had for the last 26 years, of course you [inflict] hurt.'

Mourinho is finally charged with bringing the game into disrepute by UEFA. Assistant manager Steve Clarke and security officer Les Miles are also in the dock for 'wrong and unfounded statements' after the tie in Barcelona. The trio face fines or touchline bans; who saw what, in a tunnel, is normally a petty issue, but the UEFA hierarchy is furious as Mourinho keeps casting doubt over the integrity of its staff.

On the eve of Mourinho's hearing with UEFA, a five-game ban to include the Champions League final is being touted. But Chelsea stick to their line that Steve Clarke and Les Miles saw Frank Rijkaard in an area forbidden to coaching and playing staff and reported their concerns to Jose Mourinho. They are also claiming that there are many inaccuracies and discrepancies in UEFA's report.

In the event, Mourinho is handed a two-match touchline ban and a 20,000 Swiss francs (£8,900) fine, Clarke and Miles are reprimanded and the club receives a 75,000 Swiss francs penalty (£33,000). Significantly, UEFA withdraws its key allegation that the club manufactured a conspiracy that 'created a poisoned and negative ambience.'

Meanwhile, rumours spread that Mourinho is set to quit Chelsea over the club's failure to appeal against UEFA. The club are not appealing against UEFA's decision, believing that this would almost certainly lead to a longer ban for their outspoken coach. Roman Abramovich flies in to London to talk with Mourinho, something he always does before a game. But this time the headlines shout, 'Crisis!' Mourinho's agent, Jorge Mendes, joins the talks to provide even more 'evidence' that Mourinho's future is on the line.

Mourinho, though, is not genuinely considering resigning and Chelsea do not want to lose the coach who has taken them to the brink of a first title in fifty years. Mourinho, equally, prefers to remain at Stamford Bridge, despite numerous other offers.

Baltemar Brito reveals that Mourinho will watch the Bayern

111

game in a 'private place' on television and that there will be no contact with the bench via mobile phone or any other means of communication. When asked about the manager at the pre-match press conference, Brito says, 'When Jose comes to a club or starts a new job, he gives 100 per cent and expects 100 per cent back. Jose is not too happy because he feels slightly hard done by around the ban situation.' Mourinho is keeping his thoughts to himself.'

WEDNESDAY, 6 APRIL 2005
CHELSEA 4, BAYERN MUNICH 2

Mourinho is supposed to be the man who isn't there, but his presence is everywhere on a night of mystery and intrigue, cloaks and daggers. He is there in the banners, then in the boos that greet the playing of the UEFA anthem before the tie, and in the words of support from John Terry in the programme. Chelsea add to the melodrama by refusing to give any clues as to his whereabouts, except to say he is 'in a quiet place'.

Notes are being passed around among Mourinho's assistants in the dugout. Where is Jose? Is he in a health club a mere 50 yards away? Someone says he is in the Chelsea Village Hotel, holed up in a room overlooking the pitch. No one knows for sure, although one paper manages to snap him leaving in a baseball cap and tracksuit top.

Mourinho's ban has created a siege mentality at Stamford Bridge, which is immediately evident when Chelsea fans boo the UEFA anthem before the game and chant Mourinho's name to drown it out. A giant banner says, 'Jose, They May All Hate Us But We All Love You.' Another reads, 'Jose Is Simply the Best.'

Soon, Frank Lampard shows there are leaders on the pitch as well as off it. And two left-footed goals demonstrate how he is maturing into arguably the best midfielder in Europe. After substitute Bastian Schweinsteiger capitalises on a rare instance of fallibility from Petr Cech to cancel out Cole's deflected early opener, it looks as if the absence of Mourinho could prove costly. At this point, it looks as if the remainder of Chelsea's season hangs in the balance. Enter Lampard ... His first, which puts Chelsea back in front just seven minutes after Schweinsteiger's equaliser, is simple in construction; Glen Johnson's high ball is knocked down by the head of Drogba, for Lampard to take a step back before steadying himself and directing a low accurate shot past goalkeeper Oliver Kahn.

The next is even better, as Makelele clips the ball into the box. Lampard controls it on his chest, then spins 100 degrees to produce a thunderous finish on the half-volley – a special strike. The Germans are unable to deal with the long-ball tactic, with Drogba making life a misery for the centre-backs Robert Kovac and the Brazilian Lucio and, when the Ivorian forward forces the ball home from close range with only ten minutes remaining, things are looking good for the Blues.

But deep into stoppage time, Ricardo Carvalho's tug sends Michael Ballack into sufficient histrionics to alert referee Rene Hemmink. Terry later accuses Ballack of diving to win Bayern's late penalty, which the Germany international successfully converts, as Chelsea become embroiled in yet another Champions League refereeing controversy.

Was there any communication between Mourinho, Rui Faria and Silvino Louro? Fitness coach Faria, rarely on the bench, wearing a 'beanie' hat, was scribbling notes and speaking to

Clarke and Brito. During the second half, UEFA press officer Hans Hultman was seen standing by the home bench keeping watch on the trio and, in the seventy-fifth minute, he asked fourth official Pieter Vink to question Faria. Later, Brito denies having any contact with Mourinho during the match.

One mystery is solved soon after the game. It transpires that Mourinho watched the Bayern match on a huge plasma-screen television inside the Chelsea Club & Spa, which is part of the Chelsea Village complex. Chelsea can now claim some justification over their account of what happened in the Nou Camp during the Champions League first leg on 23 February. The club always insisted referee Anders Frisk spoke to Frank Rijkaard outside his room, and remain adamant that such a conversation took place – a claim now supported by UEFA. Chelsea's version of events is now backed up by the venue director's own report to the UEFA disciplinary panel.

It really is astonishing that UEFA apparently did not include the written testimony of the man at the centre of the dispute. The twenty-five-page report compiled by investigator Edgar Obertuefer for UEFA's Control and Disciplinary Body does not appear to contain a single reference to the referee's version of events.

Chelsea contacted UEFA to ask for Frisk's report and, when it arrived a day later, they discovered that the Swede had bolstered their version. Frisk said that Rijkaard approached him on three separate occasions until he finally lost patience and told him to return to his own dressing room. Although UEFA confirm that Chelsea have 'waived the right to appeal', the club are discussing whether or not they can pursue other avenues to seek redress.

Chelsea deliver another snub to UEFA by putting fitness coach Rui Faria and fringe striker Mikael Forssell up for the pre-match press conference. The event degenerates into farce, as Faria fields questions about his infamous woolly hat and launches a scathing attack against UEFA's touchline ban on Mourinho. Faria denies he passed on mobile-phone messages to Brito and Clarke at Stamford Bridge and adds that he had nothing to hide under his hat! Faria is dubbed 'Mini Mo' the next day in the press, and shows he is a chip off the Mourinho block as he declares himself a 'Special One' in his own way.

TUESDAY, 13 APRIL 2005
BAYERN MUNICH 3, CHELSEA 2

Mourinho arrives on the front seat of the team bus with an air of affected nonchalance: feet up and eyes shut. If his entrance is unusual, his exit is spectacular. As most of the stadium's photographers train their lenses on the VIP seats, Mourinho suddenly appears on the giant screen in the stadium; he's back outside and stepping into a beige Munich municipal taxi for the short ride back to the team hotel. A Chelsea spokesman later announces that Mourinho's 'privacy' had been invaded at the stadium. He fully intended to watch from the VIP area but felt harassed by cameramen and left the ground minutes before kick-off.

Before the half-hour, Chelsea take a daring lead. The goals Lampard keeps scoring, and the games he has dominated, mean that his triumphs are no fluke. But when he strikes his fifteenth of the season, the ball goes in after a big deflection off a defender, just like Cole's first last week. The equalizing goal arrives on sixty-five minutes and, by then, the home side are in control. Sagnol crosses from the right and Ballack, who has established himself as the match's most influential man, produces a stunning header. Cech is equal to it, but turns the ball against the inside of the post and, as the ball ricochets back along the line, it is turned in by Pizarro.

Bayern pour forward. But out of nothing, Chelsea appear to seal the tie with eleven minutes remaining. Cole makes the crucial breakthrough, running unselfishly to keep the ball by the corner flag. As the defence expects him to waste valuable time, he crosses from the left for Drogba to power-flick his header past Kahn into the far corner.

Bayern manage to rouse themselves from the depths of a display that sees most of their supporters exit before their winning goals go in. The first comes from Jose Paolo Guerrero, who turns in Schweinsteiger's cross from the right at the near post. Then, in injury-time, Mehmet Scholl scores with the last kick of the game. It is the first time that Mourinho's Chelsea have conceded three goals, but they are through. In the semi-finals, Mourinho's team will play against either Liverpool or Juventus.

While the game is going on, UEFA officials confront fitness coach Rui Faria during the half-time interval to prove he is not in communication with Mourinho. Faria is ushered into a side room and told to remove his hat after allegations he has been passing on messages from Mourinho to Brito and Steve Clarke during the first leg. Despite protests from Faria, who claims such a request is not in UEFA rules, the Chelsea coach duly removes his hat to prove he has no communication device attached to either ear.

Can Mourinho become the first manager in the modern era to win the European Cup with different teams in successive seasons?

After the match, he joins his players and staff for a celebration party thrown by Abramovich at Munich's trendy Cafe Roma restaurant, a regular haunt of the rich and famous just 400 yards from their hotel, the five-star deluxe Hotel Kempinski. As he makes his way out through the hotel lobby after the game, Mourinho is applauded on his side's victory.

The tone for the night was quickly set. The clattering of Kahn by Terry and the long balls to Drogba in the first leg had been part of a successful tactical ambush by Mourinho; then Terry and his team-mates did a remarkable job of subduing a Bayern side intent on revenge.

The following evening Liverpool seal a first-ever all-Premiership semi-final against Chelsea, which also guarantees that an English side will be in the final.

Benitez knows Chelsea are overwhelming favourites to make it through to Istanbul. But his side's own European pedigree must disturb even the single-minded confidence of Mourinho. It has taken foreign leadership to make English football a Euro force again. Mourinho claims, 'English football needs to adapt to Europe in certain aspects. English managers are very good. But maybe the mentality of me and Rafa Benitez to play in a more tactical way gives us a little bit of an advantage.'

Mourinho is ready for an ear-bashing from the Scousers, who will be within touching distance behind his dugout. After Gerrard's own-goal equaliser in Cardiff, Mourinho was sent down the tunnel for putting his finger to his lips and telling their fans to be quiet. He also had a running verbal battle with

Jamie Carragher, who did not like Mourinho shaking hands with the Liverpool players.

Mourinho adds, 'My reception is always bad from rival fans and always negative. I think that is normal; it's not just Liverpool fans but every fan. They sit behind me and can almost touch me. I think we are a special club because we give opposition fans the best seats in the stadium. When we go to Liverpool, Newcastle and Manchester United our fans are stuck up on the moon at the top. But they come here and get the best. That shows we are special. They always try to disturb me a bit but I try to calm them down and be nice to them.'

WEDNESDAY, 27 APRIL 2005
CHELSEA 0, LIVERPOOL 0

At 5pm Damien Duff fails a fitness test on his hamstring. Arjen Robben is in a slightly better condition but his ankle problem means he can only come on for the last half-hour and, lacking these two creative forces, the game heads towards a goalless draw as Liverpool dig in.

The game is tactical, rather than end-to-end. Throughout its ninety minutes, goalkeeper Jerzy Dudek makes no noteworthy saves but Petr Cech has to pull off two to avoid a perilous away goal before the trip to Liverpool. There is no sign of panic from Mourinho at the end. He slaps hands contentedly with Steve Clarke at the final whistle. Mourinho's conviction that Chelsea will secure passage to the final is unswerving. 'We need to be strong mentally but I think the pressure is on them. At this moment 99.9 per cent of Liverpool people think they are in the final but they are not. It's an easy thing to come and play for a draw, and they defended well, but it will be different in the second leg. I like this situation very much because it is now like an FA Cup tie with the result being decided over 90 minutes.

'Don't forget that Manchester United drew 0–0 here in the first leg of the Carling Cup semi but we went up to Old Trafford and won the second leg. And in last season's semi-final with Porto, we were held 0–0 at home by Deportivo La Coruna but they lost Mauro Silva through a booking late in the game and we beat them at their ground. Tonight Liverpool have lost Xabi Alonso for next Tuesday's game so there are a lot of similarities.'

It transpires that, before the first leg with Liverpool, Mourinho asked Arjen Robben to begin the match after Duff failed a late fitness test, but the Dutch international declared himself not fully fit, despite being cleared by the club's medical staff. The media interpret this as a conflict between the star and coach, which is strenuously denied. Although frustrated, Mourinho understands Robben's predicament and has resolved to concentrate his playing time until the end of the season.

Steven Gerrard warns that, when Chelsea visit for the return leg, Anfield will be no place for faint hearts. As the war of words grows, Rafa Benitez tries to turn the tables on his Chelsea counterpart by insisting all the expectation lies with Mourinho. 'Chelsea are saying that we are too confident, but I think that only goes to show that they are worried. What they are trying to do is put the pressure on us because they know that in reality it is them who are under all the real pressure.

'When you have the most expensive team in the world

then you need to win titles to justify that. Chelsea have spent £200 million. They should be expected to win the Champions League after spending that kind of money and that's why they now feel under so much pressure.'

Mourinho invites the Kop to make as much noise as they can. The new Premiership champions, their manager says, are unafraid to claim their European Cup final place in one of the most imposing football stadiums in the competition's history. Both Mourinho and Benitez insist that the pressure to triumph in the Premiership's private European battle is weighing more heavily on their opponents, and yet neither can deny that defeat will irredeemably scar their season.

Duff and Robben are both consigned to the bench after failing to fully recover from injuries, while several other players are shattered following their efforts in winning the Championship at Bolton on Saturday. But Mourinho says, 'Motivation can make miracles. Chelsea are tired but ready to go to the final. Liverpool rested six or seven players this Saturday, but with a little more effort we can get to the final. We played our best team at Bolton because winning the title would help us forget our fatigue. We're confident that we can win.

TUESDAY, 3 MAY 2005
LIVERPOOL 1, CHELSEA 0
(LIVERPOOL WIN 1–0 ON AGGREGATE)

After the stalemate at Stamford Bridge, the last thing anybody expects is an early goal, but Liverpool seize the initiative after four minutes. Steven Gerrard plays a delightful first-time ball over the top to Milan Baros. Petr Cech collides with the striker as he rushes out, but referee Lubos Michel allows play to continue. Luis Garcia hooks the ball towards goal and the linesman rules his effort has crossed the line, despite Gallas's desperate last-ditch clearance.

Having given his side the lead, Garcia almost gifts Chelsea an equaliser midway through the first half. He is caught in possession on the edge of his own box by Frank Lampard, who feeds a ball through to Joe Cole, but the angle is acute and he lifts his shot over Jerzy Dudek but wide.

It is the same at the start of the second half, as it becomes blue attack against red defence. Jamie Carragher is awesome at the back as Liverpool see off wave after wave of Chelsea attacks. Two minutes later, Didier Drogba curls a free-kick just over the bar as Dudek waits to make his first save. Liverpool concede a free-kick in a dangerous position on sixty-eight minutes and this time Dudek is called into action. Lampard's free-kick is sweetly struck and heading for the bottom left-hand corner, but the Pole makes a superb save at full stretch to turn the shot round the post.

In a last act of desperation, giant centre-back Robert Huth is sent on up front in place of Geremi. Chelsea have a glorious chance to level deep in injury-time. Terry launches himself to win a header in the box and Dudek flaps at the ball, gifting Gudjohnsen an incredible opening at the far post. But staring at goal, he snatches at his shot and it goes inches wide. The final whistle sounds soon afterwards.

Mourinho, who congratulated all the players and Liverpool staff individually on the pitch, backs Liverpool to lift the European Cup. 'They were lucky and the best chance came in the last minute, when, if we had scored, we would have killed Anfield. So maybe it was good not to happen.'

Despite this Champions League semi-final defeat, Mourinho insists that Chelsea will rightfully still be hailed by their fans for their title success. He is frustrated, claiming the 'best team lost' as Benitez's side benefited from a controversial refereeing decision when Luis Garcia's fourth-minute goal was allowed to stand, even though Gallas appeared to clear the ball before it crossed the line.

'My players are still heroes, for sure. They have done what nobody at this club has done in 50 years. They won the Premiership. So for me, they are heroes. They can lose and lose, but if our group is so solid and so strong, for me they will always be my heroes. I think the fans have the same feeling as I do for my players.'

Mourinho adds, 'What can I say? Just that the best team lost. No doubt, that is for sure. The best team didn't deserve to lose. But football is sometimes cruel and you have to accept the reality. Sometimes it goes for you and sometimes it goes against you. Now I hope Liverpool can win – with all my heart I hope that.'

DOMESTIC
CUP ACTION

The late Brian Clough was Brian Laws' manager at Nottingham Forest. Laws, now boss of Chelsea's third-round FA Cup opponents Scunthorpe, considers it a privilege to have served under Cloughie at the City Ground for five years. Laws can see many similarities between his old boss and Jose Mourinho. 'They used to call Cloughie "Old Big 'Ead", but Mourinho should be known as "Young Big 'Ead" because he is only 41!' says Laws. 'And having heard Jose in interviews, he does remind me very much of how Cloughie used to act. But that is not just about being big-headed. It is more of an arrogance or confidence – not only in himself, but also in his players. Cloughie had a great belief in us and he was prepared to upset people with it. He just didn't care. And I think that is where Mourinho has shown his colours. He marched into Stamford Bridge and said straight from the start that he knew his team were going to win things this year – and I find that really refreshing.'

Laws adds that he felt like he had 'won the lottery' after drawing Chelsea. He was doing his Christmas shopping in Sheffield with his wife when the draw was made but managed to watch it in an Keeper Paul Musselwhite is sure Steve Clarke, Mourinho's assistant coach, will warn his superstars about the perils of facing the League two side. Former Scotland international Clarke was Chelsea's right-back when they were hammered 4–1 in a League Cup clash at Glanford Park in 1988. Musselwhite played in goal for the Humbersiders that day as a teenager. Seventeen years on he cannot wait to get to grips with Clarke's Chelsea. He says, 'Obviously it's a bit different from 17 years ago because Chelsea are now a team full of superstars. But they still had a very good side back then with Kerry Dixon up front. But Stevie Clarke will remember that game. So I'm pretty sure he will have revved up his squad and told them not to take us too lightly.'

SATURDAY, 8 JANUARY 2005
CHELSEA 3, SCUNTHORPE UNITED 1

Jose Mourinho presents Brian Laws with the five-page dossier he has had compiled in preparation for the tie to show that Chelsea are taking nothing for granted. Yet the match proves even tougher than the score-line suggests. Striker Paul Hayes' smart eighth-minute turn and shot through Cudicini's legs puts the 6,000 travelling fans into ecstasy. Then, after Kezman's volley and a cruel own-goal by Crosby have restored the natural order, substitute Cleveland Taylor is the width of the post away from putting Laws' men back on level terms.

Only a late close-range strike by stand-in skipper Gudjohnsen kills the game off and Laws says it is a day his side can be proud of. 'Chelsea treated us like kings – but we nearly took a ransom. We showed that they're only human beings and not from another planet – even if they can play like they are. Jose came in and gave me the scouting report he'd compiled on us.

Goalscorer Hayes is also full of praise for Mourinho. 'Scoring that goal was a dream come true – I just assumed I was going to wake up. But the whole day was fantastic, thanks to Jose Mourinho. He was brilliant towards us. He showed us around, let us go into both dressing rooms, and after the game he said "well done" to each of us on the pitch and came into the changing room as well.

'Jose told us that we could go into the home dressing room and talk to anybody we wanted to and get any autographs and shirts. I got Joe Cole's, which is the one I really wanted. He didn't have to do any of that, but he did. I've seen him called arrogant and rude but he couldn't have done more to make our day great.'

As Manchester United begin to plot a route to Exeter after surprisingly being held at Old Trafford, Mourinho suggests that such trips should become compulsory. 'When it comes to the cup, the Premiership sides should always play at the stadium of the lower division side if they're drawn against one,' he says. 'If we'd played our game at Scunthorpe, I can imagine we might have lost it. I can understand that maybe it was a great feeling for them to come to Chelsea and play in front of 40,000, especially as their fans made the atmosphere magnificent. I guess it was the same for Exeter when they went to Old Trafford. That would have been a big day out for them. But I think we should all have to play away. It would give the smaller sides a bigger opportunity of winning and give the fans the chance to see Premiership football players which they normally don't.'

Mourinho admits, 'We needed a lot of luck. Scunthorpe had a great chance to equalise but were unlucky to hit the post. They played not only with commitment but also with a lot of quality and we had to work hard for the win. The atmosphere was fantastic and I hope the experience inspires them to get promoted.'

Mourinho adds, 'I can see what the FA Cup means now and I think it's fantastic. The good thing was that Scunthorpe came to Chelsea with a dream of winning, not just to look around the stadium and try not to lose too heavily. If we'd had to play at Scunthorpe, I couldn't have afforded to play the team I did at home. I'd have been pushed to play a better team because I'd be afraid of losing. I have respect for these guys.'

Back at Glanford Park, Laws glances through the Mourinho Report: four pages of computer-generated Technicolor triumph, fronted, of course, by a glossy corporate cover. 'The main thing was that he guessed correctly at our formation and how we would play,' Laws says. 'He knew that sooner or later we would give the ball back to them and the dossier is all about our weaknesses.

The fourth-round draw pairs Chelsea with Birmingham. Mourinho approaches the FA Cup with the same attitude he had towards the early rounds of the Carling Cup. 'There, we played every round with a stronger team, and when we reached the semi-final we used our best XI. In the third round of the FA Cup, against Scunthorpe, we rested a few players, now against Birmingham we'll field a stronger side. Fortunately, all our players are up to it, and I don't think three or maybe four changes will make us weaker.'

SUNDAY, 30 JANUARY 2005
CHELSEA 2, BIRMINGHAM CITY 0

John Terry's goal ten minutes from time spares Chelsea a nervous finish, with the team effectively down to ten men and only a goal ahead. Mourinho has already put on Lampard, Drogba and Robben as substitutes when Huth, scorer of the opener, is injured. The centre-half eventually goes off straight after Terry's strike. 'In the first half I think we played very, very, very well and we should have been two or three or four goals up,' says Mourinho. 'In the second half we didn't. It was our fault and they improved a bit. The most important thing is to be in the next round.'

In just the sixth minute Terry's cleverly executed block on Taylor gives Huth the space to head home from a corner. Terry heads the second from a Lampard cross ten minutes from time – his seventh of the season.

With all the off-field controversy surrounding Chelsea's alleged illegal approach for Arsenal's Ashley Cole, the FA Cup draw seems to go ahead virtually unnoticed. Chelsea are drawn away to Newcastle, who they beat en route to the Carling Cup final. Celestine Babayaro, who won an

FA Cup winner's medal and the European Super Cup with Chelsea, talks about the prospect facing his old boss in the cup and how meticulous his preparation is, no matter who the opposition are. 'Mourinho's approach to the game is so professional – the most thorough manager I've worked with. We used to watch videos before every game, but Mourinho made us watch the same video three times. A couple of days before the game he puts down notes on each player's peg of who you're playing against so that everyone knows their job. There's this incredible feeling of togetherness and belief that they're going to succeed.'

But against Newcastle Mourinho has Robben, Parker and Drogba injured and Terry suspended. Lampard and Bridge have flu, while Cech, Makelele and Duff are rested with the Champions League blockbuster against Barcelona to follow in midweek. Mourinho says, 'We will go to Newcastle to play against a strong team with my second team.' He adds, 'If the match had been on Saturday, as I believe it should have been, I would have played my strongest side. I don't have supermen here, and it would be asking too much of them to play on Sunday, then travel to Barcelona and arrive in the early hours the next morning.

'Nobody can say I don't respect the cups in England, because when others were playing reserve teams in the Carling Cup I was fielding our best team. Ourselves and Manchester United played our strongest sides in the semi-finals, which was the biggest compliment we could pay the tournament. But this time I cannot do it.'

SUNDAY, 20 FEBRUARY 2005
NEWCASTLE UNITED 1, CHELSEA 0

Chelsea's quadruple dream collapses after Mourinho's double gamble backfires spectacularly. Mourinho, who already has Terry suspended, chooses to rest six more key players ahead of the Champions League trip to Barcelona: a decision he is forced to rethink after seeing Patrick Kluivert head the home side into a fourth-minute lead.

Duff, Gudjohnsen and Lampard all come off the bench at the break, but 'Plan B' is ripped up within two minutes when Bridge is stretchered off with a suspected broken ankle. Chelsea end the game in disarray, with Duff a virtual passenger for a long spell, and even Gallas limping after a collision with his own keeper. With Cudicini sent off in injury-time, Chelsea actually finish with nine men on the field – two of whom are injured. It's little wonder that Mourinho starts shaking the hands of Souness and his coaching entourage a minute before the end of the five minutes of added time!

It is Chelsea's first defeat in sixteen games and only their second in thirty. 'You can put a big headline: "Mourinho Guilty Of The Defeat",' the Chelsea manager admits. 'Putting three on at half-time is a risk. But I don't regret it. My life is a risk. I have done it before and would do it again. I am the manager and I make decisions. I am responsible for the defeats; my team are responsible for the wins. I thought the subs would be the best thing for my team. We had ten men for most of the second half and we were better than them. Imagine if we had eleven.

'But the domestic competitions are more difficult to win

here in England. The result is not fair for us. But I have to be fair and say at Stamford Bridge they did better than us in the first half and we won 4– 0, so that was not fair. This is football. We played really well for the team I put on the pitch.'

Mourinho says, 'Today is not a good moment but there is no time for dramas, especially as we're in a fantastic position to win what we really want to win: the Premiership trophy. I have only good words for my players.'

The Carling Cup campaign begins when Chelsea are drawn against fellow Londoners West Ham at Stamford Bridge. A trio of former West Ham players – Frank Lampard, Joe Cole and Glen Johnson, all once idolised at Upton Park – are expecting to run a gauntlet of hate.

Chelsea will field a strong team because Jose Mourinho is aiming to make the League Cup his first piece of silverware in English football. During his final two seasons with Porto, Mourinho won five of the six available trophies and he is intent on ingraining the same winning mentality at his new club. 'The only difference between Porto and Chelsea is that at Porto we won everything but not at Chelsea,' states Mourinho. 'When you win things together, it makes you stronger. We had two and a half years at Porto of winning and winning and winning and winning …'

Last season Chelsea lost in the quarter-finals of the Carling Cup to Aston Villa and Clarke says Mourinho has already spelled out what he wants this time around. 'He has told the group that he expects us to win this game and then to go all the way in the League Cup. That is a shift from previous managers.'

WEDNESDAY, 27 OCTOBER 2004
CHELSEA 1, WEST HAM UNITED 0

The game sees Mateja Kezman's first competitive goal for Chelsea – something which has taken an inordinately long time to arrive. In the fifty-sixth minute he gets the reward he deserves for sheer perseverance. Joe Cole plays him in and the striker's shot just evades the groping fingertips of goalkeeper Jimmy Walker to shave the inside of the upright and go in. After the game the Serbian's relief is palpable.

The game degenerates in the last fifteen minutes after Kezman, who has just been awarded a penalty, is struck above the eye by a coin thrown from among the 6,000 West Ham fans massed behind the goal. With blood pouring from a wound in his forehead, the former PSV Eindhoven striker receives treatment for the cut. Former Hammers favourite, Frank Lampard, is then pelted with more coins before missing the spot-kick.

Chelsea's next Carling Cup opponents are Newcastle United.

WEDNESDAY, 10 NOVEMBER 2004
NEWCASTLE UNITED 0, CHELSEA 2 (AET)

Until extra-time Mourinho cuts a frustrated figure in the dugout. Plan A – with Joe Cole up front, Damien Duff down the left and Tiago in midfield – isn't working, so Mourinho switches to Plan B, unleashing Frank Lampard and Arjen Robben on Newcastle with twenty minutes to go. The game is transformed.

Robben immediately looks the greatest threat on the pitch,

and so it proves when he jinks down the left wing and dinks a ball to Eidur Gudjohnsen, who has only been on the pitch for three minutes but still manages to power home a drive low past Shay Given in the hundredth minute of an absorbing game. It marks the end of the home side's challenge. Twelve minutes later it really is all over after a superb individual effort from wonderboy Robben. He picks up the ball 45 yards out and dribbles at the heart of Newcastle's defence before flashing his shot across goal and into the far corner.

In the post-match press conference Mourinho admits, 'We were ready for penalties. But I told them Newcastle would be more tired than us in extra-time and we would get the space. The answer was magnificent again.'

After watching his skipper guide the club into the Carling Cup quarter-finals, Mourinho insists that John Terry is worth every penny of his lucrative new contract. The England international has just signed a new five-year deal, worth £80,000 a week, and Mourinho is convinced it is money well spent. 'He's ready for everything; he's a top player. To be fair, in this country, maybe you have the best central defenders in the world – John Terry, Sol Campbell, Rio Ferdinand, Ledley King and Jonathan Woodgate. But John Terry is the one for me, partly because he's a Chelsea boy – he grew up here, he was born in Chelsea and he feels Chelsea like nobody else – besides he's a big influence in the dressing room and he deserves every coin.'

This is Chelsea's tenth win in eleven games and their seventh victory in a row: a sequence which has seen the Blues concede just four goals in eighteen games with only one defeat. With Fulham next up in the quarter-finals, Chelsea are taking the Carling Cup seriously because they want to lift *all four* trophies this season.

Ahead of the tie Mourinho muses, 'You can have the top stars; you can have the best stadium; you can have the best facilities and the most beautiful project in terms of marketing, but if you don't win, all the work these people are doing is forgotten. You have to win and especially, as I have, you have to win a trophy for the first time.'

After scoring four goals in each of their last three away Premiership games, only Arsenal have a better goalscoring record than Chelsea. It would underline the opulence of Chelsea's resources if they were to succeed in the Carling Cup while maintaining a push for the Premiership, the Champions League and FA Cup glory.

TUESDAY, 30 NOVEMBER 2004
FULHAM 1, CHELSEA 2

In the first half, Fulham's four-player midfield gives them a man over and it is only after a half-time change of formation that Chelsea start to open up their hosts. Chelsea look to be on their way when Damien Duff's fifty-fourth-minute shot from the edge of the box takes a horrible deflection off Ian Pearce's outstretched leg and hops past the wrong- footed Edwin van der Sar.

Yet Fulham are determined to make a fight of it and gain their reward in the seventy-fourth minute, when Ghana-born striker Elvis Hammond, only on the pitch a matter of seconds, whips an inviting low cross past John Terry for Brian McBride to force his way beyond Ricardo Carvalho and shoot home.

Unfortunately for manager Chris Coleman, his team do not have the finesse to break down the meanest defence in the business. In the end, substitute Frank Lampard strikes the winner with just two minutes to go, after van der Sar fumbles in his 20-yard shot. Lampard nearly didn't play because he is in mourning for his grandfather, Bill Harris, who died the previous weekend. Before the game, Mourinho offers to leave him out but Lampard refuses, insisting he wants to help the team. After the game Lampard comments, 'That goal was for my granddad. Now we want to go on and win this tournament and get a cup in the bag by the end of February.'

While the Carling Cup remains at the bottom of Mourinho's list of priorities, he believes that winning his first trophy as Chelsea boss will enable his side to cross the last remaining mental hurdle. 'I have told the players that this is a competition which finishes in February. It doesn't go on until May or June. If we can reach the final, it would be great for all of us, and especially for the club as they haven't been involved in big occasions for a few years. If you can get through to the final, you go. If we can win, we win.'

The Carling Cup semi-final draw pits Chelsea against Manchester United. Manchester United thus get a chance to spoil Chelsea's perfect season and repair their own at the same time. United have been second best to Chelsea since the very first league game of the season, when Mourinho's fledgling side ground out a 1–0 victory over them at Stamford Bridge. Twenty-one matches later, Chelsea are brimming with confidence, having cast an inconsistent United eleven points adrift in the title race. Not only have they left United third in the table, dropped champions Arsenal to second and qualified for the FA Cup fourth round, but Chelsea have also been resolute in Europe and are the first club into the Champions League knockout stages after qualifying with two matches to spare and without conceding a goal in the first four games.

Fergie abandons his policy of playing his second string in the Carling Cup and recalls his star names. With Chelsea and United not due to meet again in the league until 16 April, Fergie knows this is one of his last chances to land a psychological blow on the team everyone is chasing. 'Chelsea have had a great season, you can't deny that.'

WEDNESDAY, 12 JANUARY 2005
CHELSEA 0, MANCHESTER UNITED 0

A goalless draw at the Bridge ensures it will be advantage United when the teams square up again at Old Trafford for the second leg.

Fergie has said the Blues cannot win all four competitions – and he may be right. But United are fortunate. Twice they clear off the line in the second half and, after the game, Mourinho is furious at the performance of referee Neale Barry after the break.

Mourinho is heading for trouble when he claims United got all the decisions because Fergie 'got at him'; he cites a shocking high tackle by Quinton Fortune on Drogba just before a mass brawl that went unpunished. In his cool, calculated style, Mourinho controversially alleges, 'There was one referee in the first half and a different one after the break and I suggest he didn't walk alone to the dressing room at half-time. He should go to his dressing room with two linesmen and the fourth official but somebody else was with him and, if the FA ask me about that, I'll tell them.

'Maybe one day when I am 60, when I've been in the same league for 20 years and I know everyone and they respect me, I will also have the power to speak and people will tremble a bit. The second half was fault after fault and diving and more diving. There were dozens and dozens of free-kicks; the ball went into the Manchester United end a number of times and he awarded only two minutes of stoppage time. I'm not questioning the integrity of the referee. I'm sure he is a nice man. It was a question of a big personality influencing another person without as much prestige in English football. I told the fourth official what I felt at the end. It was very important for me to understand a few things of what I saw, what I heard and what I felt at half-time.'

Fergie does not deny his chat with Barry but insists, 'Well, I certainly didn't influence him in the first half!' The United boss says his team should have had a penalty when Saha went down. 'I've seen it on TV and it certainly looks a foul. But we were at Chelsea and it was always going to be difficult to get a penalty.'

Mourinho retorts, 'Manchester United should be forbidden from speaking about referees for at least a year after what happened against Tottenham [Pedro Mendes's last-minute, 40-yard shot, which crossed the line – a fact never acknowledged by match officials at Old Trafford] last week. That was the most ridiculous thing I've seen for a long time.'

Mourinho initially escapes punishment from the FA for his comments but referees' chief Keith Hackett wants him to apologise. 'What Jose Mourinho has said is rubbish. The truth is that at half-time Alex Ferguson shouted to the referee, "There are two teams out there." Neale is one of our most experienced referees and was not influenced by that. The facts show that in the second half there were 19 free-kicks – ten of them went to Chelsea and nine to United. I'm hoping that Mourinho might reconsider his comments. Managers do not go into the referee's dressing room at half-time and neither did so on Wednesday. Referees are impartial and Neale Barry is one of the best. On this occasion, it is the comments of a manager who didn't get the result he wanted.'

Mourinho renews his war with Ferguson by branding Manchester United 'cheats'. The Chelsea boss is now in deep trouble with the FA after taking his outburst a step too far. Mourinho says, 'Sir Alex was really clever, if you can say that, at half-time by putting some pressure on the ref. In the second half, it was whistle and whistle, fault and fault, and cheat and cheat.'

Mourinho makes his remarks on Chelsea's own TV channel and his use of the word 'cheat' is likely to enrage both Ferguson and the FA. Arsène Wenger was fined £15,000 earlier in the season for branding Van Nistelrooy a 'cheat' and the FA will be under pressure to haul Mourinho to Soho Square.

The Scot is annoyed enough to recall Porto's diving antics during last season's Champions League clash with United, then to set his sights on John Terry's claim that Barry refused to listen to him during the game. 'I think Mourinho has opened a can of worms for himself. We remember what happened in Porto. Look back a couple of weeks to the penalty decision that went their way against Liverpool and how Rafael Benitez handled that. But I don't think his comments have anything to do with what happened on Wednesday. It was more about trying to influence the referee for tomorrow's game against Tottenham.'

Mourinho unrepentantly insists he will go mob-handed to Soho Square to fight any disrepute charge and maintains he has no feud with the United boss.

'I know I could be punished for pointing out that someone else has done something wrong. So if the FA do it, I think it will be unfair. I don't think they should punish Sir Alex for what he did; I think they should just tell referees not to allow it whether they are the top manager in the country, [or] a guy has who just arrived or a lower-division manager. I always say what I think and feel and I am not worried by the consequences. If Sir Alex can do that in the Stamford Bridge tunnel – and the tunnel at Chelsea is only ten metres long – I can only imagine what he can do in the Old Trafford tunnel, which is 30 metres. If the FA want me to go there and say what happened in those ten metres, I will go.'

Mourinho's 'cheat' comments were not, it seems, directed at referee Barry but at what Mourinho perceived to be the tendency of United's players to fall down at the first touch. He admits that the use of the word 'cheat' may have been wrong in the circumstances, yet he still hints that United's players were diving.

The last time Mourinho visited Old Trafford he ended up tearing joyfully down the touchline after his Porto side knocked Manchester United out of the Champions League with a late goal. This time he hopes to be celebrating more than just his forty-second birthday, which falls on the day of the game. Ferguson has not beaten Mourinho in four attempts and Chelsea have lost only three of their twelve visits to Old Trafford in the

Premiership. But Chelsea are aiming to win their first cup tie at Old Trafford in seven attempts. However, Ferguson has never lost a domestic semi-final in his eighteen years at the club.

For an entire week, Sir Alex is full of praise for Mourinho and Chelsea, but the compliments stop when it is put to him that the London club could one day be bigger than Manchester United. 'That's the most stupid question I've heard this year. You should be apologising for even asking it.'

WEDNESDAY, 26 JANUARY 2005
MANCHESTER UNITED 1, CHELSEA 2
(CHELSEA WIN 2–1 ON AGGREGATE)

When Mourinho shakes the hands of the Manchester United players in the tunnel before kick-off, they look confused, sheepish and puzzled. Only Ronaldo smiles and grasps his countryman's hand of friendship.

United find themselves trailing to Frank Lampard's strike just before the half-hour. Lampard delivers a straight pass forward from inside his own half to Robben, who in turn feeds Drogba in the United penalty box. He holds the ball up, then picks out Lampard, who bursts past Roy Keane before controlling the ball with his first touch and dispatching the shot with his second past Tim Howard into the far corner.

United have legitimate claims for a penalty not long before half-time as Bridge sticks out a foot to bring Quinton Fortune down from behind. Fortunately for Chelsea, referee Rob Styles may be unsighted by Lampard and he waves play on. Some heroics from Howard save the Red Devils from conceding a killer second not long before Giggs magically brings United back into it.

Giggs then produces another semi-final beauty to add to his solo effort against Arsenal in the 1999 FA Cup. Gary Neville clips a curling ball into the box from the right touchline. With Terry back-pedalling and Cech advancing, Giggs slips between them and chips a first-time volley over the goalkeeper and into the unguarded net.

Chelsea respond by rising above the frenzied atmosphere and clinically looking for a second. They get it, although they benefit from Howard's misjudgement as Duff swings a dead-ball in from the right that eludes everyone to find the net.

United rally and it needs a goal-line clearance from Bridge to deny Mikael Silvestre, as well as a brilliant Petr Cech save to thwart Ronaldo before Mourinho is able to celebrate yet another famous night at Old Trafford.

Mourinho says, 'This was perfect. I'll never forget it. We have given everyone a message that we are really strong. The boys were magnificent and we're ready to win the Premiership now. If you can finish your day with such an important victory, it is the perfect day. The plan was just to win the game and be in the final but we knew, with the opponent and the atmosphere that a semi-final is always difficult and we were ready for anything.' Ferguson has now failed to beat Mourinho in five attempts.

Asked about whether giving Fergie a £240 bottle of Portuguese vintage red was a fair swap for claiming his proud eighteen-year-old unbeaten semi-final record, Mourinho graciously insists, 'I would love to lose my records at his age, for his records are absolutely magnificent. I would be very pleased if I kept winning and winning and winning and then I lose one semi-final in 20 years.'

A date at Cardiff is the first tangible reward for all the investment and hard work that has been put in at Stamford Bridge. Mourinho says, 'This final is a great gift for Roman Abramovich who has given so much to this club. From the beginning I thought we could achieve good things.'

Mourinho seems genuinely pleased that Liverpool and Rafael Benitez will provide the opposition in Cardiff. 'It's fantastic for Rafa because he had a difficult week and now he's in the final. It's not easy for managers to adapt to a new country. Liverpool is Liverpool, and Liverpool is history, so it's a fantastic final for the clubs, for the pros like we are and for the supporters.'

Mourinho believes the opposition will be all the stronger by the end of February when the final is played. 'When we went to Liverpool they had no Morientes, and Baros was injured. In one month's time, maybe they have both and will have a lot of power. And of course there is Steven [note the first-name terms!] and a good defensive organisation.'

Mourinho is charged with improper conduct by the FA for his 'cheat, cheat, cheat' comments after the semi-final first leg with Manchester United. Mourinho denies the FA charge of improper conduct and requests a personal hearing to defend himself.

In a major break with tradition, Mourinho wants to treat the final like any other away match, so there will be no designer suits. Mourinho doesn't want his players distracted; he orders his players and staff to make sure the build-up is low-key.

The biggest week in Mourinho's first season begins in the worst possible way, FA Cup defeat at Newcastle, before the team head off to Barcelona for the Champions League with a series of injuries and lose 2–1. Wayne Bridge is left behind with a suspected broken ankle and Carlo Cudicini is ruled out of the final after being sent off against Newcastle.

Last summer Steven Gerrard's dad, Paul, a straight-talking Scouser, warned his son that he was about to become the most hated ex-Liverpool player in the club's history and that his family would become outcasts in their beloved home city if he joined Chelsea. After hearing his words, Gerrard stood in the Anfield trophy room and announced he had no intention of joining Chelsea and that his future lay at Liverpool. The club had managed to hold on to its favourite son for one more season at least.

Liverpool deny it, but Chelsea insiders speculate that a deal will eventually be agreed to sign Gerrard. Liverpool chief executive Rick Parry is believed to have held at least two private meetings with Paul Gerrard at the exclusive Royal Birkdale Golf Club to convince him that Steven's future lay at Anfield. John Williams, of Leicester University's Football Research Centre, who is also a Liverpool season-ticket holder and closely monitors events at Anfield, says, 'The board mobilised his [Gerrard's] family to work on him. It was emphasised that this was more than about football and money; this was about family and loyalty and the fact that Liverpool is where Steven belongs. The family, particularly Gerrard's father, implored him to stay.'

Gerrard leads his side into the final believing that a major upset is on the cards after Chelsea were knocked out of the FA Cup at Newcastle and then stumbled to a disappointing Champions League reverse in Barcelona, with a sending-off in each game. Liverpool hope to make it a treble of misery.

Mourinho will not receive a win bonus if he leads the club to a first trophy in five years. Although Mourinho's contract includes scope for generous bonus payments on top of his basic £2.25 million-a-year salary, they do not cover the Carling Cup, providing a revealing insight into the club's attitude towards the competition. Mourinho will receive huge bonuses if Chelsea win the Premiership, FA Cup or Champions League, but the Carling Cup is not deemed important enough to merit additional remuneration.

But Mourinho is desperate to collect his first trophy in English football and will select a full-strength side. Defiant Mourinho, who ordered a media blackout after the Barcelona game, holds a press conference ahead of the final in which he taunts Sir Alex Ferguson and Arsène Wenger, insisting both would want to swap places with him.

And asked about the importance of his first piece of silverware, he says, 'I'm not the point. I prefer to analyse it as Chelsea's first trophy of a new regime. People speak a lot, and rightly so, about all the money this club has invested in buying players, but the reality is that we are talking about a process – the process of building a team and a football club – and Chelsea are nowhere near a finished product. We are at the beginning of the process. If you can win trophies during our stage in that development, it is fantastic, because normally you have to wait until it is finished. To get a trophy now would be fantastic, and I'm sure Liverpool feel the same. They have not spent the same sort of money, of course, but they have the same ambitions as us. My friend Rafa Benitez hasn't come to England just to visit; he's here to make Liverpool a winning team again. Maybe he has more time to do it, but they also want to win a trophy.

'We're on top at the moment, but not because of the club's financial power. We are in contention for a lot of trophies because of my hard work, coaching sessions and the team ethic I have instilled here. My philosophy is that you don't win a game during 90 minutes. A winning team is made day by day, training session by training session, minute by minute. Winning the Carling Cup will be a testament to that. A team has to play in the image of their coach. They have to be able to do things with their eyes closed. That isn't about money or having people working together for years. It is about me making them work hard and putting on good training sessions. Then the success will come.'

SUNDAY, 27 FEBRUARY 2005
LIVERPOOL 2, CHELSEA 3

Mourinho shows another side of his character before kick-off, when Carlo Cudicini leads the team out, despite being unable to play. However, first-choice goalkeeper Petr Cech finds himself picking the ball out of the back of his net with just forty-five seconds gone, as Fernando Morientes arcs over a searching deep cross. John-Arne Riise is unmarked at the far post and produces a thunderous first-time volley to leave Cech rooted to the spot.

Sami Hyypia, already booked for bringing down Joe Cole, comes close to being sent off just after the break. Referee Steve Bennett looks set to issue another yellow card, but Hyypia escapes. Mourinho starts to lose his temper when he berates both Luis Garcia and Jamie Carragher from the touchline as the match grows in intensity.

Second-half substitute Eidur Gudjohnsen re-energises his team as Chelsea lay siege to the Liverpool goal, even if Jerzy Dudek conjures up a fantastic double save first from Gudjohnsen and then from William Gallas. Gerrard then comes agonisingly close to putting his side 2–0 up, only to divert Antonio Nunez's cross inches wide from close range.

And after Didi Hamann brings down Frank Lampard in full flight, the Blues duly equalise from the free-kick. Gerrard jumps highest, challenged only by his own players, to meet Ferreira's mis-flighted delivery but succeeds only in diverting the ball past Dudek. At this point, Mourinho cannot contain his celebrations and is dismissed from the touchline.

Just a minute into the second period of extra-time, Hyypia fails to cut out substitute Glen Johnson's long throw and Drogba bundles the ball over the goal-line from close range. Then Dudek fails to hold Gudjohnsen's fierce cross and Kezman succeeds in prodding the ball just over the line before the keeper can react in time. Liverpool rally immediately, with Nunez just beating Cech to a header as he flicks the ball into the net, but after this there is no more scoring and Chelsea run out 3–2 winners.

Mourinho is guaranteed a hero's reception from the Chelsea fans when he finally reappears after the final whistle. In his first season, Mourinho has just brought the club their first trophy in five years and only the tenth major success in their entire history.

But he has endured a controversial afternoon. He was shocked that it was a policeman who intervened to send him off after he appeared to gesture to Liverpool fans following Chelsea's seventy-ninth-minute equaliser. After Gerrard's own-goal, Mourinho turned to the crowd with his finger to his lips and then was ordered from the dug-out by fourth official Phil Crossley, in conjunction with the head of the national group of referees, Jim Ashworth. 'For me it is unusual to be sent off by the police and not by a fourth official. The policeman told the fourth official Mr Mourinho has to go off, so this is a special situation for me. But again if I made a mistake, if I do something I cannot do in English football, I have to adapt.'

Earlier, Mourinho had been warned for berating Liverpool players – notably when he pointed an accusing finger at Jamie Carragher – and he was then censured, seemingly for inciting Reds fans by putting a finger to his lips after Chelsea's late equaliser.

He later tells a news conference the gesture was not to Liverpool fans but to his critics in the media. 'It was a gesture to be cool, to put your pens back in your pockets.'

In the end, it was Didier Drogba who persuaded Mourinho to go back out on to the pitch to celebrate with his players. 'I had to do this for my team-mates,' says Drogba. 'I told him that we win together, we lose together and we celebrate together. It was me who went back for him but it could have been any of us. That is the spirit of this team.'

Mourinho says Chelsea, who dominated possession through-out, deserved victory. 'We were the best team. They fought a lot. They defended a lot and well and they were very well organised. They did their best. But when we scored with ten minutes to go, at that moment we had a big advantage from the psychological point of view. 'The attitude of my players was magnificent and we deserved to win, no doubt about it.'

Gerrard's face is a mask of suppressed rage when his name rings around the Chelsea areas of this magnificent stadium: after his own goal, the idea of his defection to the West London club is mingled deliciously with implied gratitude for his contribution to the cause. The clear implication of the chants was that this was his first significant contribution to his 'new club'!

Gerrard is distraught at the end of the match and tries to

avoid Mourinho, only to be pursued by the Chelsea boss for a handshake. The significance of that is not lost on fans, but Mourinho says, 'I didn't see Gerrard move away from me; he was feeling very down because he had scored the own goal and I was trying to console him. I went to every member of the Liverpool staff and I didn't see that as a negative thing. I didn't single Gerrard out, I just felt for him.'

During the game, Roman Abramovich could be seen willing the ball to cross the line, fidgeting and then jumping for joy as the goals went in. This is the beginning: the first trophy for the owner and the new manager, but it won't be the last.

In an interview with Portuguese television, Mourinho continues to insist that he was banished to the stands by the police. 'I wasn't sent off by the fourth official but by the authorities. This country is different and has its good and bad stuff. It was all because of a gesture to shut up the British Press. For them, this is First World and Portugal is Third World. I won't shut up because Chelsea needed a Third World manager to win a trophy – something that didn't happen in the last five years.'

Inevitably, Abramovich's riches have brought envy and resentment. Terry says, 'We don't get irritated by people having a go at us. It is frustrating at times, because we have done really well this season, but it is up to us to stop people from talking. There is only one way to do that, which is on the pitch. We have shut a few people up. It is a great win for us and hopefully that will stop people talking for a little bit.'

As he toasts his first winner's medal, Frank Lampard offers further insight into Mourinho's mentality. 'The manager can handle the pressure. He reacts to it in a positive way. He likes a fight, he likes a battle and he stands up to it.'

PART TWO
SUSTAINING SUCCESS

BACK TO BACK CHAMPIONS / CARLING CUP FINAL 2007

SATURDAY, 29 APRIL 2006
CHELSEA 3, MANCHESTER UNITED 0

Mourinho's team save the best until last as Chelsea seize back-to-back championships against the only club to have similarly won successive Premiership titles. After fifty years without winning the League, two titles came along at once: one for each of the two years of Jose Mourinho's reign.

Chelsea start with William Gallas's fifth Premiership goal of the season. Frank Lampard swings the corner over, John Terry jumps early and Didier Drogba, lurking behind his captain, nods goalwards. Gary Neville, positioned by a post, would probably have stopped it, but is helpless to keep out a more powerful header from the intervening Gallas. Terry, having come off worse in a challenge with Wayne Rooney, overcomes the pain, but is one of two defenders embarrassed by a thrilling surge from the former Everton man, which gives United hope. Finding Louis Saha from deep, he sprints and turns the striker's lay-off into a one-two; Terry, diving in, is left on his bottom and Ferreira is nutmegged before Rooney advances on Petr Cech, only to pull his shot wide. Later, with a sudden low drive from 20 yards, Rooney brings an outstanding save from the Blues goalkeeper.

Chelsea, though, are in overall control and, when Drogba flicks on a long clearance from Cech, the nimble feet of Joe Cole prove too much for both Rio Ferdinand and Nemanja Vidic, whom he leaves in his wake before shooting past Van der Sar. Rooney is cautioned for a foul on Drogba, before Ricardo Carvalho rounds matters off in style. From his own penalty area, he feeds Lampard and surges forward into attack. He never stops running as the ball moves on to Cole, who spreads it to Carvalho on the left. Carvalho cuts in and sends a smooth right-footer into the far corner.

Even in the seventy-eighth minute, with United three down, Rooney remains in brilliant defiant form until he collapses in agony after a tackle from Paulo Ferreira. Rooney's England team-mates – Lampard, Terry and Cole – are visibly anxious when the striker is stretchered off.

Then come the celebrations. Before the ninety minutes are up, Mourinho shakes the hands of all the United staff, including Sir Alex Ferguson, which leaves him free to stride triumphantly on to the turf at the final whistle, a Portugal national team scarf wrapped around his neck. This is more to do with patriotism than a subtle dig at the FA over the Luiz Felipe Scolari debacle.

Mourinho remains as unpredictable as ever. He carries a magnum of Barclay's finest champers with him out on to the pitch, sipping as he walks. Without warning, he goes over to the crowd and throws his personalised club blazer into the chanting crowd, followed by his gold medal and then, when handed a replacement gong, he pitches that in among the fans too. He is showing his appreciation, but in a way that only the idiosyncratic boss of this Chelsea team is capable of.

Indeed, he turns out to be in one of his enigmatic moods. Instead of recognising the great teams he has built, he tells the post-match press conference that his critics can only see 'coins, pound signs, big numbers and transfer fees'. He has, he says, come close to quitting Chelsea twice this season because they are 'the worst club in the world' to be the manager of. 'You can achieve, you can win leagues,' he says, 'but it is never enough.'

His achievements, Mourinho says, have only been recognised by the award of the Manager of the Month trophy, which he has received twice in two years. But there are enemies in Portugal he describes as 'rats', who are out to get him, and every club Chelsea tries to buy a player from, he insists, charges an extortionate price. That elaborate explanation is made with a glass of water as a prop. 'To everybody else this glass is £2 million,' Mourinho says. 'For Chelsea £200 million.'

Sir Alex Ferguson is magnanimous in defeat. As well as praising Mourinho and his team, he says, 'For the history and for the stats in terms of winning the League, Chelsea have got all the credit. Because it's not easy to win the League and they've deserved to win it because they don't lose goals at home. We had opportunities today and missed them and, if you miss chances against Chelsea, then with the record they've got at home you deserve to be beaten.'

But Chelsea have taken the title in a manner that banishes any doubts as to whether they deserve it or not. Their stirring performance emphasised the margin between the teams. Knowing they only needed a draw to win the League, Chelsea set out to attack to ensure there was no chance of a slip-up. 'The result doesn't show how difficult Manchester United made it for us. They were fantastic today,' Mourinho admitted, continuing, 'It is a fantastic feeling. This is my second title in England and my fourth consecutive one if you include Porto. One day we'll lose, but for now we are the best team in the country and we really deserve this moment.'

In Europe, they might have failed against Barcelona and in their FA Cup semi-final against Liverpool, but since Mourinho arrived at Stamford Bridge, he has been master of the Premiership. Out of seventy-four matches, they have won fifty-eight and lost only four. At home, they have dropped a mere two points all season: a record which Mourinho refers to as he explains why he hurled his medal – preceded by his jacket – into the Matthew Harding Stand. 'I think the people behind that goal are the best supporters we have,' he says. 'One of the reasons we are champions is that we have a very good record at home and they are a part of that, so I wanted to share the moment with them. The person who got the medal is a lucky guy. He has a great souvenir – or he can go on eBay and make a fortune!'

Mourinho may be wearing his Portugal scarf as he salutes Stamford Bridge, but he praises the English backbone at the club: players who encapsulate the spirit of his team. 'The next jump for JT is for people to look at him as the big player he really is. And for me he is the best central defender in the world. I could not have inherited a better leader of my side.' But is he a better chief lieutenant than Lampard? 'Frank is a different kind of person,' says Mourinho. 'He is a fantastic JT shadow. Frank is not so emotional, but in the day-by-day squad life he's a fantastic shadow for the captain. I cannot separate them.'

Mourinho joins Liverpool and Manchester United in the exclusive club of back-to-back title winners and remains keen to see his men maintain Stamford Bridge's status as a fortress. They have only dropped two league points at home all season. Mourinho comments, 'The home record is amazing, yes. One of the reasons why we are champions is because we didn't drop points at home. We lost just two points out of 57. For me, it is now four years without a defeat at home. It is unbelievable. Two titles for Chelsea and four consecutive years as champions here and at Porto.'

But this is also an occasion for Mourinho to get all his grievances off his chest in one go. He blames the press for his team's exit from the Champions League and rails against a system that punishes his players, but lets off big names such as Ronaldinho. 'When Barcelona played Benfica, there was a free-kick and Ronaldinho went to measure the 10 yards for the wall,' Mourinho says. 'If another player did that, yellow card, goodbye, disappear. Ronaldinho, a walk, a smile, a laugh and it's done.'

Meanwhile, Roman Abramovich loves nothing better than to mix with the players in the dressing room, enjoying their highs and sharing their lows. Relaxed in jeans and pullover, the club's Russian owner is there as usual, this time to bask in the glory of back-to-back championships.

Clearly, Abramovich's ambition is still to land the biggest prize of all: the Champions League. But, in their second year of glory, Chelsea end up with twenty-nine Premiership wins to their name, equalling their own record from the previous year, with four draws and three defeats. Their points total is ninety-one and their goal difference an impressive fifty. Their early season form was exceptional with fifteen wins in the first sixteen games and, but for a dip in March, they would have cruised to the Premiership title. As it was, Manchester United hit a hot streak, winning ten matches in a row and cutting down the Blues' lead from eighteen to seven points, before succumbing to the men from the Bridge.

Jose Mourinho triumphed again in the Carling Cup thanks to Didier Drogba's two expertly taken goals as substance succeeded over style. The first twenty minutes were all about Arsenal, whose precision, skill and movement dominated in Cardiff, but Mourinho proved that winning brings its own thrills.

Petr Cech had turned away powerful Fabregas and Baptista shots when, in the eleventh minute, he had to pick the ball out of his net. Walcott collected a sloppy clearance 35 yards from goal, fed Diaby at the edge of the area and dashed into the box for the return ball, which Diaby duly delivered. As Cech raced off his line, the 17-year-old kept his composure to slot it past him into the corner.

But then, in the twentieth minute, Chelsea suddenly drew level. Drogba peeled away from his markers in the centre and found space on the right – but had seemingly strayed slightly offside when Michael Ballack aimed a dainty chip over the top to him. The flag stayed down, however, and the Ivorian took one touch to tee himself before firing expertly past Manuel Almunia.

156

One of Chelsea's biggest setbacks of the season occurred in the fifty-fifth minute, when Terry attempted to head goalwards from a corner but was caught, accidentally, in the face by Diaby's boot. The England captain was knocked out cold and, after several minutes' treatment, was stretchered off and taken to hospital.

When play resumed, Chelsea lost the forward momentum of Essien, who retreated to defence in place of Terry as John Obi Mikel came on in the middle before Lampard struck a spectacular shot from 25 yards off the crossbar. Seven minutes later, Chelsea took the lead. Essien pounced on a loose ball in the middle and instantly fizzed it wide on the right to Robben, who took one touch, looked up and arrowed a wicked cross towards Drogba in the box. The Ivorian masterfully directed his header into the far corner. Chelsea almost snatched a third when Shevchenko controlled a Drogba flick on and walloped a shot past Almunia and back off the bar.

As the match ticked into the first of eleven minutes of injury time, Mikel tugged Touré's shirt; the Ivorian reacted by pushing the Nigerian in the chest – and then the other twenty players joined the melee. Amid the pandemonium, Wayne Bridge was sent sprawling to the ground, and both managers and several officials had to separate jostling footballers. It took several minutes to restore order. Referee Howard Webb dismissed Mikel, Touré and, after a tip- off from his assistant, Adebayor too.

Chelsea clinched the first trophy of what promised to be a thrilling bid for a historic Quadruple-winning season. But the after-effects of the blow to Terry's head can be pinpointed as one of the reasons Chelsea surrendered their Premiership crown to Manchester United. Mourinho had run out of centre-halves.

Terry swallowed his tongue, stopped breathing and was left

concussed; his injury was so serious that players immediately summoned medical assistance from the bench and he was treated for five minutes before being carried off on a stretcher. Yet he recovered enough to leave hospital a short time later and join in the celebrations after the game.

Mourinho urged that there should be no witch hunt after the eighteen- man brawl that marred the final. 'What happened is not my responsibility or Arsène Wenger's responsibility. If sometimes mature, adult people – managers – lose our emotional control and do things sometimes that we shouldn't do, we cannot kill a player because something happened.'

Mourinho and Wenger had marched on to the pitch in time added on because they feared the fighting would escalate. Mourinho said, 'When I was there I could stop some Chelsea players and when Wenger was there he could help control the emotions of his players. It is what we have to do. We have to try to help.'

Mourinho, who celebrated his fifth trophy of his two-and-a-half- year reign with a five-finger gesture to the owner, Roman Abramovich, was pleased to have emerged victorious. 'We fought hard,' he said. 'We were losing, they had a much better first half than we had, so to be 1–1 at half-time was good. They were much better than us. The second half was the opposite. We controlled the game and we had two shots hit the post, we scored the winning goal and had control of the game.'

Carling Cup match-winner Drogba was named African Player of the Year for 2006, beating Barcelona's reigning three-time winner Samuel Eto'o by just five votes.

JOSE'S DILEMMA
AND DAY OF
RECKONING

With a historic Quadruple challenge still very much on the agenda as the 2006/07 season is drawing to a climax, Jose Mourinho wants to focus solely on footballing matters. However, the on-off saga over his future at Chelsea refuses to resolve itself, no matter how hard Mourinho pushes the club's board to clarify his position.

He is clearly agitating for a declaration of support from his board when he says, 'I think, in the same way as I take the pressure off my players by speaking, if the people at the top of me could also speak and leave me free of this pressure in my life, it would be better and easier for me. If I could choose I wouldn't speak. If they speak I wouldn't speak so much. So please speak and give me some free time. Unfortunately, football is like that. Managers and players have an obligation to speak to the public through the media, but the other people, they can make their own choice. From me the supporters know everything. I have said I want to stay. Imagine if at the end of the season I tell them, "Goodbye, I go." What do people think of me then? This guy is a liar? So from me no doubts. I make everything very clear. If at the end of the season I am leaving the club, you then have the right to come to me and say, "Jose, f**k off. You're a liar." I say two hundred times, I want to stay. So every Chelsea supporter believes me.'

The subsequent public declaration of faith from Chelsea chief executive Peter Kenyon is intended to end months of speculation, rumour and counter-rumour. Designed to stabilise the dressing room on the eve of the Champions League semi-final first leg with Liverpool, as well as the showdowns with Manchester United for the Premiership and FA Cup, it sadly doesn't achieve the desired effect: the back pages are still awash with intrigue.

Yet, following the statement of intent from Kenyon, Mourinho is at pains to point out that, if it is up to him, he is certainly going to be around next season.

For some time, rumours of profound disagreements with billionaire owner Roman Abramovich have left Mourinho's position shrouded in doubt. However, after seeing his side fail to take advantage of Manchester United's draw with Middlesbrough by beating Newcastle – they draw 0–0 – the Portuguese manager is happy to talk about the resolution of his situation and acknowledge his feelings for the club. 'Of course it is more than a job for me. Maybe the country is special, maybe the country's football is special. Chelsea is my first club in this country and I do not think it would be easy for me to leave Chelsea and go next door [to another club in this country] because we have become part of Chelsea history with the first title for 50 years, the connection with the supporters, the feeling with the supporters, everything together. I like the club; I like the players very, very much; I like the way I work with Peter Kenyon – I think he is top and the way we work together pleases me very, very much.'

Mourinho confirms his commitment to the job, adding, 'I am not saying it was easy, easy, easy, but I am not saying it was difficult, difficult, difficult. I have a job to do and I was always focused on the job. Now you think about the future – that is normal. But it helped me that I opened my mind, I opened my heart and told them I wanted to stay. I was only focused on my job. For the board to say they wanted me to stay and the story was over, that was important.

'It is good, it feels good. Now we can work together for the future. If any story comes again from the media, for me it is not a problem. What mattered for me is they wanted me to stay and my decision was made. I was not thinking much about my future or another club. At that moment I thought nothing because I knew I would be at Chelsea.'

Despite the public utterances from both Mourinho and Kenyon, there is no doubt that Abramovich and Mourinho have brokered a fragile peace as long as Chelsea stay on track for the Quadruple. The timing of Kenyon's backing for the manager, whose future had been the subject of daily doses of media hype, came after news of a meeting with Jurgen Klinsmann at a summit in Los Angeles was leaked. The club then, and only then, issued their first formal declaration about keeping their manager. The announcement, brief, as it was, came as a big surprise to many people, even if it did not entirely end the uncertainty. Kenyon said, 'We are not going to sack him [Mourinho]; he has the club's support. That's the situation and we are agreed on it.'

According to the club, the 'we' includes Abramovich himself. However, there remains serious scepticism in some quarters, principally because so much will depend on how the team does at the end of the season in the Premiership, the Champions League and the FA Cup, even allowing for the fact that the Carling Cup was secured back in February.

And yet, after so much controversy, there are still real areas of doubt, irrespective of the supposedly unequivocal statement from Kenyon. The 'deal' is also widely reported to be conditional on the Portuguese coach agreeing to potential new measures implemented by Abramovich. Mourinho himself denies there are any strings attached, but it soon emerges that there could still be problems once the owner and the coach eventually sit down face to face to discuss the new set-up for next season.

The crux of the latest twist in one of football's longest-running soap operas comes when Abramovich realises that Mourinho is such a huge talent that it will be very difficult to replace him. And Jurgen Klinsmann has shown no signs of wanting to leave his stable family existence in LA.

Equally, it is pretty clear that Abramovich will not tolerate any further public sniping from Mourinho, otherwise the fragile truce will be off and the Cold War back with a vengeance. Besides, Abramovich and his extensive entourage are still considering appointing another senior figure to the club's football staff, with the Israeli coach Avram Grant the clear favourite to be chosen.

Mourinho's conciliatory words after the extraordinary Champions League quarter-final second-leg victory over Valencia, stressing how much he wanted to stay at the club, also helped enormously as Abramovich was fed up with his press-conference criticisms. Given that Abramovich missed the game, it is felt by those around the Russian that some kind of compromise needs to be reached in order that the man who has spent over £500 million on building the club's success will be present as Chelsea approach a historic end to the season in three competitions. It is felt that every effort should be made to reach a situation where Abramovich will want to attend games.

Kenyon has long been a supporter of Mourinho and it is his decision to go public with the news that the Chelsea manager will be staying next season. 'I would like to be clear on one thing: we support Jose as manager, fully support him, and, given the level of speculation, where we are now is an even bigger achievement,' he says. 'Whatever you have read or heard, no lists of candidates have been drawn up; no one has been offered the job. So let's put that to bed straight away. Jose has a contract to 2010 and he wants to stay. We are not going to sack him – he has the club's support. That's the situation and we are agreed on it. I think we're up to 14 managers we've been linked with, but we haven't got a list. We haven't made any offers and Jose Mourinho is our manager.'

This is the public affirmation of confidence that Mourinho has asked for in recent weeks and the Russian hierarchy are intent on the loquacious coach delivering his side of the bargain by tempering any public comments that can be interpreted as slights against the owner.

As a result, Abramovich attended the game against Newcastle United at St James' Park and, given the latest rapprochement, the atmosphere is clearing to enable him to once again visit the dressing room after games: a tradition he tellingly gave up as hostilities intensified after the home match against Wigan on 13 January.

At this point, Klinsmann, who managed Germany to the World Cup semi-finals last summer, is still being linked in the press with the Stamford Bridge job. But now, with the Klinsmann option exhausted, Kenyon has staked a great deal of his own credibility on Mourinho staying. If Abramovich later decides that he has had enough, the Chelsea chief executive will be seriously undermined. At the very least, it will become increasingly difficult for him to tell prospective new managers that he is fully aligned with the most powerful forces within the club.

As well as Mourinho's future, Kenyon also moves to play down suggestions that Frank Lampard and John Terry have become unsettled by the delay over new contracts. Terry, who has just confirmed that negotiations over his new deal have broken down, is contracted until November 2009. Lampard is signed up until July 2009, but can buy himself out of his contract this summer under new FIFA rules. Mourinho retains his position as the No. 1 media darling, his every word, action and deed filling acres of newspaper space. In the build-up to the semi-final, Andriy Shevchenko makes it known that he wants Manchester United to lose the other semi because he prefers the idea of facing his former club AC Milan instead of completing a hat-trick of epic showdowns with United. The Premiership title and the FA Cup already hinge on the outcome of these. If both clubs reach the European showpiece in Athens on 23 May, Chelsea will meet their Premiership-title rivals three times in fourteen days.

Shevchenko maintains that he wants to shut out all memories of Liverpool's 2005 Champions League victory over Milan in the semis. Talking to *Gazzetta dello Sport*, Shevchenko adds, 'There will not be any sporting revenge, why does everyone speak about the past? For me the word is future. I will play against Liverpool without thinking about what happened in that cursed Champions League final. It's going to be difficult. Liverpool are very strong, especially in the Champions League.'

The Ukrainian striker has endured a difficult first season at Stamford Bridge and has been criticised for his poor performances – particularly in the Premiership. The thirty-year-old admits having had problems adapting to a new style of football and concedes the criticism has upset him. 'I have had my share of problems but they have all been related to having to adapt to a different reality, a new language, the different style of football, it is not easy. Here you play very competitive football. I am only saddened that so many people have criticised me at the start of the season when things weren't going well.

Even before Peter Kenyon came out with his statement that Mourinho was staying, it was clear that Chelsea's fans, who constantly sing the name of the manager and the players during games, stand firmly behind the Portuguese coach. Meanwhile, John Terry makes it clear that he hopes the club 'will do the right thing' by the Special One and Shevchenko. But, when asked about Mourinho's future, Shevchenko will not be drawn.

'It's not for me to say. I am just a player and I do my job. The rest only serves to create controversy. We are united and we are stronger than everything. He is able to charge up the group in a different way. He has a lot of confidence in himself and his ideas have been very clear to me since the beginning, despite what others say.'

In the week preceding the Kenyon accord, there were numerous hints that Mourinho's days were over. Now the man at the centre of the storm publicly declares that his task is not being made any easier by the number of managers who have been linked with the Stamford Bridge job, the position which carries the biggest pay cheque for any manager in the world. In remarks reported by the Spanish newspaper *Marca*, the Portuguese boss says a number of other managers have been mentioned as possible successors to him at Stamford Bridge – even though he insists he wants to stay at the club at least until the end of his contract in 2010. 'It is harder to work and to achieve results for a team that does not have peace,' he says. 'At Manchester United, there is tranquillity; Arsenal will not win anything this year, but they also live in peace and without any doubts over their future; the same can be said for Liverpool, who have new owners and everyone is talking about their future in positive terms, focusing on the amount of money that Benitez will have to strengthen the team. By contrast, the other day I was calculating the number of coaches who have been named as Chelsea's new manager for next season. We're up to 13. The latest name was Mark Hughes, who appeared last week.'

Mourinho suggests that he will not stay in the Premiership if he is forced to leave Chelsea in the summer, adding fuel to the media's belief that he is definitely on his way out. Mourinho gives an indication of his thinking should he find himself out of work – although he also plays down speculation linking him with a summer move to Real Madrid. 'I don't want my name linked with Madrid or with any other club because I want to stay with Chelsea,' he says. 'I've got a contract until 2010 and I want to carry on.'

But he adds, 'If I have to leave for some reason or because someone wants me to, that's life in soccer. And, if I leave, I want to keep coaching next season at another European club. I like English soccer and I'd like to coach another club in the Premiership, but not now. I don't imagine leaving Chelsea and going straight to another English club. It would be a very strange situation and I don't want it to happen.'

It transpires that Peter Kenyon offered him warm congratulations in the dressing room after Chelsea progressed to the Champions League semi-finals with a momentous victory in Valencia. Kenyon is a huge admirer of Mourinho and it is clear even now that he always wanted him to stay, but that his ultimate loyalty is to Abramovich. 'I have spoken a lot to Peter Kenyon, we meet him a lot,' Mourinho says. 'He is on my side, of course, since the first day, more than ever as always. Fantastic. Peter told me, "Great, I'm very happy with your decision [to stay]."

'What I've said at least 20 times is that I want to be here, and I can't do more than that. I'm not a liar, I'm honest, so when I say 200 times to my players, my supporters, my board, to you and to everybody in the last two months that I want to stay at Chelsea, that I want to honour my contract, I mean it. I love the club and want to be here. I love English football.

I've forbidden my agent from speaking to other clubs. I don't want my name to be linked with other jobs. When I say this 200 times in the last two months I cannot do more than that.'

Mourinho praises Abramovich for providing the best facilities in the country and illustrates his continued personal commitment by saying that he has reserved school places in September for his two children. 'I think leaving Chelsea would hurt me more than leaving other clubs. What I did in Porto was big history, but I wanted to move. I would like very much to honour my contract. I feel everything is great as I am happy in every aspect and families are important. For example, we have made a reservation for next year – we have told the school that we want to keep their place at the school. Everything at Chelsea is the best. If you go downstairs, it's the best health club in the country, amazing facilities. The future of the club is fantastic because the working conditions will be great. What is happening here is the board's job and the boss [Abramovich] is responsible for that.'

THE WAR
OF WORDS

Mourinho is always keen to renew his war of words with Rafael Benitez, who claims that the Chelsea manager only befriends rivals he can beat, with Mourinho stoking the flames of enmity by taunting the Liverpool manager for being on holiday – a reference to the fact that Liverpool are left with only the Champions League to play for while Chelsea continue their quest for the Quadruple. 'If I was on holidays and only playing Champions League matches, I would answer and would think how to make it nice. But I'm not on holidays. Since January, every game is a final for us, but they have had time to think about this kind of thing because they have only had the Champions League. I have no time and have a big game on Sunday.'

This is the FA Cup semi-final against Blackburn managed by yet another of those thirteen names who are supposed to be in line for his job, Mark Hughes. After putting Hughes and Blackburn to the sword in extra-time, Mourinho goes on to suggest Chelsea's quest to win four trophies could play into Liverpool's hands. 'One of my assistants went to watch Liverpool on Saturday and he left after 60 minutes because it was like a testimonial match, and he saw the Champions League game against PSV and it was no different. It is clear they are preparing for the Champions League semi-final. But, at Chelsea, after two hours of playing Blackburn we have a game in two days we have to win and another one at the weekend we also have to win. This is what we fight for though – to be in this position. We can't complain about it.'

Rafa Benitez cranks up his rivalry with Mourinho by admitting he won't be having a post-match glass of wine with Chelsea's boss. He gives a clear indication that the Cold War between the pair is unlikely to thaw during their upcoming meetings, but he refuses to be drawn on whether he likes Mourinho as a person. While Premiership title rivals Sir Alex and Mourinho often share a bottle of expensive red wine after games, Benitez has never sat down for a drink with Chelsea's boss. 'I don't know if he goes for a drink after a game with other managers, but I was with Gareth Southgate the other day and David Moyes, so I don't have a problem with other managers,' reveals Benitez. 'After the game, I meet some managers and we talk for five minutes, but you cannot chat for half an hour because usually there is too much to do. I don't expect to go for a glass of wine with him after the match on Wednesday because we have never done. But with Arsène Wenger or Alex Ferguson and other managers we invite them into the boot room for a drink at Anfield.'

It's clear there is still an edge between the pair, which stems back to the debate over Liverpool's alleged 'ghost goal' in their Champions League semi-final, second-leg win at Anfield in April 2005.

The goal still rankles with the Chelsea boss and he brought up the issue again when the teams were drawn against each other. Benitez believes it's just sour grapes and he is keen to move on. 'We don't need to talk about this anymore. They can talk about the goal, we can talk about the penalty and the red card! We can talk about it for days – but it's better to think about a new game and a new semi-final. We will see what we can do in these games and that is all that matters to me and my team.'

For a time, the pair refused to shake hands at games and Benitez still won't pretend they are best buddies. 'We shake hands now – so we have finished a debate which made no sense,' he adds. 'It is better to talk about the quality of Steven Gerrard or Frank Lampard or some of the other players than talk personal things together.'

Benitez resists the urge to further ratchet up the tension between the pair when asked if he thinks Mourinho will still be in charge next season. 'I'm not surprised people say he may leave in the summer. I have experience of that in Spain when a manager was eight points clear at the top of the League and he got sacked. But I don't want to start a war with Chelsea. If they are under pressure, I don't know. We have our own pressure, which means we want to win every game and every trophy. I don't get any extra satisfaction for beating him. The joy would be just to be in the Champions League final, not because we have beaten Mourinho and Chelsea – it would be the same with Ferguson or Wenger.'

Michael Essien is suspended for the first game against Liverpool, while Joe Cole, Ballack, Diarra, Robben and Drogba are all one booking away from missing a game. Mourinho is most fearful of losing his prize centre-forward. 'It wouldn't surprise me if they chase Drogba for 90 minutes and try to get him suspended for the second game.'

Benitez dismisses the Portuguese's attempts to 'play games'. Mourinho then accuses Benitez of reducing once-great Liverpool to little more than a cup team. 'History speaks for itself and, historically, Liverpool are not even a big club, they are a monster,' says Mourinho. 'But in the last years you can see that they play only one competition and they succeed in knockout competitions. I am not a statistics man, but I think that in the Premiership Chelsea can have 60 points more than Liverpool. I don't know – 50, 55 or 60 – but I would go with 60 points. That's a lot. They are a great team in knockout competitions. We have to admit that and praise them for that: they've won the Champions League, FA Cup, again they're in the Champions League semi-final. But, since January, they have played only one competition: Champions League.'

Liverpool currently trail Premiership leaders Manchester United by fifteen points, having played one game more. According to the Chelsea manager, that luxury of single-mindedness has afforded them freshness he can only envy. 'Liverpool are the favourites because in the year of 2007, three or four months, we have played 27 matches [in fact 24] and Liverpool four,' he says, with a sardonic reference to Liverpool's Champions League exertions. 'Before the game in Barcelona, Liverpool had a week in Portugal preparing for the game. In that week we played three matches. We played the Carling Cup final. We had the FA Cup and two matches against Tottenham; we played 24 hours after a Premiership game. We had Blackburn in the semi-final and extra-time, two games against Valencia. We didn't play PSV. It's a completely different power to fight. But we think we can win.'

Benitez scoffs back that Chelsea's financial resources far outweigh his own, but Mourinho keeps making the same point. 'Liverpool have also played 22 or 21 matches, but they rest players. Do you think Gerrard and Frank Lampard have the same conditions to compete tomorrow? I don't think it will be a fair fight.' When asked if Benitez would be granted the same patience extended by Liverpool's hierarchy if he was Chelsea's manager, Mourinho expresses his doubts. 'Three years without a Premiership title? You would have to ask Mr Buck,' says Mourinho, looking over to his watching chairman, Bruce Buck. 'But I don't think so.'

At this stage, Chelsea's Quadruple is still possible. However, the goalless draw in the League at Newcastle, and with it the missed opportunity of closing the gap on Manchester United, who had dropped points to Middlesbrough the night before, might prove significant.

Saturday, 28 April 2007 turns out to be decisive in the chase for the Premiership as second-placed Chelsea take on Bolton at Stamford Bridge and leaders Manchester United travel to Goodison Park. Before the whistle sounds at 12.45pm for the start of each game, the difference between the two clubs at the top of the table is a mere three points.

For twenty glorious minutes, Chelsea are effectively level on points with Manchester United as they sprint into a 2–0 lead against the Trotters. For the following quarter of an hour, they trail the Reds by only two as Bolton pull back the deficit. But ten minutes later, the gap has grown to five points. The ever-changing scores on the giant electronic scoreboard offer Chelsea a lifeline, but eventually condemn them as Bolton Wanderers draw 2–2 on the same day Manchester United come back from two down at Everton to win 4–2. Two set-piece Bolton goals lead to Chelsea's first points dropped at home since the turn of the year. Frank Lampard, Joe Cole and Didier Drogba are rested, but all three are called upon before the hour mark. Michael Essien starts in midfield, but within half an hour he is filling in for the injured Carvalho in defence.

One of the country's outstanding midfield players is again required to patch up the Chelsea defence at Anfield as the cracks begin to show. 'Of course it's too much, but I always told you that it's very, very difficult to compete in every competition at the same time,' Mourinho says. 'Of course my players are devastated, but Liverpool should also be devastated because they are third, and so many points behind that they lost the title in January. I want my team to remember where we are and what we are doing and what we have to do. They still have a big chance to do something incredible for their careers and for this club.'

Mourinho prowls the touchline clapping and urging every ball on, but his team cannot match the result 200 miles away at Goodison Park on the day the title disappears and Benitez fuels his feud with Mourinho by claiming that tinkering with his team 'cost him the league title'. The Chelsea manager has also been critical of Benitez's decisions to rest players ahead of Liverpool's Champions League clashes. In response, Benitez claims that, by trying to do the same in the 2–2 draw against Bolton, Mourinho lost Chelsea their Premiership crown.

Two years earlier, Chelsea clinched the title with victory at Bolton just three days before losing the second leg of a Champions League semi- final at Anfield. Overcoming Liverpool this time will be harder because Michael Ballack has just undergone ankle surgery, while Ricardo Carvalho will also be missing with knee problems. Chelsea's last defeat was at Anfield in January, when Peter Crouch and Dirk Kuyt took advantage of a depleted defence and Mourinho quickly points out the fact that Carvalho was missing that day too. Mourinho also notes that both Crouch and Kuyt are missing from the Liverpool shadow team beaten at Portsmouth.

For the first time in his three success-strewn seasons in charge of Chelsea, the destiny of the Premiership title is beyond Mourinho's control, leaving his immediate priority what he calls 'the most important game in the history of this club.' The European return with Liverpool will be a defining moment in Mourinho's Chelsea adventure. 'If we can reach the Champions League final, finish second in the Premiership and reach three finals, that's an unbelievable feeling,' he announces at the end of a turbulent afternoon partnering Bolton on the Premiership-title see-saw.

Mourinho has been critical of Liverpool's fans, but Benitez hits back by saying that, unlike Chelsea, Liverpool do not need to hand out free flags to get their fans in the right mood. He adds, 'At Stamford Bridge, we showed that our supporters won their battle, even though Chelsea had their fans all with flags to wave. But our supporters were there with their hearts. We do not need to give away flags for our fans to wave –

our supporters are always there with their hearts and that is all we need. I aim to be concentrating on one competition after the semi-final, and I do not worry whether Chelsea have one or two to think about. They will know that Anfield is a difficult place for them. I know they can say it is not a problem and they have experienced it before, but we know it will be a problem for them. Our supporters, they are the special ones, that is clear. Chelsea know why.'

Two years earlier, the Anfield hordes roared their team into the Istanbul final on a memorable night against Chelsea, and Benitez believes they can do it again, though the Merseysiders are 1–0 down from the first leg. He says, 'We can use the memories of two years ago to our advantage because we know what the players and fans can do working together. I remember, before the game in 2005, the Chelsea players spoke a lot about being ready for the Anfield atmosphere, but when the game was played they could not handle it. It's very difficult for any opposing team to prepare to play against 12 men. Our fans cannot give red cards or award penalties, but they can score goals. I like this about our supporters because we know they will show they are the best in the world again tomorrow night.

Mourinho is sure to be further antagonised by the appointment of referee Manuel Mejuto Gonzalez for the game against Liverpool. The Spaniard was in charge during the 2005 Champions League final, when Liverpool beat AC Milan on penalties. It was Mejuto's perceived leniency during that shoot-out that some commentators believe helped Liverpool to success after they had trailed 3–0 at half-time.

Benitez argues that the complexion of the match is already

significantly altered by Chelsea's dwindling hopes of retaining the title while Portsmouth manager Harry Redknapp expects the luxury of extra rest will be a key factor. 'Chelsea are running on empty at the moment. I don't know how they have kept going. Lampard, Terry and Drogba have played week in and week out and they have all been massive games and they have come back from the World Cup. It's got to take its toll at this stage of the season and that's the big advantage for Liverpool.'

Liverpool win the 2005 Champions League semi-final on penalties and head triumphantly to Athens by the same route in 2007 – for their seventh final. Pepe Reina saves penalties from Arjen Robben and Geremi and it proves enough. Only four Liverpool spot-kicks are needed, with Dirk Kuyt converting the decisive one. Shoot-out specialists Liverpool take their tally to eleven victories in twelve competitive penalty shoot-outs. 'We have the best goalkeeper in the world,' says Steven Gerrard. 'We saw his penalty saves before he came, so we knew all about him.'

Reina follows his father Miguel in reaching a European final – he kept goal for Atlético Madrid in the 1974 European Cup final. In his last season at Villarreal before joining Liverpool, the Anfield penalty specialist saved seven from nine spot-kicks, going on to make the decisive stop from Anton Ferdinand in the FA Cup Final shoot-out last year. Chelsea could have settled the Champions League tie in London, but were restricted to a 1–0 win. At Anfield, Liverpool level the tie on aggregate with Daniel Agger's goal in the twenty-second minute.

After Joe Cole's foul on Steven Gerrard, and in the absence

of the injured Carvalho, Chelsea anticipate the routine high ball aimed at Crouch, but a well-worked free-kick catches them out when Gerrard pulls the free-kick back along the deck and the onrushing Agger side-foots a low shot first time into the net at the near post. Liverpool are outstanding at the back, but there is a shortfall in creativity from Chelsea.

Drogba, inevitably, has the best chance. After thirty-two minutes, a pass from John Obi Mikel slips the Ivorian striker in behind Agger, but his first touch takes the ball half a yard too far, the angle narrows and he blasts straight at Reina, who is well placed to push out the fierce drive. For Liverpool, Kuyt hits the bar and has a goal disallowed for a marginal offside.

Andriy Shevchenko sits watching from the stands but, given his form, it is doubtful whether he would have made an impact if he'd been fit. Carragher diverts an Ashley Cole cut-back over his own crossbar after seventy-six minutes. In extra-time, Mourinho finally makes late changes – first Robben, then Wright-Phillips – for pace down the flanks, and the latter's low cross is almost met by Drogba in a rare opening for Chelsea.

So, as Liverpool reach a seventh European Cup final, Chelsea have yet to qualify for one, and still no London club has won the biggest prize of all. When the final whistle blows, Terry and Gerrard, England captain and vice-captain, respectively, hug each other, with the Liverpool captain offering words of consolation. Terry sportingly offers his own generous congratulations. Deep down, though, the emotions are more basic.

Chelsea have fallen to their second Champions League semi-final defeat to Liverpool in three years. 'The first time was special but to do it again from being a goal down against a magnificent squad like Chelsea is fantastic,' says Gerrard. 'The manager's tactics were spot on. We crossed that line and stuck together out there. The players fought for every ball together. If we are through to the final, it has made all of that hard work worthwhile.'

Mourinho had dismissed Liverpool as 'historically a monster', and insisted that their limitations this season make them a little club. After the game, Gerrard admits Jose's words had spurred him on. 'The players read the press,' he says. 'We understand it, but that's Jose Mourinho. He has been a credit to English football. He makes us laugh, but for him to say that we are a little club was a bit disrespectful. Two European Cup finals in three years is not bad for a little club, is it? But credit to Chelsea. Frank Lampard and John Terry were magnificent after the game. They wished us well for the final. I take my hat off to them.'

Mourinho is unapologetic, claiming his team sought to win the tie while a physically fresher Liverpool played for penalties. 'I felt that, even against a team who has only been playing in the Champions League, we were very strong. Physically in the second half and extra-time we were the only team that tried to win in 90 and 120 minutes. But penalties are part of the game. They scored and we didn't score and they are in the final. Chelsea showed more appetite to win the game. We could speak about the first match when we were the best team by far, but history will not remember that we were the best team in that game, the best team tonight, the best team in extra-time.'

With the Premiership slipping from their grasp, Mourinho's players have only an FA Cup Final left to play for, even if the Carling Cup is already sitting snugly in the trophy room. Anywhere else, this would be a fair old return but, for Chelsea, it is no longer acceptable. There will be renewed questions about Abramovich's commitment to his manager, especially if they lose to Manchester United at the new Wembley in the FA Cup Final.

Asked what Benitez possesses that he does not, Mourinho is typically blunt. 'What we have they don't have? We have two Premierships in the last three years. They have none.' The inevitable question about his own future is dead-batted. 'The speculation?' he asks. 'Again? More?' Cue for him to depart.

But Mourinho has faith that he will be in charge next season. 'We believe always there is a next chance,' he comments before leaving Anfield. 'Next year is another year. This is heartbreaking because we deserved to be in a final but penalties, penalties … Sometimes football is not fair. It's difficult, but we are strong characters. Next season the group will not be very different to the squad we have now, with maybe one or two changes. Our intention is to keep a big percentage of the players. I've won this competition and I'm very, very sad. I know what the players are going through. The Champions League is important for everybody.'

Rick Parry, Liverpool's chief executive, takes one final swipe at Mourinho. 'I don't care what he says, I don't listen. I guess when you've invested £500 million it's a fantastic season to win the League Cup. He's welcome to his opinions. We only care about Liverpool.'

The fall-out from this defeat is sure to linger, however, with renewed speculation about Mourinho's future prospects. The question of players continuing to play despite injuries is a major issue with Mourinho, who makes a subtle point in his post-match press conference. Using the unlikely example of Robben, who was making his first appearance since 19 March, the Chelsea manager says that the Dutchman had made himself available, despite not being completely fit. 'Arjen came here to help the team, he trained for two or three days and he told us, "You have no players, I want to help,"' Mourinho says. Wayne Bridge delayed an ankle operation to continue playing, while Ballack made the decision to undergo surgery in Munich on his ankle.

Chelsea's dreams of a Quadruple have been shattered by Liverpool's victory and they are falling behind in the battle for a third successive title. If Manchester United defeat rivals City at the weekend and Chelsea lose to Arsenal at the Emirates Stadium, the Blues really will have just the FA Cup left to play for. But Kenyon declares.

Chelsea's players are to sport black armbands against Manchester United at Stamford Bridge next week after the death of the Blues honorary vice-president, Phillip Carter. Carter, forty-four, was killed in a helicopter crash on his way home from the Champions League clash with Liverpool. Carter's son, Andrew, was also killed in the crash, along with Chelsea fan Jonathan Waller and pilot Stephen Holdich. Chelsea play Arsenal, Manchester United and Everton in the League, and face another meeting with United in the FA Cup Final at the new Wembley.

Sir Alex Ferguson draws a line under the row with Mourinho and suggests that the Premiership will be a duller place next season if Abramovich dumps him. Ferguson refuses to jump on the anti-Jose bandwagon. 'I don't pay attention to all the talk about Jose's future, I really don't. Just look at the way Abramovich has conducted himself since he came to this country – he never says anything or comments on anything. So how you get information about Jose's future is beyond me and I don't think there is a great deal of substance to these reports that he's going. I think he will probably be there next year and I would like him to be.'

Fergie believes Mourinho's mischievous barbs offer a colourful touch to managerial life in the Premiership. 'Obviously, there should be a challenge amongst the different groups of players, but sometimes with Jose's continual dialogue as a manager you occasionally quite enjoy having a go back, you know. Maybe it adds a bit more to the game sometimes because you can get too intense and focused about the game itself. Jose maybe brings another agenda and it's one that you can join in if you want to, or just sit back, admire and enjoy what he has to say. But nonetheless I do believe he'll still be at Chelsea next season.'

Despite Chelsea's failure to reach a Champions League final in Mourinho's three years in charge and United's Premiership superiority this season, Ferguson believes the Londoners will continue to be a force because of their financial muscle, while also insisting the Premiership race isn't over until it is mathematically impossible for Chelsea to fight back.

Sir Alex joins forces with Mourinho in criticising Liverpool for discounting the Premiership title in favour of Champions League glory. Mourinho has belittled the achievement of Rafa Benitez in reaching the Champions League final by saying Liverpool have only had eyes for one trophy since January. Fergie agrees. 'Rafa's achievement of two European Cup finals in three seasons is fantastic, but sometimes athletes can prepare for one big event. I think he made up his mind in January that he wasn't going to win the League and that Europe would be his target – and he was helped in that when Liverpool got knocked out in the FA Cup third round by Arsenal. His target was simple and his preparation and tactics were very good. There is nothing wrong with that, but it requires patience from your fans and courage to do it.' Chelsea need to win at Arsenal to keep the season alive, but can only manage a 1–1 draw, with Essien equalising after a Gilberto penalty has put the home side in front.

Mourinho labels his players 'heroes' after they reluctantly relinquish their title quest with only ten men at the Emirates. Mourinho strides on to the pitch at the end, walks over to the Chelsea fans and points enthusiastically to his players; the fans cheer the Blues off, despite seeing the Premiership title head for Old Trafford. Shirts are flung into the stands, hugs and high fives are exchanged and congratulations are offered all round. Chelsea give up their title for the first time since 2004 with heads held high.

Asked if the best team has won the title, Mourinho says, 'It doesn't matter, what matters is the team with more points is the champion. I have to congratulate the champions, the players, the manager, the fans, the board, all the people that help them be champions. I have to say that maybe I'm prouder today than when I was champion. My players are heroes. All season, against absolutely everything, they did brilliantly. The season was magnificent and I think today is a game to remember. It showed how big Chelsea players are and I couldn't be happier with the way it finished for us.'

Mourinho promises Manchester United a guard of honour at Stamford Bridge next Wednesday, but pledges the new Premiership champions can expect a major battle to retain their crown in 2007/08. Two years ago Sir Alex Ferguson famously ordered his players to applaud Chelsea on to the Old Trafford pitch following the Blues' first title triumph under Mourinho. And now, after Chelsea's lingering hopes of a championship hat-trick have died, Mourinho confirms the gesture will be reciprocated when Ferguson takes his team to Stamford Bridge. 'They did it for us and we shall do the same for them,' says Mourinho.

Even though he left Drogba, Ashley Cole and Carvalho out of his team, Mourinho claims he never abandoned hope of winning a third successive championship until Alan Wiley sounded his whistle for the final time. Certainly, his team have not let him down. Asked how the triumph rated against the previous eight, Ferguson says, 'All of them were good. Maybe the fact that for two years Chelsea dominated the Premier League and we had a big job to do to catch them. The key was a good start to the season and we did that very well. It gave us momentum and from that moment on we did not lose it.'

Shevchenko's miserable season is hit by fresh mystery after he has groin surgery. This means he will miss the FA Cup final. Initially, it was stated that the Ukrainian would have his operation at the end of the season, but it soon turns out he has played his last game of this campaign.

Shevchenko has been dogged by difficulties since his £30.8 million move from Milan last summer, scoring only fourteen goals all season. His signing is widely believed to have been initiated by Abramovich, and Shevchenko himself is frustrated by his loss of form.

Drogba is the manager's preferred striker and in January it emerged that Abramovich wanted the Portsmouth technical director, Avram Grant, to be brought in to work directly with Shevchenko. That idea was strongly resisted by Mourinho, although Grant is still lined up to arrive at the end of the season in the position of director of football. The Chelsea manager clearly believes that losing players through injury contributed to the fact that the Premiership title has left Stamford Bridge for the first time since his arrival in the summer of 2004.

Rio Ferdinand responds to Mourinho's suggestion that Manchester United only won the Premiership because Chelsea lost key players through injury, and Petr Cech, John Terry and Joe Cole were badly missed by Mourinho. But Rio says, 'There's no bad way to win it. You win the trophy and it's as simple as that. It doesn't matter what anyone else says or reckons what's happened to their team. Everyone's going to have their opinion, but I think we're more than worthy winners.

Ferguson, whose newly crowned champions are about to visit Stamford Bridge for a game that will end goalless declares, 'I kept saying to people, "Will somebody please shoot Drogba!" His performances were unbelievable. He carried their team, I thought, and he kept getting these incredible goals. Like the one at Everton with almost the last kick of the ball. He had to play all their games, as they couldn't leave him out.'

Jose Mourinho issues the strongest indication yet that he will be in charge of Chelsea next season by revealing his plans for the first- team squad. Mourinho will not require a bigger squad for his next campaign, despite player fatigue and injuries being widely blamed for Chelsea's failure to win the Champions League or retain the Premiership title. 'It is impossible to have a squad of 35 players,' says Mourinho. 'What we have to do is pray a lot because the situation we have in terms of injuries is not possible to be repeated. We had, I think, seven surgeries and 14 players with traumatic injuries, not muscular or tendon strains – everything we had was a broken bone, a knee ligament, a skull fracture, everything was really bad stuff and we cannot have a bigger squad. Maybe next season I have big, big problems to choose a team because I have 24 players ready to play and everybody is fit. It is something we cannot control and I think the numbers we had this season were correct.'

IT'S A DOG'S LIFE

Perhaps it could only happen to the Odd One. Jose Mourinho's FA Cup final build-up is interrupted by a shaggy-dog story. He admits to being cautioned by police after an incident involving his pet Yorkshire terrier, but pledges to co-operate fully with the authorities.

Officers are concerned the dog has been abroad and has then been brought back into Britain without the required jabs. Reports suggest that Mourinho refused to let police take the dog away and got into an argument with officers. He received a caution for obstructing police.

Scotland Yard say the dog was to be seized for alleged offences under the Animal Health Act of 1981 and the Rabies Order of 1974. Mourinho, forty-four, was at Chelsea's Player of the Year awards when his wife Tami telephoned to tell him the dog was being taken away.

All in all, it's just another 'ordinary' day in the colourful world of Jose. But in football terms, the Special One is quickly back focusing on a final that is back where it belongs at Wembley. Mourinho is particularly proud to be taking his Chelsea team to his first FA Cup final on this historic occasion.

Mourinho discusses the issue of the 'responsibility' both sides have to make sure the FA Cup final is a fitting occasion. 'The game should be correct – I would be very disappointed if the players were diving and provoking, and trying to get people red cards,' he says. 'I think Mr [Steve] Bennett has enough experience and had a very discreet season. To be low profile is the best quality a referee can have – when you don't remember the referee, it is because the referee was perfect and I think Mr Bennett has been low profile during the season.'

Mourinho pays due deference to tradition, remembering the days he watched the final as a child in Portugal, incredulous that 'the small team could always win it.' Mourinho can remember watching Coventry City in 1987, but not that it was Tottenham they beat 3–2 after extra-time.

'This is something we chased a lot,' Mourinho says. 'It's something that, from the first day, we said we wanted to be there for, to play at Wembley in the first FA Cup final. Chelsea was in the last final at the old Wembley and we wanted to be at the first of the new one.'

Sir Alex taunts Mourinho by claiming that the pressure is all on Chelsea because Manchester United have already won the title. Fergie claims Chelsea will find it hard to raise their game after losing the title – just as United did in 1995 when they lost the title to Blackburn and then the FA Cup to Everton six days later.

Mourinho is determined to end up having the final word on the season. 'From a selfish point of view,' he observes, 'you like to win new things instead of repeating yourself. The point is that it's an FA Cup final. It's the only title this group didn't win in the years we've worked together. And I can imagine it's a special final because it's the new Wembley. I can imagine that has a lot of meaning for everybody. I'm not English, but for me it means a lot. For me it means remembering my youth. There were a few things I always dreamed of winning and the FA Cup final was one of those.'

Despite assurances from Peter Kenyon only a matter of weeks ago – and irrespective of Mourinho finishing the season loudly insisting he will be around for the start of the new one – the rumours inevitably resume, with speculation growing that Mourinho's future at Chelsea will only be decided after the final. So victory over Manchester United takes on even greater significance than simply winning a second trophy in the season.

Roman Abramovich has yet to have a full and frank discussion with Mourinho, who is making it clear that he wants to stay and see out his contract, which expires in 2010. On the plus side for Jose, Abramovich is aware that Mourinho will be difficult to replace and candidates such as Jurgen Klinsmann, Barcelona's Frank Rijkaard and Juventus's Didier Deschamps show little desire to move to Stamford Bridge.

The likelihood is that he will stay, but Mourinho has to accept changes, including the expected arrival of Avram Grant from Portsmouth, plus the fact of having less money to spend on transfers than in previous years. Mourinho acknowledges this when he says there will not be great changes in the squad this summer. 'No big investments, not involved in the big market.'

He acknowledges that mistakes have been made during a season in which Chelsea surrendered the Premiership title and again failed to lift the European Cup. Shevchenko will miss the final following a hernia operation. It hasn't been a great season for the Ukrainian. England's most expensive player scored fourteen goals, but only four in the Premiership. Mourinho cuttingly observes, 'Hopefully, he's not happy with the season he has given us. I hope he's not happy with what he gave to this team. If he's not happy, then that's a good start.'

After Chelsea won the Carling Cup in February, Mourinho made reference to an incident in United's game at Tottenham when Ronaldo won a penalty, intimating that he dived. Later, Mourinho claimed Ronaldo was 'ill-educated, disrespectful and immature' after the twenty-two-year-old had said the coach could never admit a mistake. Mourinho later apologised and now calls on all parties to come together to make the return to Wembley memorable.

'The fact that it is Wembley, with 90,000 people there when they could have sold 180,000 [tickets], means that socially and as a cultural event it will be a day to remember, a historical day.'

The final against United also gives Mourinho the chance to complete the third part of his dream to win four prizes – the Premiership title, the Carling Cup, the Champions League and the FA Cup. Chelsea have missed out on a Quadruple, but Mourinho still wants the full set of trophies. 'If we can win that trophy, we can say we have won every competition in domestic football. As a kid you are more focused on finals, on one-off matches. For me the matches were the Portuguese Cup final, the FA Cup final – because it was a game everybody was waiting for all year to watch on TV – the European Cup and the World Cup final. If I can realise this dream, then it would be fantastic. But I don't think we can say this game – will make us forget what happened in the season.'

Mourinho is still hurt by his failure to complete a hat-trick of Premiership titles, as well as again missing out on the Champions League at the semi-final stage to rivals Liverpool. The FA Cup, he insists, is being taken seriously. 'It's something that, from the first day, we said we wanted to be there, to play at Wembley. All through the competition we always played good teams and good players. I never made rotation. I think we have to enjoy the fact that we are there and we have to play the final with happiness, not with any pressure.'

This will be Mourinho's third visit to Wembley, where he has nothing but good memories. 'I was at Wembley only twice. One was to see England versus Scotland in Euro 96, when Gazza scored that goal. The other time was with Barcelona [as assistant manager]. We played Arsenal in the Champions League and won 4–2. Those were the two moments I was there and both of them were absolutely magnificent.'

Apart from one brief week in September, United have led Mourinho's team for the whole of the Premiership campaign. The final is Chelsea's big chance to prove that Manchester United are not the superior side. It will be the Clash of the Titans; not since Liverpool beat Everton twenty-one years ago have the clubs finishing first and second in the League disputed the Cup Final as well.

Ferguson, fresh from lifting the title trophy for the first time in four years, adds, 'We are going to go bouncing into Wembley. Winning the title has certainly helped us and now we are looking forward to the FA Cup. It will be great to play in the first final at the new stadium. Terry plans to sit down with Mourinho in the summer to give his views on the way forward. 'There will be a bit of an inquest. Certainly, myself and Lamps will have chats with the manager. We've got a lot of time pre-season amongst ourselves, so discussions will be had – little changes and little things to be done to improve ourselves and improve everything around the place. Credit to the manager because he's willing to listen to his players as well.'

Joe Cole plans to fulfil a boyhood fantasy by lifting the famous trophy. 'For me, the FA Cup final is as big as the Champions League, if not bigger. I was driving along the Westway the other day and I looked across and could see Wembley with that huge arch, and suddenly I got tingles all through my body. Everyone knows what Wembley means.'

Ashley Cole needs an anti-inflammatory injection in his troublesome ankle and will then undergo a small surgical procedure three days after the final that will rule him out of England's games with Brazil and Estonia. Ballack had a similar problem, but elected to have an operation back in Germany. Although this was successful, the stitches have not healed sufficiently to withstand full-on contact and Ballack is ruled out.

Whether Ashley Cole starts remains to be seen, as Wayne Bridge has shone at left-back, but Mourinho is impressed by Cole's determination to make himself available despite the discomfort from the inflammation surrounding the arthritic bone spur outside the ankle joint. Ashley feels as if he has let down Mourinho and his team- mates with some of his performances. The England defender has not been at his best since his controversial transfer from Arsenal to Chelsea last summer, with his efforts hindered by an ankle injury that troubled him during much of the campaign.

Mourinho has said as much by describing Cole's season as 'not superb', but the Portuguese maestro praises him as 'one of the heroes who has played injured the whole season.'

Ashley Cole has sat out the last three matches to rest his ankle, even though he has returned to full training. Cole is the only member of the squad to have won an FA Cup final after lifting the trophy three times with Arsenal, but that is discounting the winner's medal John Terry picked up while sitting on the bench as Chelsea beat Aston Villa seven years ago.

Alan Hansen suggests England now has the best league in the world thanks to Mourinho and Chelsea. The Scottish pundit says, 'The fact that England had three semi-finalists in this year's Champions League is proof that the Premiership is now the best in the world. That is all down to Chelsea. They have raised the bar in this country and forced the other ambitious English clubs to respond. In the 1980s and even in the 1990s, you could win the English League with a better-than-average team. But not any more. To be Premiership champions these days, you have to be top, top class. Chelsea have brought unbelievable quality since Mourinho became their manager and this season United have risen to the challenge and matched them.

When the time comes to pick his team, Mourinho opts not to risk Ashley Cole but to gamble on Mikel. Cole trained but is still left on the bench as he has not been as consistent as Wayne Bridge. Despite starting twenty-six matches, he was not considered match-fit. A Cup Final place is Bridge's reward for sticking it out. Gary Neville loses his fight for final fitness. After attempting a return to training, it quickly becomes apparent that the ankle injury he suffered against Bolton on 17 March is still too sore to let him play.

SIX-FINGER SALUTE

Chelsea claim a 1–0 victory over Manchester United at the new Wembley thanks to Didier Drogba's extra-time goal. Mourinho, who threw his Premier League winner's medal into the crowd last year, promises he will treasure this one. Mourinho comes down the 107 steps at Wembley holding up 6 fingers to underline how many trophies he has won during his time at Stamford Bridge. Referring to the fans who are chanting his name, he says, 'They are in my heart – in the bad moments and the good moments. I love these people.'

Asked if he had felt under tremendous pressure going into the game after missing out on the title and the Champions League final, Mourinho replies, 'Only the pressure you put on yourself to win… nothing else. We know the game plan and how to beat them and I think the boys deserved this great moment.'

The big moment of controversy came in the first half of extra-time when Giggs slid in to meet Rooney's cross, but failed to get decent contact on the ball, deflecting it into the body of Cech before the winger's momentum took him crashing into the goalkeeper who carried the ball fractionally over the line. Ferguson feels Giggs should have had a penalty for Essien's challenge on the Reds veteran and blames referee Steve Bennett for not spotting it.

Mourinho ends the season of turmoil on a winning note and isn't slow to make sure everyone knows. 'I learned that it's very difficult to kill me, very, very difficult,' he says. Victory was imperative, given the pressure that he was under, and he makes no secret of his tactics; he gathered his players together at the start of the week and presented them with two choices. 'I asked them, "Do you want to enjoy the game or do you want to enjoy after the game? A pretty football match or do you want to win?"'

Mourinho predicts that Chelsea will resolve their contractual issues with Terry and Lampard and he will almost certainly have to compromise over personnel on the coaching side too. Avram Grant, the former Israel manager, was watching from Abramovich's private box with his arrival as director of football imminent.

Meanwhile, John Terry dismisses suggestions that he is about to hand in a transfer request in a bid to force Chelsea's hand over a new long-term contract. Terry's future at the club has come under increasing speculation in the build-up to the big game, with Terry reported to have rejected Chelsea's latest offer.

Terry's remarks over talks are echoed by chief executive

Peter Kenyon, who says the club's message to both Terry and vice-captain Frank Lampard has always been positive. Lampard, also the subject of difficult negotiations over a new long-term deal, insists he wants to remain at the club for life, and his comments have also been noted by Kenyon.

Lampard repeats his statement that he wants to stay at Chelsea, despite reports suggesting contract talks have broken down. In the end, the country's top two clubs were not able to serve up the thrilling final predicted but Drogba savours his moment, having scored the first goal at the new stadium to prevent the match going into extra-time. 'I feel great,' says the Ivorian, who struck in the 116th minute. 'If we didn't win this cup, we would be very, very frustrated. I'm just happy to score the first goal in the new stadium.'

Drogba also takes the chance to pay tribute to Mourinho and Abramovich. 'This [another trophy] is what Jose has shown in his three years with us. Special congratulations to him and Roman.'

As for his exit down the tunnel at the final whistle, Drogba says, 'I chased Jose Mourinho down the tunnel because he means a lot to me. The reason I'm here is because of him and Roman Abramovich. They gave me the chance so I have to say thanks to them.'

Mourinho has never forgotten the Garcia 'ghost goal' for Liverpool, but now, after Giggs' disallowed effort, he has had the benefit of the goal-line decision in the final. Mourinho isn't concerned either with 'putting on a show', as he doesn't care how he wins. Bringing off Joe Cole so early surprised many, but it was the right decision because Ronaldo wasn't offering much defensively on that flank and the introduction of the flying Robben suddenly gave Chelsea a threat they had been lacking.

In the press there is immediate analysis of the season and whether it has been good enough or not in the eyes of Abramovich. Shevchenko's contribution is still a matter of great debate. The Ukrainian, who missed the final victory because of a groin injury, insists he should not be branded a flop.

While headlines rage that winning two domestic cups is 'not good enough' for Chelsea, Mourinho has had the final word over United and he doesn't mind rubbing it in. 'We deserved to win totally and it has been a great season for us. We have won two cups, lost on penalties in the Champions League semi-final and have finished second in the Premiership. They have made history, not only by beating Manchester United, but by beating them in the first game at this magnificent stadium.'

Mourinho defends his three-year reign further, saying, 'We have dominated domestically in this country for the last three years and that is why I held up six fingers to show the trophies we have won in my time here. Manchester United have been champions this season, but I can see the same fight between us next time.'

Mourinho thanks his players for rescuing what had threatened to be a disappointing season. 'My first season was very important because we won the title 50 years after we had last won it, and we won it again the second season, but I think this third season was better than the second with the problems we had. I'm not a magician, I cannot predict things, but if we did this with players limping and losing an important player every week, what would the season have been like if Petr Cech and John Terry were not out for four months, if Ricardo Carvalho had not been out? We had Arjen Robben playing with injury, Ashley Cole the same. We deserve this happiness at this historical moment for the country. Chelsea made history by winning the last cup at the old Wembley and special regards to all the boys that won that cup, and a big, big, big hug to every one of my boys because they were brilliant.'

Mourinho's Chelsea become just the third team to win an FA Cup and League Cup Double – following on from Arsenal in 1993 and Liverpool in 2001. If you add the Premiership titles of 2005 and 2006, the inspirational Portuguese manager has now been a winner in all three of English football's domestic competitions in three seasons, but he admits there is something special about lifting the FA Cup. 'It's amazing,' he says. 'I had heard a lot about the FA Cup, about the tradition, about the finals, but this feeling is just amazing. It's such an important victory – it's not just an FA Cup, it's more than that; the first FA Cup at the new Wembley, the FA Cup against Manchester United, and we have now won every competition in English football and six trophies in three years. It's especially amazing after this difficult season when we've been chasing all four trophies. We lost a semi-final [in the Champions League] on penalties, we lost the Premiership at the last moment, so this is a great achievement.'

Asked when he will be speaking to Abramovich, he says, 'I will speak with him. There is no problem. He does not need to be at the club day by day because he has people to do that for him. But I mentioned him in the programme and he was in my heart because I knew winning at Wembley was a big target for him.'

PART THREE
RETURN OF THE KING

Top: Mourinho and players Petr Cec (*left*), Frank Lampard and John Terry (*right*) gaze down at the trophy after being crowned Premiership champions in May 2005.

©*Adrian Dennis/AFP/Getty Images*

Middle left: Carling Cup victory after beating Liverpool at the Millennium Stadium in Cardiff.

©*Rebecca Naden/AFP/Getty Images*

Middle right: Mourinho proudly lifts the FA Cup trophy, presented by Prince William at Wembley.   ©*Getty Images*

Left: John Terry and Frank Lampard celebrate the amazing achievement of winning back-to-back Premiership titles – Chelsea are the only club besides Manchester United to do so in the Premiership era.   ©*Getty Images*

The evident respect and admiration between the Chelsea players and manager: Mourinho celebrates victory against Barcelona with Frank Lampard (*above left*), sharing a joke with striker Didier Drogba (*above right*) and embracing Lampard and John Terry following a Premiership match against Arsenal (*below*).

Above left: Jose Mourinho addresses the press as he returns to Chelsea for a second managing stint in June 2013. ©*Getty Images*

Above right: Mourinho's legendary status among Chelsea fans made him a popular choice to replace Rafael Benitez. ©*Getty Images*

Below: Back in action: Mourinho watches from the sidelines during a Premier League match between Chelsea and Norwich City in May 2014. ©*Getty Images*

Back where he belonged?
Whatever the future holds,
Mourinho undoubtedly
left his mark on Chelsea.
©Getty Images

SO SPECIAL IN ITALY, SPECIAL OR NOT SO SPECIAL IN SPAIN?

Jose Mourinho transported his winning mentality to Italy and then on to Spain in the 'gap years' away from the Bridge and continued to collect the usual profusion of trophies, enemies, alongside media-fuelled rows and endless controversial headlines.

He is, to date, the only manager to win the league titles in England, Italy and Spain. He also won in Portugal, claimed the Champions League twice with arguably the weakest teams (Porto in 2004 and Inter Milan in 2010) to lift the trophy in the last ten years. He has won cups, super cups and holds a remarkable record, which he transports from club to club, of never having submitted to defeat in home fixtures until, unexpectedly, right at the end of his first season back at the Bridge.

To his detractors, Mourinho is a man prepared to sacrifice style to win, with exuberance, mind games and disrepute charges – a multi-faceted genius. To the players who worship him and talk of incredible relationships, to his proven CV, he is a genuine genius.

Away from the Bridge, he was still never far from the hearts of Chelsea fans, who longed for what seemed an unlikely return, considering the manner of his break-up with Roman Abramovich. But the headlines he created in Italy and Spain reverberated back in England, where the Mourinho brand was sorely missed.

With the public utterances of Mourinho as direct and uncompromising as the teams he creates, he is always a headline waiting to happen, whichever the country, or whatever the language. While some foreign managers come to English football struggling with the language – and often ridiculed as a consequence – Mourinho's use of it is colourful, explicit and cutting. He uses language to his advantage. It is important for him to be word perfect, so, arriving in Italy, it was vitally important that he commanded Italian and he worked relentlessly to achieve his goal.

Mourinho gets into the mind of his players, to communicate directly and personally, as well as to manipulate the media in a side- show, to perpetuate the so-called managerial mind games. The players are the 'Important Ones' for Mourinho and his personal style of man management. The 'Mourinho Method' is based on being up close and personal with the players, forging relationships, which often linger beyond their time together at a club. A clip of Ronaldo and Mourinho crying on each other's shoulders is typical of the bond he forges with his players, irrespective of the furore he creates and the controversy that often surrounds him.

His former players reveal that constant attention: persistently calling their mobiles, sending texts, wanting to know how they slept, making sure they are 'happy', whether they are eating correctly. Even the girlfriends and wives are under the Mourinho spell as important conduits for his mission to know the ins and outs of his players, so they, too, are made to feel part of his 'team' to ensure his players are happy. Mourinho's mission is to motivate his players to give their all. When it was announced that Mourinho was returning to the Bridge, Ramires was informed by the new boss that he tried to sign him during his spells as coach at Inter and Real Madrid. This is typical of the 'Mourinho Method', making personal contact with his players even before he meets up with his new squad.

On returning to the Bridge, those rows in Italy and Spain continued to follow Mourinho. On the eve of his new Chelsea playing Galatasaray in Istanbul, accusations flew from one camp to the other. The Turkish team was now managed by Mourinho's predecessor at Inter Milan, Roberto Mancini, once of Manchester City, and the background to Mourinho's appointment at Inter continued to gall Mancini, who was sacked by Inter in 2008, less than a fortnight after winning Serie A for the third time in a row. Mourinho had taken over the job at Inter Milan and, within two seasons, had outshone him by winning the Treble and transforming Inter into European champions for the first time since 1965.

Mourinho was soon adored by the Italian club. He made history at Inter by winning the league and the Coppa Italia, the Italian Super Cup and the Champions League during his two-year spell at the San Siro after leaving Chelsea in 2007. Along with Chelsea, the Italian club remains in Mourinho's heart. He still owns the house in Milan where he lived during his spell there, providing President Massimo Moratti with the hope that he might one day return.

Now at Paris St-Germain, Swedish striker Zlatan Ibrahimovic played under Mourinho at Inter in the 2008/09 season before being sold to Barcelona. In his autobiography, *I Am Zlatan Ibrahimovic*, he offered a fascinating insight into how Mourinho motivates and into his work ethic. 'He worked us twice as hard as all the rest to get us ready. Lives and breathes football 24/7. I've never met a manager with that kind of knowledge about opposing sides. It was everything, right down to the third-choice goalkeeper's shoe size. He built us up before matches. It was like theatre, a psychological game. He might show videos where we'd played badly and say, "Look at this. So miserable! Hopeless! Those guys can't even be you. They must be your brothers, your inferior selves." And we nodded, we agreed. "I don't want to see you like that today," he would continue. No way, we thought, no chance.'

Mourinho responded, 'It's not obsessive. I think details are important: details make players better; details make the team better; details help to win. Of course, there are a few players in the world who by themselves can make a team look better than it is. But basically, football is about teams and teams are better if you care about the details. So it's not an obsession, my experience tells me that details can make a difference.'

One of the highlights of Mourinho's Inter reign was the 'almost perfect' – as he put it – display of winning 1–0 on his return to the Bridge to dispatch Chelsea out of the Champions League, 3–1 on aggregate in the 2009/10 season.

Mourinho received a warm welcome from the Chelsea supporters prior to kick-off at his first competitive match after returning to the club. Drogba was sent off in the eighty-seventh minute for kicking Thiago Motta as Mourinho's side produced a dazzling display, and Chelsea fans were left with the enduring image of Mourinho doing his best to tone down his celebration of Eto'o's second-half goal, which secured Inter's quarter-final place. Mourinho indulged in some fairly low-key fist pumping but the rest of Inter's backroom staff and players celebrated wildly. Inter came with a slender 2–1 lead. Mourinho ditched his normally defensive tactics for an attacking formation. 'The team accepted the risks that I took – and you don't always get that as a manager. I don't think it was tactics, it was attitude on the pitch.'

Mourinho's affection for Inter, and theirs for him, was cemented when they beat Bayern Munich 2–0 to win the Champions League final, ending the club's forty-five-year wait to regain Europe's top prize. Argentinean striker Diego Milito scored both the goals in a game that was won by brilliant defending and individual magic. Inter became the first Italian club to win the Treble. Mourinho outfoxed his mentor Louis van Gaal. They had worked together in the 1990s at Barcelona, where Mourinho had started his career as a scout and interpreter. This earned him the nickname of 'The Translator', with which Barcelona fans had taunted him during their Champions League contest.

No one predicted that Inter would become the Champions League holders again after such a long time, let alone beat Premier League champions Chelsea, Spanish La Liga champions Barcelona, and the Bundesliga Champions Bayern Munich, to enable Mourinho to become only the third man ever to have won the Champions League with three different clubs.

For Mourinho, though, his management pattern persisted. There followed yet another season of personal vindication, a frosty relationship with the Italian media, and he often admitted to being unhappy in Italy. As usual, the media was awash with speculation that he would move on and his destination was rumoured to be Real Madrid – a rumour that soon became fact.

It was the perfect send-off that his last victory at Inter Milan should come at the Bernabeu, Real's home stadium. The final whistle at the Champions League final saw a warm hug between the protégé and the professor as Mourinho went on to celebrate with his team and lift the trophy, while Louis van Gaal waved impassively at the supporters.

But the switch to Real was not going to be what Mourinho had anticipated. During his three years as Madrid manager, he appeared determined to undermine Barcelona – arguably the finest club side in history – and their coach Pep Guardiola. In 2011 things actually got physical when Mourinho appeared to poke his finger into the eye of Guardiola's successor, Tito Vilanova, during a post-match scuffle.

Mourinho, some time later, admitted he was wrong to poke Vilanova in the eye: 'I should not have done what I did, obviously not. The person who messed up there was me.'

For Mourinho, the constant discussion of his off-the-field behaviour and his 'dark-arts' tactical mind games is vastly overstated. 'In football, the only game I know is the 90-minutes game. It's not mind games; I don't try to do that. The period before the game can be important to influence opinions, characters, personalities, feelings, and, of course, I use that to touch my players, to touch opponents, to touch supporters. But for me, the only game in football is the 90-minutes game.'

Mourinho bemoaned the 'worst season of my career' after seeing his Madrid side slip to a 2–1 extra-time defeat to capital rivals Atlético in the final of the Copa del Rey. Widely tipped to return to Chelsea, he made his feelings clear to the media after seeing his last chance of silverware that season slip away, as Real lost the semi- finals of the Champions League to Borussia Dortmund, and Barcelona clinched the Spanish La Liga title. A season that had started with such promise after beating Barca to win the Spanish Super Cup petered out. 'This is the worst season of my career with a title that is not sufficient to satisfy Real Madrid and therefore it is a bad season. With a final, a semi-final, second place in the league and the Supercup, what for many would be a good season, for me is the worst.'

Pressed on his likely move to Chelsea, Mourinho refused to be drawn. 'I have a contract for three more years [with Real Madrid] and I have still not sat down with the president to talk about my future. I have to be honest. Until the day that the president sits down with me and the club does something official it has to be like this.'

His swansong in the Santiago Bernabeu wasn't the best of nights for Ronaldo either, as he saw red in the dying minutes. Mourinho was ordered by the referee to leave the touchline for protesting a decision late in the second half as Atlético won their first Copa del Rey in seventeen years and beat their Madrid rivals for the first time since 1999. Mourinho was teased by the Atléti fans. 'Mourinho, stay!' they implored with heavy sarcasm.

Mourinho believed that his team should have lifted the cup and had been plain unlucky. Several of his players cared more about their public appearance than about winning trophies, according to Mourinho, who, after three years in charge at the Santiago Bernabeu, was not impressed by their attitude.

'Lots of times at Real Madrid, the players would be queuing in front of the mirror before the game while the referee waited for them in the tunnel, but that's how society is now. Young people care a lot about this: they are twenty-something and I am fifty-one and if I want to work with kids I have to understand their world. How can I stop my players on the bus doing, er, what do you call? ... Twitters and these things? How can I stop them if my daughter and my son do the same? So, I have to adapt to the moment. I'm a manager since 2000 so I'm in my second generation of players. What I feel is that, before, players were trying to make money during their career, be rich at the end of their career. But in this moment, the people who surround them try to make them rich before they start their career. They try to make them rich when they sign their first contract, when they didn't play one single match in the Premier League, when they don't know what it is to play in the Champions League. This puts the clubs in difficult conditions sometimes. You have to find the right boy: the boy who wants to succeed, has pride and passion for the game. His dream is not one more million or one less million, his dream is to play at the highest level, to win titles, because if you do these things you'll be rich the same at the end of your career. So we are working hard to give the best orientation to young players, to follow examples of guys from the past – the Lampards, the Terrys – who were always fanatical for victories.'

For the first time in a decade, since he took the reins at Porto, he endured a term without a trophy (bar the Spanish Super Cup).

Newspapers reported an alleged falling-out between Mourinho and two of the 'galácticos': Iker Casillas and Sergio Ramos, globally revered goalkeeper and defender, respectively. After a defeat to Barcelona, stories appeared that Ramos had sniped at Mourinho, ,'Because you've never been a player, you don't know that that sometimes happens.' It was suggested that Mourinho and Ronaldo barely spoke to each other at the end of his time in Spain.

Conversely, Ibrahimovic felt his manager made him 'feel like a lion'. Dutch playmaker Sneijder went even further: 'I was prepared to kill and die for him.' When Lampard's mother died in 2008, Mourinho phoned him every day, commiserating and offering advice. Mourinho wasn't even his manager.

Mourinho was interviewed for the Barcelona job in 2008 but they opted in the end for Pep Guardiola. Johan Cruyff didn't like the style of football, and others find Mourinho arrogant. Manchester United should have pursued Mourinho to replace Sir Alex Ferguson but they went for David Moyes for the long-term, preferring someone far less controversial. Mourinho denies that he cried when he learned he'd been passed over at Old Trafford but he also denies that he was ever approached.

While Mourinho was celebrating winning the Spanish title in 2012 with Real Madrid, Andre Villas Boas, following in the footsteps of Mourinho, departed FC Porto with a domestic double and Europa League triumph after a gap of just under four years to take charge of Chelsea Football Club at the age of just thirty-three.

AVB was a self-confident young manager at the Bridge, with the brief to perfect a 'project', often referred to as 'transition', which was inevitably going to lead to personality clashes and conflict within a group still dominated by the senior players loyal to Mourinho. But after an undistinguished start, the inevitable sacking was the chance for Roberto Di Matteo to take over the reins and lead Chelsea to an improbable Champions League triumph.

Chelsea's decision to axe their eighth manager in eight years came on the brink of elimination from the Champions League – clearly the defining moment in AVB's short reign as manager. It also came immediately after the 1–0 defeat by West Brom, which put their qualification via the league in jeopardy, with a disastrous run of three Premier League wins in twelve games. Abramovich had to act fast to save a rapidly disintegrating season. Di Matteo was put in charge on an interim basis until the end of the season.

The club had taken soundings from a couple of vastly experienced managers but to take the job on a temporary, virtually trial basis until the end of the season didn't fit comfortably with the likes of Rafa Benitez. So Di Matteo – who played for Chelsea from 1996–2002 and had helped win two FA Cups, scoring inside forty-two seconds in the 1997 final against Middlesbrough (the fastest goal in a final at the old Wembley Stadium) – was handed the interim post. He also helped win the League Cup, the UEFA Cup, the UEFA Super Cup and the Charity Shield while at Stamford Bridge.

Di Matteo, though, pulled off one of the most incredible managerial feats when least expected to do so. Chelsea succeeded for only the fourth time in forty-five attempts to overcome a first-leg deficit of two or more goals in the Champions League as the Blues won 4–1 after extra time, winning 5–4 on aggregate on 14 March 2012. Chelsea joined

Manchester United's class of 1957 and Leeds United's 1992 vintage as the only English team to progress in the European Cup after losing the first leg by two or more goals.

Chelsea overcame Benfica to reach the semi-finals against Barca and recalled how unfortunate it was to be knocked out by Guardiola's side in 2009, complaining bitterly about a succession of decisions made by Norwegian referee Tom Ovrebo. The two legs of this semi- final were the ninth and tenth times these two teams had met since that dramatic win in Camp Nou in 2000.

Drogba was determined to land the elite prize in Europe, as this was his final season. He answered the critics who said he was over the hill, after scoring the winner in the hugely impressive 1–0 win over Barca at the Bridge. The thirty-four-year-old found the net with his team's only shot on target. Few, if any, thought they would survive the barrage of attacks that awaited them in the return leg.

Chelsea were sixth in the Premier League. Their ability to qualify for the Champions League via the league was in such doubt that it increasingly looked like the only salvation to the season would be actually winning the Champions League, despite having to overcome Barcelona, and then take on either Real Madrid or Bayern Munich.

Chelsea produced one of the greatest escapes in the history of European football, as they withstood the sending-off of Terry to win a place in the final on a night of drama at the Nou Camp. After surviving a Barca siege from start to finish, which saw Messi miss a penalty, Torres came off the bench to score a stoppage-time breakaway goal as Chelsea avenged their 2009 defeat in the most remarkable manner possible. Terry's indiscretion ruled him

JOSE: FAREWELL TO THE KING

out of the final in Munich. Meireles, Ramires and Ivanovic were also suspended after picking up yellow cards.

So no magical final showdown with the 'Special One' after all. Mourinho was naturally supporting his 'Chelsea heroes' against Bayern in the final after he was denied a reunion with his former club by a dramatic penalty shoot-out defeat in the second leg of the semi- final. The then Real manager rounded on critics of Chelsea's tactics, telling them, 'You know nothing.'

Ronaldo and Kaká had penalties saved and Ramos blasted his over the bar as Madrid were beaten 3–1 in the shootout after a 3–3 aggregate draw. Mourinho, as usual, defended his players, highlighting the 'brutal' pressure and praising them for having the 'balls' to step up. He continued in a similar vein with an equally spirited defence of his former players from Stamford Bridge over their defensive approach against Barcelona. 'John is missing but Chelsea are there and that is the most important thing. I just hope it is a good final and, of course, I want the Blues to win, even though I have a lot of respect for the reds. I have a blue rib, still. Inter and Chelsea mean a lot to me. I think Chelsea's boys were heroes, absolute heroes. Some people think they are the masters of the game and they will criticise Chelsea in the same way that they criticised Inter two years ago, but they know nothing. Nothing. They know nothing about character and personality. They know nothing about the effort or what it is to resist physically, emotionally and technically, with ten men. They know nothing about organisation. They know nothing. That's why my heroes at Chelsea are in my mind and why Chelsea deserve to be in the final. One of the great things about football is that it is unpredictable. Chelsea have fantastic fans and so do Bayern Munich so I hope they enjoy the final. And I hope Chelsea win.'

Chelsea ended the season a shocking sixth, so they would only qualify for the Champions League by beating Bayern. Equally, Bayern were under pressure to deliver the club's fifth European Cup, having been eclipsed domestically by Borussia Dortmund, losing the German Cup final 5–2 to the league champions. Bayern, beaten in the final by Mourinho's Inter in Madrid two years earlier, would be the first side to play in a Champions League final in their own stadium and it was Bayern's last chance to win silverware that season.

As Di Matteo led his players up the seemingly never-ending flights of stairs to reach the presentation podium high in the stands, he embraced the man he called 'The Boss'. 'I won it,' Di Matteo could be heard telling his boss. For the tenth time, an Italian manager won the European Cup; the first Italian to achieve the feat with a foreign club. For Chelsea, it was the first time they had won the European Cup – the first London club to win it and the second side to win the FA Cup and the European Cup in the same season, along with Manchester United in their 1998/99 treble-winning season.

However, it looked as though Chelsea were going to lose the shoot-out again when they started two goals down. Mata missed the first penalty. The German side went 2–0 up in a penalty shoot-out. Surely game over? But Luiz, Lampard and Cole were all successful. Lahm, Gomez and goalkeeper Manuel Neuer were all on target. After Robben's saved penalty in normal time, he was unable to take part in the penalty shoot-out, leaving it to his keeper, who scuffed the shot slightly but still found the corner. Cech was guessing each penalty correctly; it was only a matter of time before he saved one. The momentum shifted decisively when Cech denied Olic, and Schweinsteiger hit the post to present Drogba with his moment of destiny.

Drogba composed himself, then took three strides to strike the perfect penalty just inside the post. Signal wild scenes of elation among Chelsea's players, staff and supporters. Drogba ran the length of the pitch, swirling his shirt above his head before finally slamming it onto the pitch. Nine cup finals, scoring in every one.

For Abramovich, the Champions League was the Holy Grail: £1 billion pounds, eight managers in eight years, a penalty-shoot-out defeat in Moscow against United – finally, after all the frustrations, Abramovich got his hands on the trophy he craved; *the* trophy that had always eluded him; the one piece of silverware all the gold of the Russian oligarch's £16 billion wealth could not buy, no matter how much he threw at buying players. The wait was finally over.

THE
HAPPY ONE

Jose Mourinho described his return as a 'great moment' for him almost a decade since he was first unveiled at the club. Mourinho first joined Chelsea in 2004 and the impact of 'The Special One' was instantaneous: back-to-back Premier League titles in 2005 and 2006. He was conscious, however, of the possibility that his return might not spark the same level of success and that it might ruin the memory of his original achievements. 'When I decide to come back, there is some risk of things going wrong, but I'm not afraid. I trust myself, I think I can do it again. I'm not afraid to lose my job and when you're not afraid, you don't feel any pressures. You are not too worried, you can express yourself in a different way. It makes you better, I think.'

He embarked on the season giving the impression he had changed; that he had returned older and wiser, and that it would be less 'sexy football', but the motivation was there – the thirst for more success. His first Chelsea experience was all silverware, even if he failed to deliver the real pot of gold – the Champions League: the trophy that eluded Roman Abramovich and was, ironically, delivered in Mourinho's absence.

Now he was back, in his fifties, his hair grey. More than half the managers in the Premier League were younger than him. Mourinho was no longer the fashion icon. The media were eagerly looking for a new tag on the manager's comeback, and the man who inspires a million headlines didn't disappoint, branding himself 'The Happy One'.

But that was received with a huge dose of scepticism; contentment in the Mourinho mind is never far away from outbursts of ego, anger, moodiness and controversy. The tranquillity he sought back in West London after the turbulence of life in Madrid didn't last too long.

However, comparatively speaking, life was far easier. Mourinho was back among the Chelsea faithful that adored him and, once he had knocked his side into shape, despite their shortcomings in attack, the old Mourinho song was soon ringing out at home and away. He was back where he is loved and appreciated by the fans.

The fans, too, recognised that Mourinho had inherited a Chelsea far from the one that satisfied him and, as the season unfolded, the lack of a genuine out-and-out goalscorer within his squad was the team's ultimate downfall, as they lost the Champions League semi- final and the chance of the title in the space of five days. Apart from the Spanish Super Cup at the start of the previous season, it was back-to-back seasons without a major trophy: something that forced Mourinho into a passionate defence of his entire career record. Having branded Arsène Wenger a manager who specialises in failure, it was not the right time to fail but, given the shortcomings of his squad, it was not exactly unexpected.

Mourinho parted company with Real Madrid after three years in which he won La Liga and the Copa Del Rey and, while it seemed he might be heading to Old Trafford, he wasn't their kind of guy, with Sir Alex recommending David Moyes instead. Despite the Scot's uncanny warm relationship with the Portuguese manager, and their endless banter about the quality of red wine afforded him in previous Bridge visits when Mourinho was their coach, the Old Trafford board would have been reluctant to risk their reputation on such a controversial manager. They played safe with their chosen one. But Moyes' six- year contract was brutally cut short when it was clear he was never going to turn around the team's fortunes. United have now turned to Louis van Gaal, every bit as controversial as Mourinho.

Before Madrid, Mourinho took Inter Milan to Champions League glory and two Serie A titles between 2008 and 2010. He disclosed that he been offered the chance to manage Real Madrid after he won the FA Cup in 2007, his last trophy during his first spell at Chelsea. He stayed, however, and was sacked in September.

A fondness for Inter remains but not so for Real, where antagonism and confrontation reached an unprecedented peak. Yet Mourinho badly wanted Real on his already impressive CV and left Inter for the opportunity. Unfortunately, though, the love affair ended in an ugly divorce. The Real hierarchy were glad to get shot of a coach who had become far too high profile for all the wrong reasons. Mourinho split opinion about his merits as coach at Madrid – not necessarily about his ability to lead a team but because of the headlines that appeared at times. His time in Spain was punctuated by a series of rows with the press and issues with key players.

Mourinho's return was remarkable given the nature of the fall-out that saw him leave in the first place. Nevertheless, he signed a four-year contract, replacing the hugely unpopular Benitez, who had guided Chelsea to third place and won the Europa League after taking over the helm on an interim basis in November from the hugely popular Roberto di Matteo.

Mourinho explained on his return how he had repaired his fractured relationship with the Russian oligarch. 'I'm very happy. I had to prepare myself [to] not to be too emotional at my arrival at the club but obviously I'm very happy. It was an easy decision. I met the owner and I think in five minutes after a couple of very short but pragmatic questions we decided, I think, straight away. I asked the boss, "Do you want me back?" and the boss asked me, "Do you want to come back?" and I think in a couple of minutes, decision made.'

Having won the 'grand slam' of titles in Portugal, England, Italy and Spain, he felt it was the right time to return. He added, 'I love it here and I have big connections with the club. I think we are ready to marry again and to be happy and successful again.'

Mourinho sought stability back in West London. His insistence that he 'will stay for the long term' was interesting considering that the longest he has managed at any club is the three years and two months he spent at Chelsea between 2004 and 2007.

After seven permanent managers and two temporary appointments during Abramovich's ten-year ownership, the club could now do with stability as they set off at the outset of the second Mourinho management era but it seemed a contradiction in terms that they could possibly find it with the nomadic Mourinho.

Despite being the most successful manager in the club's history, in terms of domestic trophies, he would not rely on his popularity with the fan base to see him through. 'I'm not coming here to sleep on what I did in the past and be comfortable just because we [Mourinho and the supporters] have a great relation, and probably the first day I put my foot in Stamford Bridge again they will sing my name. I'm not that kind of person and professional. I'm very demanding of myself. I need, of course, their support, but I want to start from ground zero. I need to work hard again and build a different team from the team I built in the past.'

He spoke of his high regard for Chelsea's old guard: John Terry, Ashley Cole and Lampard – players he once called 'untouchables'. 'They have made my life easier. Some managers bring in four or five guys they know well when they first arrive at a club. I didn't need to. They were already here.'

They helped him to get his ideas across to the team because they had the benefit of playing under him several years ago. 'It was a help for me, the way they communicated with other people, the way they know me and the way they helped others understand my ideas. They are good guys, they are professional and the relationship they have with me is perfect for the time of their career because they trust me.' Mourinho inherited an evolving Chelsea, with a number of missing links and some problem areas. He had some familiar old friends in Terry and Lampard but his rock of a captain and leader, Terry, was no longer in favour. That would change, however, with his old manager back. How to integrate Oscar, Juan Mata, Willian and Eden Hazard was a conundrum.

From his own staff Mourinho brought coach Rui Faria and goalkeeping coach Silvinho Louro, who worked with him in his first spell at the club, and scout Jose Morais, keeping Christopher Lollichon, Steve Holland and Chris Jones from the existing staff. In the build-up to his official unveiling, he remarked, 'I'm not happy, I am very happy. I was preparing myself in the last couple of days to control emotions, to come here in a cool way but I'm really emotional. I feel the people love me and in life you have to look for that. Life is beautiful and short and you must look for what you think is best for you.'

Mourinho was fined £10,000 for sarcastic appraisal of officials during the season. The manager's comments did not question the officials' integrity but amounted to disrepute and improper conduct. At the same time, Mourinho also failed in an appeal against an £8,000 fine for his conduct towards referee Chris Foy at the end of a defeat at Villa. 'The Silent One' also, on one occasion, refused to give a half-time talk to his team because his players had been so bad in the first half of the match!

Chelsea's chief executive Ron Gourlay greeted Mourinho's return as you would expect, with typical boardroom speak, but he did make this valid point: 'His continued success, drive and ambition made him the outstanding candidate. He was and remains a hugely popular figure at the club and everyone here looks forward to working with him again.'

Reacting to the news of Mourinho's return, former Chelsea assistant manager Ray Wilkins said, 'Having lost from our game Sir Alex Ferguson, who has been absolutely unbelievably good, it is nice we have got another fantastic personality coming back. It is not only good for Chelsea, it is good for the Premier League as well.' Former Chelsea captain Ron Harris added, 'I think 95 per cent of the Chelsea supporters are pleased Jose is back. I feel that the supporters will be more than happy and I think it is a pat on the back for Roman Abramovich in bringing Jose Mourinho back to the club.'

The fans had wanted him back and now they had him back, turning out in their 'Special 1' T-shirts for his return game at home to Hull City. His 'signing' was more anticipated than that of any multi-million- pound player, inspiring confidence that another trophy haul was about to start.

Mourinho was greeted at the match with a sign that read 'Jose Mourinho Simply the Best'. In the match-day programme he wrote, 'The boss [Roman Abramovich] celebrates ten years of amazing work. I celebrate my return, but this match is not a testimonial! It is great to write again to my Blues brothers.'

He told Sky Sports before kick-off, 'I feel good. I want to play. I try not to feel [emotional]. But I think when I go and sit [in the dugout], there will be thirty seconds of emotion, for sure. After that I have to focus on the game.'

Mourinho tried hard to keep things low key when he finally emerged from the tunnel to take his seat. No chance. Nearly 40,000 people sang his name, some wearing Mourinho masks. He stood up and sat down three times, eventually blowing kisses to the supporters and then, as the game started, he began writing his customary notes on a pad. His unbeaten home record in the league was never going to be challenged that day.

Up in his executive box, Abramovich gave a shy wave to the supporters when his face was beamed up on the screen. Earlier, he had imparted a rare message to the fans on the cover of the programme: twenty-nine words in all, thanking them for supporting the club over his ten years in charge.

Mourinho said that the billionaire had been in the dressing room before the game to speak to the players – the first time that he had done so during Mourinho's time in charge on the first day of a season. De Bruyne was selected as the number 10, between Hazard and Oscar. The twenty-two-year-old, who was making his competitive debut for Chelsea, was impressive. He passed to Oscar on six minutes, after Hazard had carried the ball from the left wing, and the Brazilian scored beautifully.

Mata's absence could be noted. It was obvious from the start that Mata would need to convince Mourinho that he could conform to the team ethic, despite his billing as the team's best player for two years. Equally apparent was the lack of a genuine goalscoring threat, alongside Mourinho's persistent courting of Wayne Rooney. Mourinho talked around the subject of the United forward after the game because the penny had dropped that he would not be sold to Chelsea, so there was no point in aggravating the situation any further.

Romelu Lukaku was a late replacement for Torres but Mourinho was again less than convinced and the young Belgium was destined for another loan spell, this time with Everton. Without Mata and David Luiz, it was an impressive start. But as goals became hard to come by, there was a great deal of head-scratching as to why Lukaku was farmed out to Goodison, as he hit a rich vein of goalscoring form while his strikers were misfiring.

Mata was surprised when Mourinho sold him mid-season for £37.1 million to Manchester United. Mourinho was convinced Chelsea were doing the right thing and that he would also have sanctioned the sale to title rivals Arsenal and Manchester City.

To Wenger's complaint that Chelsea benefited from Mata facing Arsenal and City in a United shirt in the second half of the season, Mourinho said, 'Wenger complaining is normal because he always does. This is the market. We don't do the market, we don't do the rules ... he should be very happy that Chelsea sold a player like Juan Mata. But I think it [complaining] is also a bit of his nature.'

Pellegrini did not agree with the principle of Mata joining United in mid-season. 'I think if a player plays for a club for more than half of the season, a club with money can take the best players from the other teams. But the rules allow it, so [there is] nothing to say.' He clarified that his complaint was not because United were still to play City at Old Trafford, while they have taken on Chelsea twice already. 'I think in this transfer window, players that play more than five or six games for the same club should not change to another.'

The inevitable abrasive managerial confrontations began to dominate the agenda for the season. Sam Allardyce defused this row by suggesting that the new incarnation of Mourinho was far more sociable, as the Hammers boss brushed off Mourinho's criticism of West Ham's style. Mourinho savaged the Hammers' willingness to get men behind the ball, after the 0–0 draw at Stamford Bridge seemed, at the time, to put Chelsea's title chances backwards with a big step. Mourinho said Allardyce had his side playing 'nineteenth-century football'. Big Sam was, understandably, a trifle peeved. Surprisingly, though, he heaped some praise on his adversary by suggesting that he had mellowed.

For the next game – one of the most significant of the season – Mourinho deployed two defensive midfielders with devastating attacking effect. First Mourinho engaged in typical mind games, dismissing Tim Sherwood's assertion that Manchester City are the best team in the world after tearing Spurs apart and continuing with their mountain of goals. Mourinho took a swipe at City, suggesting a true measure of their worth would out in the Champions League. 'Maybe, for the Tottenham manager, the planet is England,' said Mourinho. 'You will see [how good City are] in the Champions League. You will see in a couple of months.'

Mourinho continued on the attack. 'They are lucky. The reality is they have many crucial decisions in their favour. Against Liverpool, the Sterling "goal". The penalty on Suárez. Against Newcastle, the goal that is a clear goal. Against Tottenham, Dawson's goal, the penalty, the [Danny Rose] red card. They are having everything. I repeat, because I don't want to be misinterpreted, [it is] just pure coincidence. The referees, they try to do their best and sometimes they make mistakes and normally during the season the mistakes are split between teams. In their [City's] case, they have everything in their favour.'

Mourinho insisted his side were not yet ready to win the title. 'Next pre-season, day one, I will say we are candidates to win the Premier League. This season, the speech is we are candidates to win the next match. It doesn't matter where, it doesn't matter the opponent. We're just trying to win. I tell you now, before Man City... I will tell you before the Newcastle game next week, and then West Brom. I will repeat this.'

City were escaping the public criticism his Chelsea had to face 10 ten years ago, according to Mourinho. 'I don't know why they are so popular when we weren't. I don't know why. In my time we were accused of buying the title, no? Because our owner was Mr Abramovich; just arrived in the country. Maybe now people see City in a different way. I'm not sure if it's because it's taken them six years to get to this stage while we won straight away. And I don't care. I don't envy the fact that they have this kind of protection, of whichever word. It's the way it is. Teams with success, people tend not to like them, no? If they want to make it impossible for us to compete with them in the market, yes, it's impossible. Financially, no, we can't compete. Back then it was a free world. There was no Financial Fair Play. If your club was a rich one, your owner a rich one, there were no rules. It was an open situation. But times change. Many things people considered wrong fifty years ago are something very normal now. Maybe ten years ago a huge investment in the club was something people hated, but in this moment it's something people accept in a different way.'

Mourinho claimed that not all clubs were showing the same commitment to UEFA's Financial Fair Play regulations as others. On the day £11 million-signing Mohamed Salah trained for the first time and nineteen-year-old Kurt Zouma completed his £12.5 million move, loaned straight back, Mourinho hinted that some clubs were finding ways to mask their spending. Of course, Abramovich personally funded the recruitment when Mourinho guided the team to back-to-back titles in 2005 and 2006; City are funded by their billionaire owners from Abu Dhabi.

When Abramovich first arrived, they would not have sold Mata mid-season and would have fought with City for Porto centre-half Eliaquim Mangala, rather than conceding defeat to sign teenager Kurt Zouma.

Mourinho was astutely removing the pressure from his players ahead of the Etihad clash with typical divisive tactics. Asked if he might have to accept second to City, Mourinho replied, 'Yes. But if we finish second it's fantastic. If we finished second doing the formation work, it's an acceleration of our process. It's good.' He suggested City had a 'complete' team in comparison to his own, which requires 'a bit more time, a little bit more players. Just a little bit. Our objective is to finish in a Champions League spot. That's the competitive objective, because the greater objective is the improvement of the team and preparing the team for the future.'

Mourinho agreed City's midfield power axis of Yaya Touré and Fernandinho provided the platform for their goalscoring feats. Touré, Dzeko, Negredo and hamstring-victim absentee Aguero all notched double figures already in goals scored, while only Hazard scored more than ten for Chelsea. City have not dropped a point at home this season, winning eleven matches and scoring forty-two goals but Chelsea were not planning all-out defence. He added, 'I don't know if other teams have been scared of City; whether it's not so much that they don't attack them and more that they can't. Maybe they can't. I want to attack them. I can tell you that. But after ten minutes, people might say I'm not attacking. If I don't, it's because I can't.'

Almost seven years before, when Stuart Pearce was City's manager, Chelsea were the side splashing millions on the world's best players, winning trophies and challenging for European glory. Pearce fielded a team made up of academy players and bargain buys as visitors Chelsea ran out 1–0 winners. Pearce's side cost just £13.5 million, compared to £160 million for a team then seeking to leapfrog Arsenal and regain top spot in the Premier League. Although Chelsea now remained one of the elite, City were now on a level playing field after a huge investment from billionaire owner Sheik Mansour.

Pellegrini's high-scoring side had attack as their best means of defence. City had found the net 115 times already this season but were without main striker Aguero.

Despite beating City at Stamford Bridge, Mourinho had long since hailed Pellegrini's team favourites for the title. 'They're complete. The players are amazing, the squad is fantastic but you also need the manager to do a good job and I think he is [doing that]. The players are experienced. They were champions two years ago and a big nucleus is the same. They have everything and we need a bit more time, a few more players, just a little bit.'

City were still smarting from a 2–1 defeat at Stamford Bridge in October. Pellegrini's side had been practically unstoppable since then, particularly at home, and victory would represent a massive step towards clinching the title.

At midday Mourinho walked into a team meeting and told his players what he was planning: Oscar and John Obi Mikel left out from the 0–0 draw with West Ham, Matic and Luiz as the holding midfield pair. The players practised something completely different before travelling to Manchester the day before, believing Willian was the odd man out in a system designed to stop City from getting a grip in midfield. Mourinho was making sure there would be no leaks of his surprising team plans. No one in the Chelsea squad believed that Oscar, with nine goals this season, could not start a game of this magnitude.

As the teams were announced, many believed Mourinho had set his team out to 'park the bus' but his team had the better of the chances, hitting the post three times. Mourinho said, 'I think they did amazing. When the team lost the ball, they all sacrificed for the team. Our record was not good against City in the last few years. This season we managed to win these two matches, especially this one. Today we won because we were the best team – I am not saying we are better, I am just saying we were today.'

Victory at the Etihad was the first time in sixty-one home-league games that City had failed to score, dating back to a 0–0 draw against Birmingham City in November 2010. Still Mourinho played down his team's chances of winning the league. 'There are two big horses and a little horse. A horse that next season can race. We can win it if they lose it.'

Mourinho's master class of tactics was universally applauded. Sky Sports expert Gary Neville praised the way Mourinho set up his team to nullify the threat of the title favourites and said that even his demeanour on the touchline had an impact on the result. 'He doesn't mind us praising him, does Jose Mourinho. He loves the attention of big matches. You saw him tonight and he was like the conductor of the orchestra. He walks out at the start of the match and sits on the bench before his team have even come out. He comes alive on big-match days and that's what the best managers do. He is the best in the world at the moment at affecting big matches, absolutely brilliant. He thinks about every small detail, things that I don't think many would think of because he's been around the block. He's shrewd, he's smart and he calls it on. He's good and he knows he's good.'

Mourinho chose to sell Mata to United and many were surprised by his treatment of the man who'd won Chelsea's Player of the Season award for the last two years, but Neville spotted how the manager was putting his stamp on the team, and an important aspect of his success this season has been using wide players who are willing to work hard.

Mourinho claimed his side were 'not ready to win the title this season' but should be considered as favourites next year. Neville agreed that Chelsea could suffer for the lack of a top-class striker, with Eto'o, Torres and Ba scoring eleven Premier League goals between them so far, but he said, 'I have a tendency not to believe a word Jose Mourinho says, but I actually believe him. I think the odds reflect where it probably still is at. In his mind there's that niggling doubt that he's just that little bit short. He was criticised earlier in the season for parking the bus in big matches, but his team are now starting to play very well in big matches and his journey is on an upward curve. His team are getting better, you are starting to see Mourinho-like performances but is he going to fall that little bit short? The bookies suggest he is and I think he possibly might because of that lack of a devastating centre-forward.'

Stung by Mourinho's typical jibes that City had been 'lucky' with refereeing decisions, Pellegrini accused him of trying to brainwash the public. Asked if he thought it was a fair assessment, Pellegrini said, 'No, it isn't. It is very easy to say every week what is best for your team, but there is a very famous sentence: "Lie, lie and something will remain [in people's minds]." In fact, the only time there has been an apology from a referee for an important mistake was when Mike Riley said sorry for the ninety-third-minute penalty that saved a point for Chelsea against West Brom after Ramires dived.'

Pellegrini ridiculed Mourinho's assertion that Chelsea were a 'little horse' compared to City and Arsenal. 'Maybe it is a small horse if the manager thinks like that but it is also a very rich one. This is the team that spends the most money in the last ten years, it is the team that spends the most money this year and the team that spends the most money in the transfer window, so a little bit rich. He shows in the last two games he has a strong team with some great players, but he thinks it is better not to talk about it. Why? Because if he wins [the title], he has all the merit, while if he loses, he does not have the responsibility. It is the way he acts. It will be very close with Chelsea and Arsenal. Arsenal is the favourite because they have a two-point lead in the table, an important advantage.'

After an emphatic home win against Newcastle, Jose was full of his impish smiles and title-avoidance, despite City drawing at Norwich, now back-to-back games goalless, while earlier in the day Arsenal were toppled from the top with a crushing 5–1 humiliation at Anfield. Chelsea were top, installed as title favourites for the first time, with Eden Hazard looking every bit the best young player in the world with a hat-trick in a 3–0 win. Mourinho wanted to kill all talk of a horse race, as he switched metaphors to cars, likening City to a 'Jaguar' wearing 'L-plates'. Interpreted as a swipe at Pellegrini, Mourinho said, 'A Jaguar: you wouldn't put an L on it.' He went on, 'It's time to kill [talk of] the horse. We are playing well. Players individually are in a good moment, we are getting results and we are top of the league. That is something that we can't hide.'

Pre-season brought demands for industry and greater professionalism, the message clear that even the team's most mercurial talents must accept more mundane duties, tracking back, marking, committed attitude to training. Mata was sold. Hazard – a prankster with a carefree approach – was reformed. A late return to training after an invite to attend his former club Lille's Ligue 1 game against Monaco in November (Hazard said he had mislaid his passport) was make or break – 'an isolated episode', according to Mourinho – but the manager left him out for the next game against Schalke. The manager now demanded more ruthlessness in front of goal, yet fourteen goals – twelve in the league – was already more than Hazard had managed the previous season.

Alan Pardew believed that this current Chelsea vintage was the best he has ever faced under Mourinho, having taken on his friend as boss of West Ham, Charlton Athletic and now Newcastle. Pardew said, 'This is as good as he's had. They've got a real chance [of winning the league].' Mourinho, however, continued to talk down chances of silverware in his first campaign back in charge.

Pellegrini's view that Chelsea were a 'rich little horse' in response to Mourinho saying his team were a 'little horse', promoted a stampede of cross-fire from both camps. Mourinho questioned his adversary's maths. 'Mata was sold for £37 million and De Bruyne for £18 million – that's £55 million,' said Mourinho. 'Matic bought for £21 million and Salah £11 million. In this window, we are plus £23 million.'

Mourinho added, 'We are building a team for the next decade and City have a team to win now. They have experience, potential, power and no worries about [UEFA cost-control protocol] Financial Fair Play, because in summer they just spent. We don't need a calculator for this.'

Former Malaga boss Pellegrini, who faced the Portuguese when Mourinho was coach of Madrid, questioned Mourinho's view and drew reference to Chelsea's spending since Abramovich bought the club. Chelsea's net spend during the previous two summer and winter transfer windows was £49 million. City did not change their squad during the winter window but had a net spend of £80 million last summer. Mourinho was interested in signing Falcao and Cavani in the summer but did not go through with the deals, to keep the Blues in line with the new Financial Fair Play rules. Chelsea did sign Schürrle, van Ginkel and Willian.

Mourinho said of Pellegrini, 'He has been speaking about winning four competitions, so there's no reason to change the speech. But the only thing that is funny [is] that he keeps saying he never responds to Mourinho; he never comments about Mourinho. He said that in Spain too. So he's changed.'

Mourinho often draws rival managers into a tit-for-tat but Pellegrini said that differed widely from his own approach. 'It is not my way to act, so I will not do it. I don't think everyone should act the same way. I answered once what Mourinho says because he was talking about the referees but I won't be answering every week because we would just continue to give an answer and get one from the other side.'

Mourinho lamented the lack of a 'killer instinct' as Victor Anichebe's late goal saw two points slip through Chelsea's hands when West Brom's striker cancelled out Ivanovic's opener with three minutes left. Ivanovic and Cech were also involved in an on-field spat. Having seen his side give Arsenal and City the chance to overhaul them, Mourinho said, 'We were comfortable in the game, maybe too comfortable. We didn't kill the game when we had the chance. A point is a point and at the end of the season we will see.' He brushed aside the row between his two players. 'I don't know what happened but I like it. I like the players to have emotion and, if someone has made a mistake, I like [that] they speak between them.' Mourinho insisted one point was still better than none on a ground where Liverpool and Arsenal drew. 'In this moment we have one more point than before. If Arsenal and City win tomorrow, they go above us but that is their job. Every game is difficult.'

Responding to Wenger's claim that other bosses are playing down their title chances because they 'fear to fail', Mourinho delivered an acidic riposte. 'If he is right and I am afraid of failure, it is because I didn't fail many times. Eight years without silverware, that's failure.'

Arsenal had not won a trophy since the 2005 FA Cup. 'He's a specialist in failure,' continued Mourinho. 'If I do that in Chelsea, eight years, I leave and don't come back.' BBC presenter Gary Lineker felt Mourinho had gone 'over the top. 'Mourinho is out of order and wrong with the Wenger comments,' Lineker wrote on Twitter. 'He's won trophies galore all over the world, playing delightful football. Yes, Wenger hasn't won anything for a number of years, but he hasn't, until very recently, had the budget of others. Arsenal is in great shape.'

Chelsea at home to Arsenal in a month was likely to have a significant bearing on the title fight. Wenger insisted the title was 'Chelsea's to lose' but said that Arsenal would 'give everything' to win it.

Mourinho highlighted the 'many, many years' Wenger has had to turn his squad into champions. Wenger admitted after a goalless draw with United that his team were 'nervous' but Mourinho believed that they should now be mature and ready to deliver. When asked why he thought Wenger was obsessed with Chelsea, he replied, 'Ask him.' When asked why Arsenal had not won anything in eight years, Mourinho said, 'Ask him. Not me.' Mourinho would not hang around at a club if he was not accumulating silverware. 'If I don't win a trophy in four years, I don't want a new contract. It's as simple as that. I don't think a manager should be embarrassed when he gives everything, tries everything, dedicates himself to the club, the project and the collective dream. If you don't get results, that's football. But for my mentality, there is a limit. And you have to be strong enough and proud enough to admit when it's enough.'

The pair have history, Mourinho having described the Frenchman as a 'voyeur' in 2005 after his rival questioned Chelsea's transfer policy. 'He likes to watch other people,' Mourinho said in October 2005. 'There are some guys who, when they are at home, have a big telescope to see what happens in other families. He speaks, speaks, speaks about Chelsea.' At the time, Wenger retorted, 'He's out of order, disconnected with reality and disrespectful. When you give success to stupid people, it makes them more stupid sometimes.'

Wenger had his moments hitting out at Mourinho, and vice versa. Wenger quoted in August 2005 on Chelsea's tactics, 'I know we live in a world where we have only winners and losers, but once a sport encourages teams who refuse to take the initiative, the sport is in danger.' Mourinho quoted in November 2007 on Wenger's foreign policy, 'Unlike Arsenal, we sought success and tried to build it through a concept of the game using English players.'

Brendan Rodgers, manager of fourth-placed Liverpool, continued the horse-racing analogy by saying his side 'may be the Chihuahuas that run in between the legs of the horses' as they looked to make a late challenge. Mourinho then compared Liverpool to a 'privileged Chihuahua', with Rodgers' side moving within four points of Chelsea. Mourinho believed Liverpool had a 'big advantage' because they were free from the constraints of European competition.

Chelsea crashed out of the FA Cup with a 2–0 defeat at Etihad Stadium but, although he had a day earlier branded Wenger a failure, Mourinho insisted that his team hadn't failed him. 'I don't say my team failed. I would say that City played much better than us and deserved much more to win. The game was simple to analyse – they were the best team and they won.' Pellegrini felt his side were refreshed because they rested instead of playing in midweek, as their home-league game with Sunderland was victim to high winds.

Elsewhere, Wenger's Gunners beat Liverpool to reach the

quarter-finals and, just before the tie, former player and coach Bob Wilson savaged Mourinho for his views on the Arsenal boss. 'I think at its best it's disrespectful, at its worst despicable. I find him boring in the extreme. I think it's personal. He is a hugely talented, amazing manager but a self-publicist and it's mainly inaccurate. He's out of order, disconnected with reality and disrespectful … It's not the first time he has singled Arsène out. A few years ago he called him a voyeur, which is a disgusting claim – albeit thankfully with a belated apology. I like people who have within them some humility as well. Bill Shankly was, in his day, like Jose Mourinho. He took every opportunity to psyche you out. He would get at you, but in a lovely, sort of competitive way.'

Wenger escalated the feud, although he stressed that he did not specifically mention Mourinho when he claimed that a 'fear to fail' was why so many managers were saying they were not contenders to win the league title. Ahead of the next game, it was a very contrite Jose refusing to answer questions beyond his own team so, after weeks of taunting his title rivals, he suddenly clammed up, refusing to comment on a number of questions put to him by the press.

Back on the pitch, and into the final ten minutes of Chelsea's 1–0 win over Everton, and with the Blues still locked at 0–0, Mourinho got so carried away with giving instructions that he walked on to the pitch, very close to where the ball was, nearly impeding winger Aiden McGeady as the Scot ran up the wing! Mourinho insisted that his team deserved the late lucky break, which saw his side consolidate their position at the top. Two points would have been dropped until Jagielka fouled Ramires. Lampard's in-swinging free-kick just cleared

Ivanovic's leap. Terry, returning from a three-game absence due to a gluteal muscle problem, slid in as the ball squirmed past Howard, then Terry ran off, claiming it for himself. But whoever scored (it ended up as Lampard's goal, direct from the free-kick), Mourinho didn't care. He was just delighted that his team had finally notched a goal.

Chelsea were still unbeaten at home in the league, extending Mourinho's overall record to seventy-four games. Mourinho, whose first objective was Champions League qualification, said it was essential for Chelsea's challenge at the top of the table. 'Any objective you have, to have a good home record is important,' he told Chelsea TV. 'We've lost four points at home – [drawing with] West Brom and West Ham – and if you can arrive at the end of the season without dropping many points at home, you have a better chance.'

Terry was a key figure for Mourinho during his previous spell at the Bridge, lifting five major trophies, including two Premier League titles, but Benitez dropped him down the pecking order. On returning to the club, Mourinho needed to be convinced that Terry was still the talismanic figure he had placed so much trust in before. He has been left in no doubt that that is still the case, with the thirty-three-year-old becoming a key performer once more. Mourinho said, 'I didn't know [what to expect]. And I told him that. I told him I wanted to understand what had happened. Some players lose form, lose their performance level and lose condition. I wanted to feel if that was the case. I wanted to see if it [him not playing] was down to other managers' options. That is something you always have to respect. So I didn't know. I started pre-season with him, analysing the situation. With me he has always played well, except when he had back surgery and lost an important part of the season. But in my first two seasons here he had a fantastic level. Now? This season he is doing very well.'

Yet another extraordinary row erupted over a series of unguarded but highly disparaging remarks by Mourinho about the club's strikers, recorded by the French television company Canal Plus in what he thought was a private conversation with the owner of the Swiss watch manufacturer Hublot. 'I have a team but no striker,' said Mourinho. 'The problem at Chelsea is that we are lacking a goalscorer. I have one but he is thirty-two, possibly thirty-five, who knows?'

The remark about Eto'o was controversial for the supposed doubt about the true age of some African players. Chelsea 'briefed' that the remarks were light-hearted and not meant for broadcast or publication, with Mourinho unaware that Canal Plus, there to conduct an interview, were filming the exchange. The conversation was then posted online, with Mourinho's comments soon being translated from French and then published around the world. The footage was subsequently removed from the Canal Plus website. Mourinho was furious that what he thought was a private conversation had reached the public domain.

With Rooney having signed a new contract at United, Chelsea were pursuing other options and, in the same 'private' conversation, Mourinho said of Falcao, 'He doesn't have a team. Who wants to play in front of three thousand supporters? If I was one day to go to Monaco it would be the end, perhaps to prepare for retirement.' Mourinho admitted that it would be impossible to prise Cavani or Ibrahimovic away from Paris St- Germain.

Eto'o was naturally said to have been 'very annoyed' following Mourinho's jibe about his age, according to former Cameroon coach Claude Le Roy. Eto'o was the last to arrive at Chelsea's team meeting ahead of the Champions League tie with Galatasaray in Istanbul, arriving fifteen minutes late. Speaking to the Canal Plus show *Talents d'Afrique*, Le Roy said, 'I had [Eto'o] on the phone just before I came on screen and he's very annoyed.' Le Roy, sixty-six, coached Cameroon twice. 'Actually, Mourinho went to see him before he saw the pictures and told him to not believe everything that was going to be said. And that he had said nothing about him. But I can tell you that Samuel didn't like it.'

Eto'o's former partner, Anna Barranca, claimed that the striker was actually thirty-nine: 'I think Samuel is not thirty-five. He is more thirty-nine. Samuel was born in 1974 and so that makes him thirty-nine now. It was evident Samuel was older than the age he said he was when he first came to Europe.'

Mourinho said at his press conference in Istanbul that the media should be 'embarrassed' by Canal Plus airing an off-the-record conversation. 'It was a funny conversation between me and somebody who doesn't belong to the football world and we were laughing. It's a disgrace that someone is taping and recording a private conversation when, obviously, we don't know. From my perspective, the comment is obviously not a good one and obviously not something I would do in a serious way; an official way in an interview. I don't make fun. I am one of the managers who really defends their players and Samuel Eto'o is a four-times Champions League winner. It was with him I had the best-ever season of my career. He is one of the few players who is working with me at a second different club and a manager doesn't do that if he doesn't like the player or the person. He has no reason to be upset. Also, a few years ago, he said Mourinho was the only manager in the world he would never play for and after a year he was playing with me at Inter and now here.'

The French TV station argued that Mourinho was fully aware the comments were being filmed. 'These are not stolen images,' Hervé Mathoux, the presenter and chief editor of the show that broadcast the Mourinho interview told *footballmercato.web*. 'The camera wasn't ten metres away, it's not on zoom. You could see the red light and he was clearly aware he was being filmed, especially as he's someone who comes across cameras so often and who is used to the media. Mourinho perhaps did not want to fully assume what he had said. He could have come and seen the journalist and asked us not to use the images. He did not make any special request.'

Chelsea became the first English team to score in the last-sixteen Champions League round of games, and a 1–1 draw was a reasonable result. 'Some other teams have three chances and score three goals. We have five and score one,' said Mourinho. 'That's not a critique of the strikers but it's the profile of the team we have. We create but, when we arrive in the final third of the pitch, the correct pass and right movement is something we don't have. We are paying for that. In the Premier League we are losing points and in the Champions League we could have had a different result.'

On their return, Chelsea won 3–1 at Fulham. Arsenal, second at the start of the day, lost 1–0 at Stoke as Mourinho's team moved four points clear of Arsenal and Liverpool, who won at Southampton, and six ahead of Manchester City, who were preparing for the league cup final. After a very poor first half, Mourinho made one of the most bizarre half-time team talks ever – he didn't talk! He later explained after Schürrle netted a second-half hat-trick, 'At half-time, I told them nothing – nothing – not a word. I walked in, then I walked out. I don't know if anyone else gave a team talk. I was not inside the dressing room. The second half was a great reaction to the worst performance of the season. The players knew the first half was really poor. I haven't had many first halves like this one – it was very bad. The second half was one of the best performances of the season.'

Mourinho later elaborated on becoming the 'Silent One'. 'Normally I give the players two or three minutes to arrive, to change boots or shirts and after that they know that I start talking, and they were there, ready for me. But I was not ready for them. I decided not to speak – because if I start speaking about the first half, I would need more than ten minutes. I think they showed they are very intelligent – without words, you understand what is in the mind of a person, especially if you know the person. I think they understood the first half was really poor and they transformed it into a fantastic second half.'

Schürrle estimated that Mourinho spent about ten seconds with his players. It was suggested he had said, 'It's your shit – sort it out.'

Mourinho is unpredictable: one game he will rant like Sir Alex, or he will be surprisingly calm. He put it this way: 'Big games are for big players. If you are a good player, go out there and win.' They did just that: 3–1. 'Simple. Nothing more to say.' The response was a brilliant second half, especially from Hazard and Schürrle.

After being named in the PFA Team of the Year last season, Hazard was enjoying a coming-of-age season: twelve goals and nine assists in twenty-eight league games. Asked by Belgian reporters about his relationship with Mourinho, he said, 'He might be called the "Special One" but to me he is the "Normal One". I prefer it if people say things to my face. I find we have a normal relationship. If there are things to be said, he says them. If you are playing well, he says so. But if you are not, you also get to hear about it.'

Chelsea went seven points clear after giving Spurs a 4–0 thrashing at home with goals from Eto'o and Hazard, and two from substitute Demba Ba. Eto'o scored first and poked fun at Mourinho's latest leaked comments about his age with a celebration mimicking an older man. Eto'o's goal marked his 300th career-club goal. The veteran striker mimicked a backache and slow walk as he bent double by the corner flag, though Mourinho enjoyed the humour, which he felt defused the situation, as he commented, 'Eto'o's celebration was fantastic. We knew he was preparing something. It's amazing how well he's coped with the situation in the last couple of weeks. I told him today he was certain to score.' Ironically, Eto'o wasn't in the starting line-up and only played when Torres hobbled off with a groin injury in the warm-up.

Mourinho was still reluctant to admit his team were title favourites, despite going seven points clear at the top. He argued, 'I think the top four is in our hands. Now the objective is the top three. If Man City win their three games in hand, we are second, not first. I would like to be in that position because, if they win those matches, they are top of the league. If we win the next nine matches, we maybe are not champions. If Man City win the twelve matches they have, they are champions. They have their destiny in their hands and we don't have ours. I just know that I would prefer to have my destiny in my hands. If you tell me you win the next nine matches and you are champions, I say "OK, great" – it depends on us. But it doesn't depend on us. It depends on them.'

Mourinho was sent to the stands in stoppage time, following the dismissals of midfielders Willian and Ramires, as the title challenge lost its momentum with a 1–0 defeat at Villa, with City winning 2–0 at Hull earlier in the day. City moved six points behind the league leaders with three games in hand.

Mourinho vented his fury at Chris Foy, as his team finished with nine men and also had their manager dismissed. 'We must be very, very unlucky to have another refereeing performance like this one. This is not about one mistake from a referee. This is about a performance from minute one to minute ninety-four.'

Villa became only the third team, after Newcastle and Middlesbrough to beat Mourinho's Chelsea more than once in the Premier League. All three teams have two Premier League wins against the Portuguese manager. Foy had now sent off six Chelsea players in the Premier League – only Mike Dean (seven) had shown more Premier League red cards to Chelsea players. The game's biggest flash-point occurred in the closing stages as Ramires was shown a straight red card for a two-footed tackle on El Ahmadi. Mourinho was dismissed in the fracas that followed, insisting as he rushed onto the pitch that he was trying to alert Foy to a push by Villa striker Agbonlahor on Ramires. Agbonlahor had already been substituted but rose from the bench to confront Ramires following his challenge.

Mourinho said, 'It is a big occasion for me to know about the character of Mr Foy because I want to know what he is going to write about my sending-off. If it was because I was on the pitch, it was two or three metres inside the pitch, then there should be ten people sent off. I don't know why I was sent off. I asked but the referee refused to speak to me. Gabriel Agbonlahor was on the bench, he jumped onto the pitch, he was aggressive towards Ramires. Then everyone jumps onto the pitch: me, Paul Lambert and my assistants, lots of people there. There are no statues in a football match, so if I was sent off, everyone should have been sent off.'

Reminded about the convention that managers should not approach referees for thirty minutes, Mourinho said, 'This is not about conventions, it's about common sense. If you see someone out of control, OK: convention. But if you see someone is calm, is not screaming, it's not the convention. Simple people from football don't need conventions.'

Mourinho denied reports that he and Terry had tried to force their way into Foy's dressing room. He did admit to attempting to speak to Foy again after the match. 'In the dressing rooms I tried to ask politely, can you give me five seconds? And he refused.'

Mourinho questioned whether Foy should ever officiate a Chelsea match again, suggesting there were 'problems' when Foy previously took charge of matches involving the club and that his players had been discussing the appointment in the build-up to the game at Villa Park. Foy had issued six red cards to Chelsea players in his last eight matches involving the club. Mourinho compared it to the controversial defeat by the same score to Queens Park Rangers in October 2011, when Jose Bosingwa and Didier Drogba were dismissed by Foy. It was pointed out that Foy officiated that match too. 'I didn't know,' Mourinho said with a smile. 'It's a coincidence.'

Mourinho commented, 'The players were speaking about it during the week. My philosophy is that I never care who the ref is, I don't want to know. If for some reason I know the referee is Mr Anthony or Mr Jon, I always think that the referee is a good referee, I look always positive. But during the week the players were speaking about the situation and I think from now on, the next time we have Mr Foy, I have to work my people in a different way because I don't want this. But do they have a reason? Maybe it is helpful that the committee doesn't send him to our matches. I don't have the right to request. It's just I think they have to analyse the situation and see if, every time he has Chelsea – or not every time – but many times he has Chelsea and problems are there, I think maybe it would be a good decision.'

He added, 'I went to the pitch, as everybody went, with one single objective, me and Paul [Lambert] and my assistants and Paul's assistants – that was to calm one situation in the last minute of the game. I was angry but calm. Completely in control of my emotions. That's why I can control myself and say I will refuse to comment. I'm completely aware that if I comment, I will be accused of bringing the game into disrepute. Donations I prefer to do anonymously and to people who really need the money. I don't think it would be a problem to make a donation to help young referees to have better conditions to improve – a referees' academy.'

Lambert laughed off Mourinho's comments about Foy. 'I know what Jose's doing – he's been around the block. If you go on about decisions, it deflects from the performance. Of course Jose thinks we didn't deserve to win. His team is trying to win the league and that's his problem. How can this team, a Villa team of young kids, beat a team that's vying for everything going?'

Didier Drogba prepared for his first appearance back at Stamford Bridge since his 2012 departure as Chelsea welcomed Galatasaray for the second leg of their Champions League tie. Mourinho anticipated the next comeback to be of a more permanent nature. 'He is a Galatasaray player. We know he is a free agent and we know he finishes his contract at the end of the season but we think it is not the right moment to speak about him. I think it has to happen one day. When, I don't know – as a player, as a coach, as an ambassador – next year, in four or five years, in ten years – I don't know. But when a person represents so much to a club and when a club represents so much to a person – and that's the case – I think he has to be back one day. Undoubtedly he is one of the most important players in the history of this club – that is not a doubt. I think all Chelsea supporters, we agree with that.'

Mourinho declared that Chelsea were back among Europe's elite after they cruised into the Champions League quarter-finals with first-half goals from Eto'o and Cahill, securing a 3-1 aggregate win over the Turkish giants. Chelsea succeeded where Manchester City and Arsenal had failed the previous week to reach the last-eight draw.

The old feud with Wenger rumbled on ahead of the Arsenal manager's landmark 1,000th game in charge of the Gunners, in what possibly amounted to a play-off for the title. Mourinho had never lost against Wenger in ten meetings. The Arsenal manager said, 'You cannot be friends. It is impossible. If I start any game, I have to win. That is our job. The real sport on that front is rugby. They do not kiss each other before the game when they walk in the tunnel. They go out and are ready for war. We are not friends. I don't know if you can be friends with somebody you see three times in a year and when you see them it is for five minutes.'

Mourinho struggled to compliment Wenger and could not resist a swipe at Arsenal's nine years without a trophy. 'I admire him and I admire Arsenal. It's not possible to have a thousand matches unless the club is a fantastic club and supports the manager, especially in the bad moments and especially when the bad moments are quite a lot. There are many ways of paying tribute. For me, to pay tribute is to say he's in a position where many people would like to be. I love my career and the experiences I've had in my career, but he's in a position where everybody would love to be.' In response, Wenger teased Mourinho's reputation for unattractive football. 'The ambition of a great club must be to win with style.'

Mourinho again played down Chelsea's title chances, despite the devastating 6–0 thrashing of Arsenal, 'City have everything in their hands,' Mourinho said, referring to the idea that Pellegrini's team could overtake Chelsea if they were to win all their games in hand. Mourinho's team rattled in three goals between the fifth and seventeenth minutes, described as 'ten amazing minutes' by Mourinho. 'As we used to say in football, we came to kill. In ten minutes we destroy... after that, easy.'

Mourinho pointed out that, of the four teams vying for the title, only Chelsea remained in the Champions League quarter-finals, adding to the strain on his players. Asked whether he thought he had any chance of winning his third Premier League crown, he finally conceded, 'Just a little.' Classy goals from Eto'o and Schürrle put them 2–0 up before Hazard added a penalty. Oscar added two more either side of half-time before Egyptian substitute Salah ran clean through before sliding the ball under Szczesny for his first Chelsea goal. To compound Arsenal's misery, Gibbs was wrongly sent off after fifteen minutes when referee Andre Marriner punished him for saving the ball on the line when it was actually Oxlade-Chamberlain who committed the offence.

Mourinho chose to disappear down the tunnel just before the final whistle, explaining that he needed to phone his wife with the score, as he regularly does, but consequently avoiding shaking hands with Wenger. Asked whether Chelsea could still win the league for the first time since 2009/10 after a shock 1–0 defeat to Crystal Palace, with a Terry-headed own-goal at Selhurst Park, Mourinho said, 'Now it's impossible to win the title. We depend too much on other results. When you depend a little it's possible, when you depend a lot I don't think it is possible. Mathematically it is still possible but one thing is mathematics and another is reality.'

Mourinho praised defenders Ivanovic, Azpilicueta, Terry and Cahill but said the others players lacked the correct 'mentality and a little bit of quality.' He explained, 'Crystal

Palace had a strong mentality, were aggressive and committed with every one of them playing to the top of their potential. Ivanovic, Azpilicueta, Cahill, Terry – they perform in the sun, on small pitches, on big pitches, against aggressive teams, not aggressive teams, possession teams and not possession teams. They perform every game from day one to [the] last day. But you have other players who are fantastic in some games and they disappear in others. It is clear to everybody that Chelsea next year want to bring a striker. What's the future for the others? The ones who are staying are competing with the striker we are bringing in. It is normal at the end of the season if players who are not playing a lot or players who are not happy and prefer a change will go. That is also part of the market. We want to improve the team and the players and make some surgical movements in the transfer window. It is also clear we want to improve our players. I can't and I don't need to improve Ivanovic, Cahill or Terry, but there are others I need to improve. We are doing that step by step. But that's not enough to be champions.'

After the defeat, Mourinho marched on to the pitch, hauled up Cahill and told him to leave with his head held high. 'I told him he was one of the guys who should not be on the floor. I told him he was one of the guys who should walk to the dressing room with pride, that he had another performance where he gave absolutely everything. I don't think it's down to courage. It's down to the qualities that make personality profiles. You have some players for everything and other players who are in their habitat in some circumstances. So Stamford Bridge is better than away. Playing away against Arsenal, City, United or Liverpool is one thing and another thing is to play at Crystal Palace, West Bromwich or Stoke City. Clearly, we have players who are up and down in relation to the profile of the match.'

In the evening kick-off, City dropped two points at Arsenal, who remained in fourth, five points adrift of Mourinho's side. Second-placed Liverpool were a point ahead of City, taking over from Chelsea at the top of the table, comfortably beating Tottenham at Anfield the next day, but City had two games in hand on the rest of the top four. City were two points adrift of Chelsea and would have gone top had they won at Emirates Stadium.

Mourinho criticised his team's sloppy defending and lack of a cutting edge after they went down 3–1 to PSG in the French capital in the Champions League quarter-final first leg. Having recovered from the loss of an early Lavezzi goal to equalise courtesy of a Hazard penalty just before the half-hour mark, the Belgian then struck the post before half-time. PSG seized the initiative again in the second period and a Luiz own-goal put them back in front before Pastore's stoppage-time effort handed the Ligue 1 leaders a potentially decisive two-goal advantage.

Mourinho continued to play down his side's title chances after they returned to their winning ways, going top with a 3–0 win over Stoke with goals from Salah, Lampard and Willian. 'It is going to be difficult.'

Mourinho first burst into prominence in this country with a touchline dash ten years ago; a brazen, fist-pumping jig of 2004 at Old Trafford. He repeated the 'Jose Dash' after Ba scored Chelsea's second against PSG. Was he celebrating or passing on tactical instructions, as he claimed? When asked what he was doing after the goal, he said, 'No, it was not to celebrate. It was to tell the players how we had to play the last ten minutes. I knew at that moment they wanted to celebrate, to think the game is over. They forget that they had three plus three or four other [injury-time] minutes to play, and the way we were playing we couldn't carry on winning 2–0. I had to go there because it would be the only chance I'd have to tell Demba, Fernando and Schürrle what to do in the last seven minutes. But you could see I can still run!'

Ba was brought on after sixty-six minutes, scoring twenty-one minutes later to turn the tie. Ba, restricted to only four starts since he joined, putting up with Mourinho's claims that Chelsea do not have strikers, turned match-winner in the most crucial of ties. Schürrle replicated Ba's trick, coming off the bench after only eighteen minutes for injured star man Hazard, to score Chelsea's first.

'Patience' was Mourinho's buzzword in the build-up and they played with it, despite being 3–1 down after the first leg. Being without Matic, Ramires and Salah was a blow Mourinho overcame. The direct ball into PSG's area also had a clear effect. Mourinho said, 'The players followed our plan, our ambition. All we win, all we lose, but without any energy to go home. We have to be, at the end of the game, either so happy with the result or so happy with ourselves. And we were lucky because we have the result we fought for. But, if for some reason we hadn't scored the second, or if they had scored from the last corner in the last moment to send us out, everybody in this club would still have been proud of the boys.'

With one of Mourinho's finest accomplishments since his return to Chelsea, he became the first manager to reach eight

Champions League semi-finals. Drawn against the La Liga front runners Atlético Madrid, who knocked Barcelona out in the quarter-finals, Chelsea had another golden chance of reaching the final. Real Madrid faced Bayern Munich. The draw set up an intriguing situation with goalkeeper Thibaut Courtois, on loan to Atlético from Chelsea.

UEFA told Chelsea they could not stop their own goalkeeper Thibaut Courtois playing against them in the semi-finals. The twenty-one-year-old Belgian, in the third season of a loan to Atlético, found himself in the middle of a huge contract row after the two clubs were pitted against each other in the draw. Atlético said there was a clause in his loan agreement stipulating they would have to pay a total of £5 million to field him in both legs. But a strongly worded UEFA statement insisted that the clause contravened their regulations and so could not be applied. Courtois was always eligible to face them; whether or not they would look to invoke the clause privately remained unclear. Atlético wanted to secure another season-long loan deal for the Belgium international, while Chelsea wanted to sign Diego Costa from the Vicente Calderon club and were also watching midfielder Arda Turan.

Chelsea's Premier League game against Sunderland was moved forward by one day to help Mourinho's quest for Champions League glory. The first leg was scheduled for Tuesday, 22 April in the Spanish capital, 48 forty-eight hours after the home game with Sunderland. It was brought forward to the Saturday at 5.30pm, affording Chelsea an extra day to prepare for their trip to Spain. The return leg was three days after Chelsea's away fixture at Liverpool.

Mourinho ordered his players to end their three-match losing streak on the road by demonstrating more of the togetherness that saw them to a famous win over PSG as the Blues travelled to Swansea on the back of defeats to Aston Villa, Crystal Palace and PSG in successive games on their travels.

Chelsea played Swansea after Liverpool defeated title rivals Manchester City 3–2 at Anfield. Salah made his second start in the 1–0 win in South Wales, following Chico Flores's seventeenth-minute sending-off. Chelsea were two points behind leaders Liverpool with four games left following Ba's winner with the title decider increasingly looking like it would be at Anfield, although City had two games in hand, despite their defeat on Merseyside.

Chelsea surrendered any realistic hopes of the title when their seventy-seven-match unbeaten home-league record under Mourinho ended with an incredible self-destructive defeat to the bottom club, Sunderland, in astonishing circumstances.

The ugliest incident erupted in the last few moments, after referee Mike Dean awarded a hotly disputed match-winning penalty converted by Fabio Borini, a Liverpool player on loan at Sunderland. Rui Faria, Mourinho's assistant coach, repeatedly tried to confront the referee as Mourinho clutched first his arm then his hair to restrain his fellow Portuguese. Three Chelsea assistants, as well as Mourinho, hauled back the furious Faria.

Mourinho produced one of his most bizarre TV interviews after the final whistle, the content of which he repeated in the main press conference, declining questions and opting for heavy sarcasm. He insisted that he would make four points and take no questions. Each point was preceded with 'congratulations'.

He congratulated Dean: 'I think his performance was unbelievable and I think, when referees have unbelievable performances, I think it's fair that as managers we give them praise. He came here with one objective, to make a fantastic performance. And he did that.'

Having congratulated both his side and opponents, Mourinho turned his attention to Dean and Mike Riley, head of refereeing body Professional Game Match Officials Limited, which represents officials. 'Congratulations to Mike Riley because he's the referees' boss and what they are doing during the whole season is fantastic, especially in the last couple of months, especially in matches involving the teams that were in the title race – it's absolutely fantastic.'

Mourinho had twice been sent to the stands this season, for his protests over Ramires' red card in March and for persistently questioning Anthony Taylor's decisions in October in the win over Cardiff. Earlier in the season, he also referred to the Premier League's 'kings of the penalties', a veiled reference to Liverpool, who had won twelve spot-kicks that season: five more than any other side in the top flight.

Mourinho has never liked losing. The idea that he had become more relaxed went out of the window along with his amazing home record. Ramires faced an FA charge after an off-the-ball punch to the face of Seb Larsson, missed by the ref, although it occurred right in front of him.

Two weeks earlier, when Chelsea were still realistically in with a chance of winning the title and on the verge of a Champions League semi-final, you couldn't stop him talking. Suddenly, there was the possibility that Mourinho would finish a second season in a row without a trophy.

Mourinho brought up Chelsea's 2005 semi-final defeat to Liverpool as an example of how his side have been unlucky in the Champions League under his stewardship. In reference to Luis Garcia's controversial winner in the second leg, before Liverpool went on to win the competition, Mourinho said, 'There's no unfinished business. I did my best, always did my best. In my other semi-finals with Chelsea one was lost on penalties [in 2007] and that was because Liverpool scored one more than us. In the other semi-final we lost with a goal that was not a goal but that's part of football.'

For Fernando Torres, it would be an emotional homecoming to a club where he started his career and the stadium where he stood and cheered his beloved Atlético to the La Liga and Copa del Rey double in 1996, with a certain Diego Simeone in midfield.

Mourinho was given a torrid time by the fans on his return to Madrid but it was a tactical master class again in the Champions League, with a goalless draw. Mourinho parked the bus. The match finished goalless. The desired result, albeit without a preferred counter-attacking away goal, came with the price of bad injuries to Cech, who dislocated his shoulder in the opening minutes, and Terry, who twisted an ankle.

It left Mourinho threatening to rest virtually his entire team and potentially hand Liverpool the title after consultation with Abramovich to pick a deliberately weakened side in protest at being made to play on Sunday, with serious ramifications for Manchester City, relying on Chelsea to beat Liverpool and throw the title race back open.

Mourinho was furious that the game was not switched to Friday or Saturday, when Chelsea had the second leg against

Atlético at Stamford Bridge the following Wednesday. He was willing to risk sacrificing their slim chance of the title unless Abramovich objected. 'I can't decide by myself,' Mourinho replied when asked how the injuries would influence his team selection at Anfield. 'I have to listen to the club. I'm just the manager and I have to listen to the club.

Chelsea were five points behind Liverpool with three games to play. City, in third spot, were another point behind Chelsea but had a game in hand and could potentially win the league on goal difference if Liverpool lost to Chelsea and City won all of their remaining fixtures.

Mourinho became the first manager to be charged for sarcasm. He was furious with the FA decision to hit him with his third misconduct case. Mourinho was tight-lipped following the charge. 'Every time I speak there is a consequence. Even if I say that a referee was amazing that was a reason to be with a charge. I can't say the truth. I don't feel free at all. If you want a better press conference, speak with the FA.'

Asked about the British sense of humour and sarcasm, Mourinho said, "So Mr Bean is in jail... I told the referee he was amazing, and I repeat: the referee was amazing. I was not surprised (by the disciplinary action). In football I'm never surprised.'

Rodgers prepared to lock horns with the man who advised him to join Liverpool. They had remained close friends since Rodgers' time as a Chelsea youth coach but that was not going to be a distraction as he focused on Liverpool's biggest domestic fixture in twenty-five years. Rodgers was also wanted by Tottenham but, after an exchange of texts, Mourinho steered his protégé in the direction of Anfield. 'Jose told me to take the job, and what a great club Liverpool was,' Rodgers revealed. 'He encouraged me about the sheer scale of the club. We have kept in contact. He has been supportive of me wherever I have been, even in my time here. We might be considered a rival but I know that if they didn't win the league, he would want us to.'

Mourinho almost took the Liverpool job, according to Rodgers. 'There is no doubt that there was a period back in the early 2000s, that this club was a possibility for him. Maybe resources were different and he had a better opportunity to go elsewhere but, make no mistake, he knows the size and prestige of Liverpool. There has been a history there, what with the rivalry, and it was a great rivalry between the clubs but, beneath it all, he knows the power of Liverpool for sure.' Mourinho was in pole position to replace Gerard Houllier in 2004 and made it known he would love the chance to manage a club he has always regarded as one of the biggest in the world.

Mourinho insisted that Chelsea were the most important English club in Europe and fans believed their team deserved more respect for their continental exploits. 'Chelsea fans would like Chelsea to be respected and get the respect they think they deserve for what they have done for English football in the last ten years,' said Mourinho.

Mourinho was worried about playing Schwarzer in Cech's absence. Asked whether, with Cech facing the prospect of shoulder surgery, he could risk Schwarzer, he said, 'It's a big dilemma. Yes. With players that are always looking for penalties and they go for contact with the goalkeeper, it is even more dangerous. When the goalkeeper comes [out] and this kind of striker [tries] to hit the goalkeeper and dive for a penalty, it is even more dangerous.'

Mourinho accused Suárez of 'doing an acrobatic swimming-pool jump' to try to earn a penalty during Chelsea's 2–1 win against Liverpool in late December – the last time Rodgers' side, who led the table by five points, were defeated in the league.

Liverpool disputed Chelsea's claim that they refused to move Sunday's fixture forward by twenty-four hours to help the Londoners prepare for Atlético. Rodgers said, 'I think the Premier League should have helped them this weekend. It's not Liverpool's fault, it's the Premier League's. They should have had the game on the Saturday. That is nobody's fault bar the Premier League. That is what happens and you have to deal with it.'

After finishing his last season at Real trophyless, another barren season was a possibility. Would Mourinho also regard that as a failure? 'No,' he retorted, 'It's different in every sense.'

It was a classic Mourinho performance on and off the pitch, his side at their imperious best to claim an unlikely 2–0 victory, while he insisted that the title was still beyond Chelsea. 'We are not in it,' said Mourinho, whose side had two games remaining. 'The champions will be Liverpool or City. We have nothing to celebrate. Today was an important three points and we need one more to finish third.' Third place would ensure they wouldn't have to play any qualifying matches in Europe's elite club competition next season.

Defeat would have ended Chelsea's hopes of winning the title they last claimed in 2010 but late goals in each half ensured they were still contenders, despite Mourinho's reluctance to admit so. 'Now we can say we have won both matches against the champions,' added the manager, whose side had beaten Liverpool and Manchester City twice in the season.

Mourinho gave twenty-year-old Czech Tomas Kalas a debut in central defence and praised 'a giant' performance from goalscorer Ba, who took advantage of a Gerrard slip as Chelsea claimed sixteen points from eighteen against the top four sides.

Rodgers attributed his team's defeat to 'time-wasting' and 'parking two buses'. He, who had worked for three years under Mourinho at Stamford Bridge, would never embrace the style that proved so effective for his old boss, suggesting it was 'not difficult to coach to play defensive.'

Mourinho dismissed suggestions that there was anything negative about his tactics. 'When a team defends well, you call it a defensive display. When they defend [badly] and concede two or three goals, you don't consider it a defensive display and sometimes they are. My team played brilliantly, every player was magnificent.'

Chelsea's players were subject to a series of crank calls at the base in nearby Formby Hall on the eve of the game, while fireworks were also set off in the early hours. Mourinho was riled by a guest appearance before kick-off of Luis Garcia, to whip the Kop into a frenzy with the reminder of the 'ghost goal' of 2005. It motivated his side.

Three days later Mourinho's men crashed to a 3–1 defeat at the Bridge to Madrid giants Atlético. Mourinho felt the game hinged on a whirlwind passage of play when Courtois made a fine save to deny Terry's powerful header and, in the next attack, Eto'o fouled Costa to concede a penalty, which the striker converted. 'The difference was one minute in the second half, where Atlético's goalkeeper makes an impossible save and, instead of 2–1 to Chelsea, a few seconds later a penalty, which I'm happy people tell me was a penalty. And they scored to go 2–1 up. In one minute, two actions decided the game. After that, there was only one team on the pitch. My team played with pride, honour and professionalism, but after that moment the game was controlled by Atlético. Complete control.'

Likely to finish without a trophy, Mourinho defended the campaign. 'We need one point to be third. You know, we know we are realistic. But at the same time we are optimistic. At the same time, when things go in a certain direction, there is a moment where you can dream and you think that things are possible, even if things are not so. Because we did well in the Champions League and in the Premier League, there was a moment where we felt we could do it. In the Premier League it was the match against Aston Villa that made me believe that we had no chance to be champions. After that we built the momentum again and we were waiting for the Liverpool match to be the title match, but we had another surprise against Sunderland. But I think the boys did a very good Premier League. In the Champions League, it's the same. We knew that there were teams with more potential than us and more ready than us to win the competition, but because you go step by step and beating PSG you build your dream. We had our chance. Until minute sixty-one we were completely in the game. From that moment, the game was over.'

Mourinho was reticent to accept that the title was possible; maximum points in their last two games with Norwich and Cardiff, plus Liverpool and City slipping up. 'The only thing we can do is win both matches. Imagine if we are not champions because we don't win these two matches. That wouldn't be a good feeling for the players. So we have to win both matches. On Sunday, Norwich are playing for their lives, to decide if next season it is Arsenal, Chelsea and United or midweek games in the Championship. They are playing the game of their lives.'

Mourinho was pursuing a 'critical signing'. He explained, 'That's what I'm going to do after the season: work, think, think about next season.' The manager was confused by relegation-threatened Norwich's defensive tactics as his side's fading title hopes ended with a tame goal-less draw with the Canaries at Stamford Bridge.

Mourinho stormed down the tunnel at half-time to blast a number of players, including Matic and Salah, for their performances, accusing his team of being 'lazy'. Mourinho told Matic he was having serious reservations about the decision to bring him back in the January transfer window. Salah was replaced at half-time and told to make sure he returned for pre-season 'ready to be a footballer.' Mourinho stormed out of the dressing room and appeared in the dugout a few minutes before the start of the second half, sitting alone until his players came out.

Despite the disappointment of dropping two points, the squad completed a lap of the field. Cole was in tears and had to be consoled by Terry. Cole, Terry and Lampard could leave as all three had contracts that expired with 1,609 Blues appearances between them. Mourinho believed they would stay. 'Will they play at Stamford Bridge again? I think so, but the summer is a long summer for us. For the players at the World Cup, it's a different story. But for us, as a club, it's a long time to be calm, to sit and discuss and analyse the market and possibilities. A long time.'

Mourinho admitted the season could have been better, 'We lost games where we had them under control but didn't kill them and we were killed. But from day one, never in danger, never outside the top four or outside the title race.' Chelsea finished the season third with a win at Cardiff, as both Liverpool and newly crowned champions City won their final games. Chelsea finished without a trophy for the first time in three years; their eighty-two-point total the worst under Mourinho. He denied being hurt by missing out on the title in his first campaign back in England, saying City were worthy champions. Evolution and transition were buzzwords, so third-placed finish 'is not a drama.'

He added, 'Next season, if we do our work in a successful way in the summer market, which I know the club is trying to do everything to make that a successful period for us, then if we do that I want to start day one saying we are going to fight for the title. We don't need a new spine, a new structure. It is there. The fundamental for us now is a couple of players of a certain level to help the team immediately go to a different level. After that the additional is if someone has to leave then someone has to come. Our work in the summer is not a big amount of work; it is just the right choice.'

He also wanted to re-establish to forge the mentality required to win matches like those against Villa and Sunderland, to which he referred six times in his press conference. 'Manchester City are champions and they deserve it,' he said. 'They have four more points than us and two more than Liverpool. They are not guilty of defeats like ours to Aston Villa and Sunderland. It has nothing to do with them. Am I hurt? No, because it is part of the process. One thing is to play clearly to win the title. Another is to be in a transition phase. It was an easier job for me to get a team ready to win [not Chelsea] and I promise you I had chances to do that, not just in this country but others. My decision was this and I am happy with that. It is part of a process in a dangerous league where you can finish fifth and be out of the Champions League. Third is not a drama, it is a position you have to accept in this transitional period. We are not asking for eight, nine, ten years to achieve success but you can't just click your fingers and success arrives. This season it almost happened.'

In his final match programme notes ahead of the Cardiff match, Mourinho penned a heartfelt message to his son Jose Junior. He would normally have used his column to discuss the defeat to Atlético but, instead, he wrote, 'I know this space is to communicate with you fans, but one of you is my son. I want to tell him thanks for being with me every second of every match, a few metres behind me, jumping for every goal; hurt by every difficult moment. Thank you, kid, for being my kid. Every time I look at you, I see you, but I also see your sister and your mum, both at home but also playing with us, both waiting for us to go home and to be what we are – an amazing family... like the blue family, supporting each other.'

Mourinho also indicated his desire to land a prolific goalscorer. 'Against the teams that are more defensive, more aggressive, more worried about trying to keep a clean sheet than really to play, we keep saying the same. We have good players, but we don't have the kind of striker able to, in a short space, to make an action, to score a goal, to open the gate. In these [kinds] of matches you just need to open the gate. When you open the gate, the gate is open and you win much more. We weren't able to do that. We have to try to win as a team, to improve as a team, but also add the attacking player with that killer instinct and the number of goals that push teams to different levels.'

Mourinho then stated that he plans to leave the game at sixty-five – normal retirement age – after a dozen years turning Chelsea into the dominant outfit in global football and then two years taking a national team to the World Cup. He views international management as a symptom of growing old. 'It's not a job I like. You have to wait two years to have a competition! You have easier matches, many friendlies, qualification matches! Training two days a month! I don't need an escape from football. I just need a couple of weeks in the summer to be somewhere, a beach. That's fine for me.'

He is very much a family man, and you can see him taking the Portuguese national job to spend more time with them. His seventeen-year-old daughter, Matilde, has a budding interest in photography. During a magazine interview, Mourinho spent the accompanying photo shoot quizzing the photographer on how much such work pays and what editing programs Matilde might need. 'In our house, it's two and two. Mum and daughter isolated of football. They like me to win and they care about my happiness, but they don't live for football. And obviously the boy [Jose Jr] is a boy, and at this age – 13, 14, 15 – he gets involved in the game, too. So, it's two for football and two who are more intelligent than the men of the house.'

JOSE: IS HE
THE GREATEST?

In terms of managers, who is The Greatest?
Ask Jose Mourinho and he will probably tell you Jose Mourinho.

Statistically Mourinho is the most successful current club manager in world football. He has won league titles in each of the four countries where he has managed, Portugal, Italy, Spain and England. He has won the Champions League twice.

I asked for views from experts; coaches, footballing legends, top sports writers, and even some football mad celebrity fans. I asked for their vote for the all-time greatest managers, and didn't specify whether that was a global or parochial vote, but there were plenty of votes cast for global coaches and managers. It must be stressed that everyone cast their votes for this book, before the unexpected second sacking.

However, two managers stood out above all others, Sir Alex Ferguson and Jose Mourinho.

And while Mourinho has some way to go to catch Fergie, the one-time Manchester United 'hairdryer' is now switched off, while Mourinho remains in his prime. If anyone is going to catch and overtake Sir Alex, it is going to be him.

Glenn Hoddle, the former England manager told me: 'Mourinho has won the Champions Leagues in different countries. Mourinho has challenged himself in new countries, and like never before has proved himself in every country he has managed, whatever the conditions, with all different types of clubs and different types of players. And it's not taken him ten years at each club to do it; he comes in and does it straight away, that takes some doing, so whatever managerial methods he uses it works wherever he goes.'

Roberto Di Matteo, the Chelsea manager who won the Champions League, put Mourinho ahead of Sir Alex. Why? 'He is a great coach, communicator and motivator. One of the best in our generation.'

Paul Elliott, while casting Sir Alex as No. 1, put Mourinho third in his list but he explained: 'Mourinho in my view [is] currently [the] best modern manager in the world, [when it comes to] modern-day coaching/tactical methodology. Brilliant man manager, delivered championships in Portugal, UK , Spain, and unprecedented treble in unlikeliest of environments in Italy with Inter Milan similar to amazing achievement with Porto winning Champions League. Only fifty-two, with hunger and desire to achieve much more.'

Ben Rumsby, sports correspondent at the *Daily Telegraph*, said it was 'tough' picking his top five, but went for Mourinho over Fergie. As he explained: 'Mourinho always wins, all the time, everywhere he goes. If Ferguson had done it overseas as well as in the UK, he'd be top.'

If there is more to management than trophies and success, if Brian Clough comes third ahead of Sir Matt Busby because of his charisma, then Mourinho is in a league of his own. 'Mourinho is also the most divisive manager in football,' Mick Brown suggested in his piece on Mourinho in the *Daily Telegraph*. 'Watching Mourinho is almost a spectator sport in itself,' he observed.

It is hard to compare like-for-like when managers were in charge of vastly contrasting dressing rooms in different eras with different standards, just as Pele and Maradona played on some churned-up grassless pitches wearing heavyweight boots and using hard leather balls, compared to the snooker-like surfaces, lightweight kit and everything modern players can use to make them look better and faster. They are also much better protected by the officials, with massive changes in the rules to protect the flair players.

Jim Lawton, one of my all-time favourite sports writers, gave me his considered opinion: 'It is easy to despise Mourinho for his vanities and his cynical tactics but so much harder to deny that he is a one-off football genius. His Champions League win with Inter was a triumph of football's black arts. He did more than park the bus. He out-thought Guardiola and disabled the team that was supposed to be the best in the history of club football. For what it is worth, Stein was the master of man management and motivation, getting eleven Glaswegians to pick off the cream of the European game and destroy the mystique of the legendary Inter coach

Helenio Herrera. Fergie had the nerve to build on Busby's legacy – and an astonishing drive to win – and Clough was a forerunner of Mourinho, a man who had a rage and an instinct to finish on top.'

Ivor Baddiel, brother of comedian David, and who among other things writes scripts for the *X Factor*, certainly believes that Mourinho has the X-factor among managers. Ivor placed Mourinho as No. 1 in his list of the five greatest ever managers with this explanation: 'Jose Mourinho is a manager who actually manages as well as coaches. In a game that is now dominated by massive egos, here is a man with possibly the biggest of them all, and one that he uses to deflect attention away from his players, allowing them to get on with their job. It's a master stroke, beautifully simple, yet effective.

'He's a man who is obsessively thorough and regimented. If you play for him you know exactly what is expected of you and you're prepared to do it to the best of your ability. Once again there's a brilliant simplicity to this. In any walk of life, clarity is vital. If you give someone absolutely clear instructions, they will know what is required of them. They can be focused, a vital part of the game.

'Ultimately though, Jose Mourinho is a man who knows how to win. He doesn't bottle, he sees the job through, no matter how hard that might be. He knows that tough decisions are part of it, but he doesn't shirk and will do what is necessary to succeed.'

It is often thrown back into Mourinho's face that he never made the grade as a player. He was a defender in the second tier of the Portuguese league, but made little progress and decided to move into coaching, enrolling at the Technical University of

Lisbon to study sports science, and then becoming a teacher. Mourinho's father – also José – was a goalkeeper, who made one appearance for Portugal before becoming a coach. The young José accompanied him to games, sometimes running the line, passing on instructions from his father to the players.

His first job was teaching children with Down's syndrome and severe mental disabilities – 'a big challenge', he admits in the insightful *Daily Telegraph* interview, 'I wasn't technically ready to help these kids. And I had success only because of one thing, the emotional relation that was established with them. I did little miracles only because of the relationship. Affection, touch, empathy – only because of that. There was one kid that refused all his life to walk upstairs. Another one that couldn't coordinate the simplest movement – all these different problems, and we had success in many, many of these cases only based on that empathy. After that I was coaching kids of sixteen. Now I coach the best players in the world, and the most important thing is not that you are prepared from the technical point of view; the most important thing is the relationship you establish with the person. Of course you need the knowledge, the capacity to analyse things. But the centre of everything is the relationship, and empathy, not only with the individual but in the team. And to have that empathy in the team we all must give up something. It's not about establishing the perfect relation between me and you; it's about establishing the perfect relation to the group, because the group wins things; it's not the individual who wins things.'

Mourinho believes in family values. When he wins, he is on the phone to his wife, the first person he calls on his smartphone. They are well connected. He and Matilde were teenage sweethearts, growing up a street away from each other in the coastal town of Setúbal, now married for twenty-six years with two teenage children, also named Matilde and José.

Mourinho's first managerial job came in 2000 as the manager of the Portuguese side Benfica, having worked as a translator and then as a coach under Bobby Robson at Sporting Lisbon, Porto and Barcelona. He lasted only three months before resigning after a row, moving on to União de Leiria and then Porto, where he won the Portuguese Primeira Liga twice, the UEFA Cup and, in 2004, the then the Champions League. That was equivalent to Brian Clough winning the European Cup with humble Nottingham Forest. That sort of thing isn't supposed to happen. The European elite tournament should be for the European elite, surely, Real Madrid, Barcelona, Bayern Munich and, before that, Ajax and Manchester United. That totally unexpected triumph, with the running down the touchline and celebrating on his knees knocking out Manchester United on the way, announced his arrival on a global basis.

Mourinho remembers his old mentor, Sir Bobby, citing the Old Etonian ethos of his Ipswich Town owners, the old-school Cobbolds. 'Bobby Robson used to say – I disagreed with him – when we lose a match, don't be so sad, just think that in the other dressing room the guys are so happy. Don't be so sad, it's not the end of the world.' That might be something to go against the grain, yet in his own career he has learned to 'respect the guy who deserves to win,' and cites the example of Crystal Palace, who inflicted a painful league defeat on

Chelsea at Selhurst Park in March: 'I wanted to kill my guys. But they [Palace] were amazing. And they needed those points to survive. So, in the middle of my unhappiness, I was mature enough to say – hey, these guys were brilliant, because they did very well. I told the [Palace] guys "congratulations" one by one.'

Mourinho first locked swords with Sir Alex in 2004, when Porto knocked Manchester United out of the Champions League. 'That was when I felt the two faces of such a big man. The first face was the competitor, the man that tried everything to win. And after that I found the man with principles, with the respect for the opponent, with the fair play – I found these two faces in that period, and that was very important for me. In my culture, the Portuguese and the Latin culture, we don't have that culture of the second face; we are in football to win and when we don't there is not a second face most of the time. But when we beat United in the Champions League I got that beautiful face of a manager which I try to have myself. I try.' Since then the two men have forged a very close friendship, and share a love of fine red wine.

Gary Neville, having played in the game, reminded him of that iconic moment, sliding down the Old Trafford touchline. 'When I remember that [knee slide], the good thing for me is that last year I did the same,' Mourinho said. 'So it was not something from a young coach, it was not something from somebody who feels that moment was my moment to change my career. Last year I did exactly the same against Paris Saint-Germain and hopefully this year I will do another one. So this is part of me. This is part of the way I sometimes don't control the emotion, the happiness.

'But going back to that day, I think I was already in important contact to leave Portugal so it was not because of that game and that moment I had the interest from Chelsea. I was already in on that.'

That Champions League triumph over Sir Alex made Roman Abramovich sit up and take notice as he bought out Ken Bates, having watched Champions League football at Old Trafford, wanting to build his dream team capable of winning it at Stamford Bridge. So, with Claudio Ranieri knowing he was 'dead man walking' even before his Champions League tie with Monaco, Mourinho was to be installed for his first stint at Chelsea, where he won back-to-back Premier League titles 2004/05, 2005/06, the FA Cup and the League Cup, again twice. As the manager of Inter Milan he won the Serie A twice, and the Champions League for a second time. In 2010 he moved on to Real Madrid, where he won the Copa Del Rey and La Liga in consecutive seasons. In June 2013 he returned to Chelsea and after one barren season, landed the Premier League and League Cup double.

Mourinho once ran through his CV: 'I had a career project. Many times you cannot follow your career project. I want to leave Portugal and come to England. Clear. When I leave England I want Italy. I'm mad to go to Italy, where people are talking about the mentality of the Italians, the tactical aspect of the game. And after that I want Real Madrid. Spain – but I wanted Real Madrid. This circle – I want very much to do it, and I did it. When I did it came [to] the [question]: where do you like more, where are you happier? Which is the biggest challenge? I made the choice. I keep saying the same. In every club I was working and thinking about that club, but I always have my next movement. This is the first time where I don't have my next movement. I want to stay. I want to stay till the moment Chelsea tells me it's over, because the results are not good, or they want to go in another direction, or they don't agree with my style of management – for any reason. This period at Chelsea is going to hang by their decision, not my decision. That was the objective, but to make that movement I had to be very sure what I was doing, especially because I didn't want to come back to my club – because I can say Chelsea and Inter are my clubs – after a very nice period I had here, and not be happy again. And not to make good things again. Mr Abramovich gave a lot of time to think about that. Also when he invited me to come back it took time for me to analyse the situation. The Chelsea team we started building in 2004/2005 is finished. We have just two or three boys from that time. We need to rebuild the team. And the perspective now is different from ten years ago, because the perspective then was about spend not-in-a-controlled-way. So me and the club found each other in a very good moment. I think the club was waiting for a manager like me, and I was waiting for my Chelsea to have this new profile. Hopefully we can hold together for many years.'

It would have come as quite a shock to the system to have ended up sacked for a second time.

MOURINHO
ON MOURINHO

You don't have to look very far to find out what Mourinho thinks of Mourinho. Self-analysis and self-proclamation come easy to him. He is not the shy, retiring type.

He drives a Jaguar F-type, which might have something to do with his many endorsements, although he says, 'I've driven many cars of similar high performance and beautiful style, but nothing is like a Jaguar. The noise of the F-Type and the speed … there is nothing like it.' He wears a Hublot King Power 'Special One' watch – again, another endorsement. 'I made it, I designed it and the company did it for me according to my needs. It's the colour I want, the material I want and the right size and weight. I designed it with the company. It's my watch.'

He has the sultry good looks, the designer stubble, and the charisma that makes him an endorsement darling, having recently launched BT Sport's new Champions League channel. Perhaps, arguably, the David Beckham of the dugout. While not a star turn as a player, he has moved up the gears as Bobby Robson's interpreter to being the greatest manager of his generation, and closing in on overtaking Sir Alex Ferguson as the greatest manager of all time.

Opinions are dramatically divided; you will either love his chutzpah and agree with the self-proclaimed Special One, or you will think of him as self-centred, conceited, arrogant and vile.

Some of the escapades he got up to on the touchline – mainly during his turbulent and sometimes violent times at Real Madrid – are either showmanship or gamesmanship, depending on your point of view.

My view is that Mourinho is pure box office; his presence in the premier League illuminates the scene and, while I am extenuating the positives, I am not forgetting the negatives in coming to an assessment of the man and the manager.
So let's hear from the man himself, and there are plenty of telling gems he has given in a selective amount of interviews that are far more revealing than the one-liners, quips and mind games from his multitude of entertaining media conferences.

I have kept a cutting from the *Sunday Telegraph*, which lingers on my desk. I probably kept it to remind me of the sheer audacity of the man. To understand Mourinho's extra-ordinary self-confidence and assurance, it is well worth reproducing some of his comments from that *Sunday Telegraph* article, headlined: JOSE MOURINHO: I AM IN A LEAGUE OF MY OWN IN ENGLAND – NO OTHER PREMIER LEAGUE MANAGER CAN COMPARE. Mourinho based his lavish claim on the fact that he is the only one who has won every competition, with an impressive haul of trophies.

Mourinho, though, needs to win the Champions League with Chelsea; he wants to win the Champions League with the West London club he has returned to with that ambition in mind more than any other. He might tell you differently. Don't believe him!

He would then create history by winning it with three different clubs in three different countries, guaranteeing his immortality as a manger anywhere in the world. Do you think Jose would like that as his epitaph? Yes, he sure would.

In the in-depth *Sunday Telegraph* article, though, he passionately dismissed the idea that he would remain unfulfilled unless he won the competition with Chelsea.

'It is wrong to assume that. People are [more] worried about me than they should [be]. They don't know what my happiness is. My happiness, first of all, is when I compare myself with the others [managers], I see just a few that are with me in terms of success, and [in] the others I see a huge difference, a huge distance, with all the respect that they deserve and this is not a fight with them and I have lots of respect for all of them. But in the Premier League, who is European champion? Me and Van Gaal. Right? In the Premier League, how many won the Premier League twice or more than twice? Mr Wenger and myself. How many won every competition in this country? Community Shield, Capital One Cup, FA Cup, Premier League. How many? How many? You go to Europe, how many won seven league titles? How many won two Champions Leagues? Ancelotti wins three, Van Gaal two and Pep [Guardiola] has two. I am not content with that, but you are too much worried about myself (sic). What makes me feel special is that I am above all of this. You think I care with some bulls**t I read? Do you think I care? I don't care.'

But, oh yes, he does care. He cares passionately about what he has achieved and what there is left to achieve. He cares passionately that he has to write his place in the history of the game. Yes, he does care.

The *Sunday Telegraph* article was published in mid-March 2015 as Chelsea were steamrolling towards the title, but had suffered Champions League elimination. That hurt Mourinho – a hurt that healed with the Double, the league and the League Cup, but that ache to win the Champions League lingers and, like a sore that he cannot help but scratch, he won't give up until he succeeds, and it will be sooner rather than later with this formidable Chelsea squad.

Mourinho cannot hide from the fact, no matter how hard he tries – and modesty is not his strong suit – that the Champions league is his Holy Grail; it is the tournament that made his name, and will be the tournament that will have him down as the Greatest if he can create history by winning the trophy for a third time with a third different club and, therefore, become the first manager to achieve it.

He demands trophies and more trophies – he is driven to success. He wants it for himself, for his team, for his players and staff, for his family. He will go to any lengths to gain it.

He is, therefore, usually meticulous with his preparation. When a trophy is at stake, Mourinho is more meticulous in his planning than usual. Except on one big occasion. He went into his first Wembley Cup final in 2007 after spending time in jail because of issues with his dog.

Mourinho recounted the extraordinary story to Gary

Lineker on his BBC documentary *The Road to FA Cup Glory*. Mourinho explained how he was arrested for preventing police officers from taking his beloved family pet away.

'I won the FA Cup but it was a complicated week for me because I was in jail because of my dog. It's an odd story. The vet thought I was taking the dog from Portugal in a private plane and without the legal situation. They sent the police to my house to take the dog, but I didn't let them take the dog. So, because they didn't take the dog, they took me for obstruction to justice. It was a difficult week – I was in that final but my family was not there because they had to stay in Portugal with the dog, for the dog not to go to jail.'

However, it didn't adversely affect Mourinho, with his Chelsea side beating Manchester United 1–0 after extra time.

In press conferences, Mourinho dominates, gives away only what he chooses, fences with his audience, enjoys the cut and thrust with journalists, loves to play mind games with them, as much as that being transferred to his rival managers. One-to-one interviews are vastly different. He then becomes very introverted in a positive way for the writer to extract his innermost thoughts and feelings.

An interview in the *Daily Telegraph* was one of those more fascinating and intimate examples of getting under the Mourinho skin. He told interviewer Mick Brown, 'I think I have a problem, which is I'm getting better at everything related to my job since I started. There has been evolution in many different areas – the way I read the game; the way I prepare [for] the game; the way I train; the methodology ... I feel better and better. But there is one point where I cannot change: when I face the media, I am never a hypocrite.'

The 'team' is the word Mourinho refers to as part of his footballing mantra. His forte is balancing individual talent to the collective team ethic.

How to motivate overpaid players is a vexing problem, which even Mourinho finds hard to find a solution to. 'It's true! Once players came to football expecting to be wealthy when they retired. Now they expect to be wealthy before they've played their first game!'

Mourinho doesn't have many close friends in English football. 'Some, we like each other and have some communication, but I cannot say so close.' Mourinho refers to the Arsenal manager as 'Wenger'. There is no love lost there. Perhaps there is even disdain. They crossed swords, a little pushing and shoving as they wondered outside of their technical areas, with a massive jibe about winners and losers. And it was a backhanded compliment, and only that, when he said of Wenger, 'But I think Wenger said something that is interesting; he is against the Ballon d'Or, and I think he's right, because in this moment football is losing a little bit the concept of the team to focus more on the individual. We are always looking at the individual performance, the individual stat, the player that runs more. Because you run 11km in a game and I run 9 you did a better job than I did? Maybe not! Maybe my 9km were more important than your 11.

'For me, football is collective. The individual is welcome if you want to make our group better. But you have to work for us, not we have to work for you. When the top player arrives, the team is already there. It's not him who comes to discover the team, like Columbus discovering America. No, no, you are coming now to help us be better. And as a manager you have to give this message every day – not with lectures or words. It's about what the players observe in relation to the behaviour and to the feedback – the way you react to this player and that player; the empathy with this one and that one.

'The only thing you cannot give to a player is the talent. But can you work the talent properly so that he understands the team's needs? Is he an intelligent, open guy waiting for you to help him be better? Is he the kind of maverick guy, the selfish guy, where it is much more difficult to persuade him the team is more important than he is. I've had all of these in every club I've ever worked at. There is no perfect group anywhere but if you ask me what's the most important thing in a player, it's the talent.

'It's harder and harder to install such working relationships with young players who have too much too soon. Young footballers are given the opportunity, but invariably they don't know how to handle it, too immature, and they can waste their God given talents.

'I know, but, remember, they're the final product of something. I had one player, for example – I won't name him – and I gave him the chance to play in the first team. A couple of weeks after he'd played his father left his job, his mother left her job; they were living with him, living his life, making decisions for him. It's very difficult. That's one example out of 1,000. They need to be lucky with the parents; they need to be lucky with the agents. They need education. I had a player once that came to me with a new car, and I told him, "Another one? Why? Do you have a house?" No. "Do you have lots of money in the bank?" No. He said, "This car, I didn't buy it; my father got it for free in leasing and I signed the document."

I said, "Do you know what leasing is?" He said, "It's free!" "No! Sit here and I [will] explain to you what is leasing." He didn't know, because nobody had explained. When I got real money in my hands – real big money – it was my second contract with Porto in 2003, I was thirtysomething. I was married. I was ready for it. These guys, they're 16, 17, 19, 20. They don't know how to react, what to do.

'In Chelsea we have a fantastic department which we call Players Support and Welfare where they help the players with everything. They have people in the bank to explain money. You want to buy a house? Let's make sure you're with the right person making the right deal. Young players coming to the first team – don't buy a car, we're sponsored by Audi and they provide the cars for the players. The players need this. This is a complicated world.'

'It's my duty!' Mourinho says to finding himself playing the role of 'father figure'. With his lately acquired greying locks, it fits him snuggly.

Mourinho says he is a great admirer of the writing of Fernando Pessoa, Portugal's most beloved poet. Visiting the Ivory Coast in his role as World Food Programme Ambassador Against Hunger has been very important to him.

'This has been a fantastic experience for me, that I shared with my wife and kids. We know about poverty, but to be directly in contact with that reality was fantastic – negative, positive, difficult to deal with, but at the same time [there is a feeling of] tremendous pride to be connected with it, to promote their works.'

He and his wife also support a Catholic food programme in Setúbal. 'But we have a principle that we do it not for people to know, or to promote our profile. We do it because we can, and we want our son and daughter to understand how privileged we are, and to understand that other people need support.'

He is a religious man: '... that I believe totally, clearly. Every day I pray; every day I speak with Him. I don't go to the church every day, not even every week. I go when I feel I need to. And when I'm in Portugal, I always go.' What does he pray for? 'For my family! For my kids, for my wife, for my parents, for happiness and a good family life. But I can say the reality is I never go to the church to speak with Him about football. Never!'

Would he describe himself as a good person?

'I think so. I try to be. And I think I am. I don't have problems with family or friends. I am a good family person; I am a good friend. I try to support people that I don't even know. Do I make mistakes? Yes. My professional area is not only very competitive – it is competitive and emotional and [you must] push people for a certain kind of behaviour – absolutely, yes. But the professional life is only part of a person; a person is much more than that.'

He does his best to separate his professional and family life. He never discusses football with his wife.

'It's not her world. Be in a club that I like. Be in a place that I enjoy. Work with people that I like. That is basically the advice [she gives] because when that happens life at home for everyone will be better. But it is difficult. Even if I can separate things, sometimes they can't. If I lose an important match, I try to go home with a nice face, tomorrow is another day, and it's just a game of football and so on and so on. But I arrive at home, and they have the bad face! They are sad for me!'

He lives in Belgravia. His family prefers it, 'and me too.' Unlike Madrid or Milan, in London he can lead 'an almost normal life'. He can walk on the street and, 'within five minutes', find a Chelsea supporter, a Tottenham supporter, an Arsenal supporter, 'even [a] Liverpool supporter or [a] United supporter. And I like that. In other places I've worked you're always walking in the middle of your club's fans. Milan, 50 per cent Inter, 50 per cent AC. Madrid, maybe 70 per cent. Real, 30 per cent Atlético. In Porto, 100 per cent. If someone comes up to me, I like to listen. Although if someone wants to give me a lesson in football, of course not! But I think people in London understand what it is to disturb and not to disturb. They have a notion that people need space, that people deserve respect. If I am disturbed it is always by non-English people. The English people in the restaurant, of course they want an autograph or a selfie, but they wait until I finish my meal. Go to a shop, they wait – they don't come when I'm choosing my socks. And walking in the street I have the same feeling. It is impossible in London that somebody would disturb because of a negative result when you are walking in the street with your family. Impossible! In Madrid, Milan – always.'

His smart phone is a BlackBerry, rather than the more fashionable iPhone. 'I like it. It is that simple. It does everything I need.' He holidays in his home country. 'It is always nice to return home. Home is home, and I don't get there enough with the busy football season.' So much so that his favourite place to dine is at home with his family. 'As a family we always eat together and, although we like many restaurants in London, we have the most fun when we eat at home together.'

Mourinho says, 'I am passionate about football, of course.

But for us professionals, if it means everything, we are in trouble; and for supporters the same. In Portugal they say that you can change everything except your mum and your football club. I understand because of football's power, socially, politically and culturally. But how can a football player be in the top 100 of the most influential people in the world in *Forbes* magazine?'

Actually, two footballers. Last year Cristiano Ronaldo was at number 30 in the *Forbes* list, and Lionel Messi at number 45. 'It's absurd! We don't save lives! I know that people can jump from a fifth floor because his team lost a game, but that person has problems. How can you compare a football player, a football manager with a scientist, a doctor? You cannot compare.'

Protecting his players is part of his managerial ethos. He works with them, wins and loses with them but, in return, he demands total loyalty from them towards him, and he will not tolerate prima donnas.

'At the centre of everything is the relationship, and empathy, not only with the individual but in the team, and to have that empathy in the team we all must give up something. It's not about establishing the perfect relation between me and you; it's about establishing the perfect relation to the group, because the group wins things, it's not the individual who wins things.'

It is true to say, perhaps, that his struggle is not always understood. The adjective that is most often ascribed to Mourinho is 'Machiavellian'.

'I don't see myself that way.'

Has he read Machiavelli? 'Yes, I know Machiavelli, of course.'

Mourinho has raised complaining to a fine art, not simply that referees are against him, but that the whole world is against him, calculated to instil a fighting 'underdog' mentality in his team. He gets under the skin of opposition players and managers. 'I agree that sometimes I can have something of Machiavelli in some of my comments, but no more than that. Not at all.'

Mourinho is only nice to people he no longer sees as a threat. 'No! I like to praise people when people deserve [it] – other managers, players. I love to say "fantastic referee", especially after a defeat.'

After all the bribes, back-handers and bungs linked to FIFA personnel, it was the perfect opportunity for Mourinho to revisit an old wound. Accordingly, he repeated his belief that he may have been the victim of corruption when he finished second to Vicente del Bosque for the FIFA World Coach of the Year award in 2012.

After finishing second in the poll voted for by national coaches, captains and journalists, Mourinho was shocked by any claims about FIFA.

Reiterating comments he made in 2013 about losing out to the Spain coach when in charge at Real Madrid, Mourinho told the *Sunday Times*, 'In 2012, I was one of the three finalists and when I was told I was finishing second with a few votes behind the first, it looked normal to me, but then the votes were made public. And my former player, a national team captain, called me: "Mister, there is something wrong because obviously, obviously, I gave you the vote, then in the list they put another coach's name and that was not me." A few minutes later my Portuguese friend, a national team coach, called me. "Mister, don't believe what you see in the list because obviously I vote for you." And a few minutes later I got a message from another national coach: "They changed my vote." Who changed the vote? His federation? FIFA? Who? It is not a drama. A drama is other things but at that time I said, "From this moment I don't go back," because obviously something happened.'

Mourinho has found it astonishing at how little recognition he has received in all his Chelsea years from the Premier League/Barclays panel, who rarely, if ever, nominated him as Manager of the Month.

After winning the Premier League and League Cup Double, it was Eddie Howe who was named Manager of the Year by the League Managers Association after guiding humble little Bournemouth to the top flight, while Mourinho was named Premier League Manager of the Year.

Howe, who was also named Championship Manager of the Year after the Cherries' title-winning season, is the first manager from outside the top flight to take the overall award since Steve Coppell, then of Reading, won in 2006. In comments reported on Bournemouth's website, Brendan Rodgers, who presented the award to Howe, said, 'He's done a fine job, a remarkable job, and done it with style and humility.'

Mourinho took the top-flight award but did not attend the ceremony in London to collect it as he was at Chelsea's own club awards event.

He had already been named Barclays Premier League Manager of the Season, despite not once winning the monthly award throughout the season. Despite the accolades,

Mourinho was still complaining about a perceived lack of recognition for his side.

In his speech at Chelsea's event, he observed, 'I don't think my players got the respect that they deserve after what they did from day one until the last day. And these are words that I really feel, serious words.'

Mourinho is often accused of playing the old Sir Alex Ferguson mind games. I feel that Mourinho is blunt, rather than manipulative. It's more about fighting your corner with him, reacting, responding, being provoked, rather than trying to provoke.

Mourinho was extremely touchy when rival managers criticised him for winning his first title back at the Bridge with pragmatic football. Parking the bus. What? That's what offended him the most; when teams came to the Bridge and parked the bus. So what an insult when managers attacked him for adopting defensive tactics. However, with his main striker Diego Costa carrying hamstring injuries, his stand in Didier Drogba on his last legs, and Loic Remy not quite hitting goals consistently and also having injury worries, he played with a 'ghost striker' now and again.

Manchester United manager Louis van Gaal and Wenger were among those to raise criticism over Chelsea's lack of possession and attacking intent in games against their sides, as well as grinding out results with a less expansive style in the latter stages of the season when they needed to.

Going on the attack, he described coaches who refuse to adopt some of the counter-attacking tactics that helped his Chelsea team win the Premier League as 'stupid'. Despite winning last season's title comfortably, Mourinho faced sniping about Chelsea's style of football, which was even branded boring.

But in an exclusive interview with the *Sunday Times*, he responded to such criticism, as well as dismissing hype about a new breed of managers who are supposedly devoted to stylish play. He said, 'When people talk about a new generation of coaches – what is that new generation? The generation will always be the ones that win. And the ones that win occasionally or never win will always be something else. There is no new generation [of managers]. What it is, is people who got some idea, some philosophy, and want to create something like, "we build very well from the back, we have a very good ball possession, we don't play counter-attack." But if you don't play counter-attack then it's because you are stupid. Counter-attack is a fantastic item of football, an ammunition that you have, and when you find your opponent unbalanced you have a fantastic moment to score a goal. So I think people are creating [illusions] and it has influenced public opinion. But football will never change. Football is to win.'

Mourinho took a highly amusing swipe at rivals Manchester United, Arsenal and Manchester City during the club's Player of the Year awards dinner.

He took to the stage at the plush Battersea Revolution venue and ripped into his critics after taking stick from van Gaal, Wenger and Manuel Pellegrini but hit back with some 'fictional' chat. 'My players did not get the respect they deserved from day one to the last day,' Mourinho said. 'These are words that I really feel, but now I have a fiction story and let's try to enjoy it.'

With a graphic on a large screen relating to Chelsea's win

over Manchester United, Mourinho added, 'This is a game with two goals, but there is one team that like to play without the ball. That team plays really well and the ball goes and goes and goes and the quality of the ball possession is good, but they don't score. No points. They asked the FIFA committee if they can win like this but they're told it's not possible. That the bigger possession is not essential to win matches and they are not champions.'

Mourinho was in his element at the £240-a-ticket event, as he dissected second-placed Manchester City, whose defensive record did not match Chelsea.

'Then, there is another team. Only with one goal, and they score a lot of goals, from players in every position, and they score and they score and they score. But they never concede a goal because there's no goal. They speak to FIFA and they say they can't be champions because there is only one goal.'

He moved on to the man he loves to hate the most in six seasons and two spells at the Bridge: Wenger. 'There is a third team, and the third team wants to play with two goals. They were scoring some, they were also conceding some. But they score really beautiful goals and then the bus comes along and they couldn't do it.'

Then, to his champions: 'And finally there is a team. They wanted to play with the normal rules and they know that in matches they have to score one more goal than the opponent. How can you do this? By scoring lots of goals, by not conceding and scoring one.'

In an exclusive and very revealing interview with Gary Neville published in the *Telegraph*, Mourinho pinpointed Chelsea's dramatic 2–0 win at Anfield in April, which ruined

Liverpool's title hopes and 'showed Chelsea's manager at his tactical and psychological best.' Neville said, 'The finest coaches are dangerous when they feel wronged. Don't back them into a corner. It was Ferguson-esque. Up in the TV gantry 90 minutes before kick-off that day, I saw signs that Mourinho and Chelsea were on a mission.'

Mourinho emphasised that he had no intention of playing 'the clown' at somebody else's party. He explained, 'I felt during part of last season that the country wanted Liverpool to be champion. The media, the press: a lot was to put Liverpool there. Nobody was saying they were in a privileged situation because they didn't play Champions League. Nobody was speaking about a lot, a lot of decisions that helped them win important and crucial points. And I felt that day was a day that was ready for their celebration. I used the word with my players. I said – we are going to be the clowns, they want us to be the clowns in the circus. The circus is here. Liverpool are to be champions.'

Neville put it Mourinho, 'You weren't having that, were you?'

'No.' Mourinho responded.

Mourinho was already wound up because of the club's request to move the fixture to the previous day, as Chelsea had a Champions League semi-final to prepare for. Mourinho was angry, perplexed and once again saw conspiracy theories when none existed. He said, 'I knew the process that hangs with the fact that we didn't play the day before. Because we wanted to play the day before – the Saturday, because we played the Champions League semi-final on the Wednesday. And I know exactly step by step. Because we went deep on it. We couldn't accept it. The title was lost for us, and we didn't understand how an English team that is representing England in the semi-final [didn't] have the right to play on the Saturday. We went deep. It was a Sky decision? We went to Sky. When people were saying it's a Premier League decision we went to the Premier League. When people were saying it was a Liverpool issue we went also to smell the situation. And the people who were involved in that decision – they were wrong. I think if we play the day before we don't play with the same spirit we did on the Sunday.'

Passion is a major part of Mourinho's persona, whether off the field passionately defending his players, his club, himself, or during a game animated on the touchline.

With the additions of especially Diego Costa and Cesc Fabregas, Crystal Palace away would no longer be so much of a challenge.

'We couldn't cope with certain moments of the game. My feeling is that obviously this season we're going to lose matches, but I don't think we are going to lose matches because we couldn't cope with a certain moment, or a specific [part] of the game. Last year we had problems when the opposite team was closed in a low block [deep-lying defence], we had problems when the other team was putting direct pressure on us with direct football, we couldn't cope very well when we had two or three or four consecutive matches, and we had to keep that high focus for one, two, three, four matches.

'When we were in a good run, I was feeling that the end of the run was coming. You know what I'm saying, because you [he means me] felt that through your whole career. Win today, and tomorrow, and tomorrow. By one side, it's a habit. By the other, you get tired, because it's the responsibility every day. My team, last year, with a lot of guys, was not ready for that.

'So my team was unstable. This season we improve "footballistically", with Diego and Fabregas, no doubt. When we analyse in tactical and technical terms, they represent the kind of player we need, the kind of second midfield player, the quality of striker. We were lucky to have in the market available for us exactly the style of player we need. But what people maybe don't realise is that the maturity of our team, the personality of our team, changed a lot.'

Mourinho likes to feel he is not handicapped by the thinking of others, or rather what others might consider acceptable.

'Obviously talent is so important. And how many points are you going to win based on talent? A lot. But how many points do you lose based on the qualities you are speaking about [character, strength]? You lose also a lot of points. So the balance is between the talent you need and these mental qualities, team qualities.'

Mourinho's relationship with the extra-star performer has always been fascinating. His man-management is of the highest level, his appreciation of extraordinary talent is second to none, but with one main difference: irrespective of how good they are – and they can be of the very best – he insists they buy into his team ethic, his team philosophy, or they have no part in his team.

Mourinho has challenged Eden Hazard to fulfil his talent. He tells Gary Neville, 'I don't know if you agree with me, but the profile of the "main player" you found in football 15 years ago is different to the majority of the players you found at the end of your career. They are different kids. I think Eden is out of context at this moment. Why? Because he's a fantastic kid. He is humble, very humble. Very nice. Very polite. Selfish – zero. Egocentric – zero. He is fantastic. I had a conversation with his father. His father told me something that I loved. I don't think it's a problem to tell you. He said, "I have a wonderful son. He is a wonderful father. He is a wonderful husband. I want him to change, because I want him to be a wonderful player. But I don't want him to change a lot. I don't want him to become – and he used the name of two or three players. I just want him to be the same husband, the same father, the same son, with a little but more tenacity, mental aggression, ambition, personal ego. A little bit more. And you are the guy to give it to him."

'We can never transform these fantastic players and men into a competitive animal, a competitive machine. Not even his father wants [that]. We have just to bring him to a different level, working hard in training, which he's doing.'

Is Hazard responding to that message?

"Yes, yes, yes. He's never afraid to play and take responsibility. But it's not about that. It's about him saying – today, I have to be decisive. What he says in that press interview, when he says, "I'm not one of the five top players in the world." – he can be, but he cannot be in a match where he doesn't do something in the 90 minutes that makes him decisive.

'The week before against Arsenal, I was on him every day – be decisive. Don't be happy with doing nice things. Don't be happy being up and down in the game. You have to do something in the game that wins the game for us. And he did. This is the point with Eden. The talent is amazing, and the human side of him – especially in the modern days, because I work with top players for 30 years – he is not from these times. He's from the old times.'

Mourinho gave an insight into what he expects: 'I had some guys in my career – they didn't want to [defend]. You try to build something behind them to protect. His [Hazard's] problem is not that. He wants. The only problem is to be focused during the 90 minutes and understand when he has to, and when he doesn't have to. I always say to him – you look to the situation. Sometimes you don't need to [track back]. And you have to learn to read the game to know when you don't have to. For example, if Matic is completely closed on the left side, and just behind him, I don't want him to come. I want Matic to cope with the situation. I love to work with him. I love the kid. He will always have my support. He knows my nature. Our relationship is at a point where I can tell him anything. He knows I like him a lot. We are fine because of that.

'Sometimes I think it's part of the players' DNA. Things that you cannot give to the players. But as a coach I always feel I have the quality to interfere. I can help, I can change. So I try. For example, Willian. Willian does fantastic work with the ball and without the ball. I say to him, "You have to finish a game of 90 minutes with three shots. It's not possible you play 90 minutes in the position you play without three shots. Three shots, two assists. It's such amazing work you do for the team, in the build-up, in the defensive transition. You do such amazing work for the team, but with a little bit of this and a little bit of that you'll be fantastic."'

Mourinho caused a stir by selling crowd favourite Juan

Mata and David Luiz, but still ended up with the Double. Proving a point.

He explains, 'With these assets or players who are not fundamental for me, it's where you – meaning my club – have to do the best possible job for me. Is this easy to say when you are talking about very good players? It's not easy. For example, [Juan] Mata to Man Utd. We are losing a very good player to a direct opponent. Would this have happened 10 years ago? Maybe not. But in the modern football and the new economic reality [for Chelsea], if Man Utd pays you an important amount of money he has to go. It is my club's vision. It's my boss, Mr Abramovich, the board. And I share it. I'm not the sort of manager that says – no, not to Man Utd. Sell Mata to Juventus or Barcelona but not Man Utd. Chelsea cannot have 20 replicas. I cannot have Fabregas and another Fabregas getting the same salary. If he can't play I can adapt and put Oscar, say, here.'

Mourinho promised at the start of the season to promote Lewis Baker, Dominic Solanke and Isiah Brown. The promotion of a greater English representation at clubs such as Chelsea and Man City is virtually important for the national team. Can he deliver on his promise?

'Me, their entourage, players, their agents, people around them. But from my point of view as a manager and a coach I think they must be Chelsea players. One of the things that stays forever in a manager's career is the kids that become great. And you were the guy that put him in. That is forever. Varane with me when he was 18 [at Real]. Santon when he was 17 [at Inter]. His second game was against Man Utd in the Champions League. Carlos Alberto scored in a Champions

League final, aged 18. These things stay forever. And I don't believe there isn't one manager in the football world that doesn't want to have this. Nathan Ake, Kurt Zouma, Andreas Christensen, Lewis Baker, Brown: we have a group of kids, I'm not afraid to play them. But at the same time we want to protect the player.'

Would winning the title with four or five home-grown lads be a better achievement than ten years ago, or now with players signed by the club? Mourinho says, 'It should be a moral commitment between the clubs and the country. I feel committed. Nobody is telling me we have a rule where we have to play five English players. But I feel [that] the difference in quality in the players we have now and the ones we had in 2004 is an amazing difference. So we have the material, and we work a lot – give a lot of thought – to what they have to do to become first-team players. Chelsea have in this moment a group of kids who will be Chelsea players. And the English ones: the moment they become Chelsea players they become an option for England.'

Which coaches does he most admire?

'I think we are in a moment of contradictions. Because there is a wave of opinion that says because the knowledge is available for everyone – the distance between you and the knowledge is a click – we have got generations of people well-informed, well prepared. I disagree. I feel a lot when I read what people sometimes write, that it's not like this, because when the knowledge is at the disposal of everybody, some people are in a comfort zone. When the knowledge is not at your disposal, you have to think. And you have to produce knowledge. If you want a good training session because you want to coach defence in a low block you have 200 sessions [pointing to the computer, where they are accessible on the Internet]. If you don't have this [the information] you have to produce it yourself. So I see lots of replicas. You got to the fifth division, or Under-10s, the two centre-halves open, the goalkeeper gives the ball to the central midfielder, the central midfielder isn't technically good, he loses the ball. But they keep going in the same direction. We are in the moment of stability because the knowledge is available to everyone and we have stopped in a comfort zone.'

What does he think of himself?

'I am not fundamentalist in football. What I mean is that in football you have your ideas, you die with your ideas. No. People ask me: what is your model of play? I say, "Model of what?" He winces when he says it. Model of play against who? When? With which players? Model of play what? I cannot answer to that. Am I too stupid [he lowers his hands to the floor] or am I too smart [raising them to the ceiling]? What is that? I don't know. My model of play is to build from the keeper to Eden Hazard? My model of play is that I have to find where is the weakness of my opponent and where is his strength. Is Diego Costa stronger than this guy [a centre-back]? The model of play. What is that? For me the model of play is the principles I establish with my team as priority principles which give us a certain DNA, but that's the depth.

'The same thing as "a project". The project has to be flexible. The project is never the same from when we start to when we end. It's like at my house. You change, I don't like this door, you change. The windows.

'I prefer my team to press in a low block, but if the opponent prefers to build from the back, and they are fantastic, it gives them huge stability in their game – I'm going to press there. Liverpool wanted to play with Suarez behind the defenders, Sterling the same thing, and Steven Gerrard in front of the defenders. So I go there, I play Lampard on Stevie G, I play my block completely low. I win. And I'm criticised because I [am not allowed to] play that way. So I am the stupid one. I'm not fundamentalist. And I think some people in football are becoming a bit fundamentalist.'

He picks out Diego Simeone's Atlético Madrid: 'What Atlético Madrid did last year is to admire, because they were champions in a league they can't win. I was there three years and it's difficult to imagine another team winning the league, but they won. A huge difference in resources. Real Madrid and Barcelona are in a different dimension. But they based it on that approach – the team spirit, the organisation, the style of play. People used to say – everybody defends, then it's a long ball to Diego Costa. No. They knew what they were doing.

'Last year, I was feeling that we could [win the league] but we were not ready to cope with that pressure. Because we had certain limitations in the team in terms of tactical qualities, technical qualities, and we were aware of that. My style of leadership is not a style. I try to have a leadership that is adapted to the reality. And last year I was feeling that they were not ready for what I call a pressure leadership – or confrontational leadership. The team as a team was mentally – and even tactically – unstable.'

His closest friend is Rui Faria, who became his assistant on his first day as the manager at Benfica, and who has followed him to every club he has managed since.

'Rui used to say, "A winning football manager is the best life in the world." It's a fact, and we try. But in this country we have so many matches that you cannot allow yourself to be affected. I lose 5–3, the next day I have a training session, and in two or three days have another match. I win 3–0 or 4–0, the next day I have a training session and in two or three days I have another match. I must try to hide my emotions. I have to live with both the victory and the defeat.

'The manager is not the most important person in the club – of course not. I keep saying, the most important person in the club is first the supporters, secondly the owner, third the players, and then I come. But it is the manager that everyone looks at. The players are watching you, analysing you; they want to see your reaction, they want to see your stability. The people that work in the club are also watching you, and they follow in a negative or positive way. Even the supporters are watching you. They want to feel that after that big defeat you are ready for the next day; that after the big victory you are not in the moon but have your feet in the earth. And I think I am good in controlling these situations, and good in trying to keep people balanced for the negative and for the positive. At home I am not good, because they know me too well. I can't hide. They get me.'

In his second spell at Chelsea, Mourinho is settled, relaxed, and on good terms with his employers. What if Chelsea offered him a six-year contract extension?

'I sign tomorrow. That's what I want. I want to stay in Chelsea and English football because I think I won the right.

My wife says many times I won the right to stop when I want. She says I won enough, I did enough, I created a good situation for the family. She says I won the right to do what I want. Unfortunately, Chelsea's not my club. I depend on the club and I depend on the results.'

Mourinho compares this year's Chelsea side with the first of his title-winning teams: 'I think the team of 2005 had one plus in relation to this team, which was killer instinct. Every time we could kill matches, we killed matches. I don't remember matches where we had the opponent and didn't kill. It was a team that never gave a chance to the opponent to survive. This team is not there. We are more artistic, I believe. We have better control of the game by having the ball, and by knowing how to move between players – the circulation of the ball. This team has more [potential] to be admired by good results but also for a certain style of play. In that team I had guys like Makelele. He knew everything about that [toughness]. These guys are still in that learning process. I think we are going in a very good direction. People like [Arjen] Robben, [Damien] Duff, even Joe [Cole] in his two great seasons with me were people with appetite to kill matches, to finish. You don't see Duff dribbling without a shot. You don't see Robben attack the space without getting a penalty or shooting. We have some guys still in the line between the artistic side and the objective side. We need to kill more matches.'

Drogba believes the team from Mourinho's first spell is better than the current side. 'I would say the first one was better because I was involved more as a player but there is a difference in the way that when I joined the team it was a bit more mature,' he told an interviewer with BT Sport. 'Frank,

Makelele, William Gallas – all these players were, I think, around 24, 25 and plus, so this time it's younger and I can see and I can feel that there is a gap, it can progress together so it's good for the players.'

Mourinho challenged his Chelsea side to achieve sustained success immediately the season concluded with a 3–1 come-from-behind win over Sunderland when Drogba bade farewell, while Petr Cech also played his final game after eleven years. The title was won with three matches to spare and there was an air of celebration as the championship-winning team was presented prior to kick-off.

Mourinho guided the club to their first title in fifty years in his first spell at the club, and last season's success ended a five-year wait for the Premier League after winning the Capital One Cup in March.

'This team is just in the beginning. This team won one Capital Cup and one Premier League. They have to win more to be better than the others. You can win something in a certain moment of your career and that's it, or during your career you can win on a regular basis. That's what makes the difference between somebody that is champion and the champions. Let's try to motivate them to go in that direction, because that's what I want for them. For me to have here today the champions of 2004/05 and the champions of 2014/15 is an amazing feeling, because I belong to both. It would be a dream to be here in 2025 and be with the champions of 2004/05, the champions of 2015 and the champions of 2025. It would be fantastic.

'My future doesn't matter. What matters is Chelsea's future and I'm working for that.'

The thirty-three-year-old Cech, displaced by Thibaut

Courtois after a decade as first choice, was to leave although he has one year left on his contract. Mourinho repeated his wish for Cech to stay, but the decision was made by owner Roman Abramovich. Cech's 'contribution was decisive,' said Mourinho.

Asked when talks regarding Cech would take place, Mourinho said, 'I hope never. But I don't know. He was always there for me and for the team. He played lots of important matches for us. For me, no problem to have both. I can cope with it. But obviously I'm not in control of Petr's decision. I have to wait.' Mourinho has had to say a number of goodbyes – Ashley Cole, Frank Lampard, Michael Essien and Drogba among them. Cech would be the hardest in the sense that he would be going to help a big rival, and Mourinho wasn't chuffed about that.

Drogba was a pre-planned substitution, but Chelsea were already behind to Steven Fletcher's header. A Diego Costa penalty and two goals in the final twenty minutes from Loic Remy saw Chelsea rally to finish with a fifteenth win from an unbeaten nineteen home games in their title-winning season.

Mourinho gave his medal to his daughter Matilde for safe-keeping, as his son – the intended recipient – was absent.

He held up eight fingers during the presentation, signalling the number of titles won in four countries.

'A lot, eh? Maybe I have no more fingers. Let's go with eight and try nine. I'm almost there,' he said.

He was pleased with the performance, in response to Monday's loss at West Brom. 'It was good to see the dynamic back. The big emotion is always when you clinch the title. When you have the cup in your hands and when the players have it, [it] is always a great feeling. [After waiting] five years at Stamford Bridge it was time for our supporters to enjoy too.'

When Cech finally joined Arsenal for a modest £10 million fee and for a pay rise to £100,000 a week, Mourinho publicly declared, for the first time, that he supported Abramovich's decision, despite not sounding as if he approved whenever he'd commented on it previously.

Clearly, Mourinho was opposed to strengthening a rival, but respected Abramovich's decision to allow a distinguished servant to choose his next destination. He said on chelseafc. com, 'I support the owner's decision to honour the player in this way. Petr has been a great servant for Chelsea for 11 years and helped this club to win almost everything there is to win. I always said I wanted him to stay but I understand Petr needed to move on to play first team football every week. Sometimes you have to respect the wishes of someone who has earned so much respect with his service and actions for your club. It is very rare in football to make a decision like this and for that reason I am proud of my club for making it. There are not many clubs in the world big enough to be able to make that decision. Petr's success at this club will always to be remembered and we thank him for everything he did.'

His 'party-line' comment on the club's website was not the full picture. But Cech was confident there was no ill-feeling between Mourinho and himself.

'I think it has been great to have a chat with Jose because he is a manager that I have worked with for the longest time in my career. He had to make his decision at the start of last season, I had to make my decision at the start of this season... and

306

obviously we're now in this situation. Last season I realised that I am not in the phase of my career that I would be happy to be a back-up goalie and sit on the bench. I believe that in all those games I played I showed that I still have the skills and the level required to play as a number one goalkeeper in the best league in the world, which is the Premier League. But I will always keep the best regards for him because I believe that we had so much success and so much respect for each other. He is one of the best managers in the world. Now, we will be opponents but it will not change our relationship, I believe. You know, I learned a lot from him and one of those things was that if you have to make a hard decision, you need to make sure that you do it if you believe it is the right choice. I have a huge respect for him and we had a good chat about it. Obviously I know he would have loved me to stay, but that's the way it goes.'

Cech vowed to play on for another EIGHT YEARS, and recalls the moment he knew his Chelsea career was over: 1 March 2015, having just won his twelfth major Chelsea honour. He says, 'The moment I knew I had to leave? After the Capital One Cup final. I knew there weren't many games left for me after that. We were out of the FA Cup and Champions League, so there were only league games, and I knew that was it. I knew then this wasn't the way I wanted to have another season. As tough as it was to make the decision, it became clear that it would be this way because I have the same motivation as I did 10 years ago. My commitment to training, the will to get better is the same. I don't want to waste that sitting on the bench.'

Cech collected thirteen winners' medals in eleven years

and will be remembered as a Chelsea legend. Cech signed a four-year contract for Arsenal and believes he can play into his forties.

'If I stay fit I can have seven or eight years at this level. Retirement is not something I'm planning for yet. I have in my head that I could possibly do it [be a manager] and maybe do the training, the travelling and staying in hotels for another 20 years. Maybe in eight years I will say I don't want to watch football any more!'

Jens Lehmann was part of the Arsenal 'Invincibles' team of 2004, and he believes Cech can inspire his new team to success, providing the emotional ties with Stamford Bridge can be cut. He told the *Sun*, 'It's not easy to suddenly go from Chelsea, where he has spent almost his whole career winning many trophies, to the other side of the capital with a rival. Before you can have it in your heart to win titles again, you have to get rid of the love you had before. At Chelsea, for Petr, it was his passion and he showed great commitment. But, as a professional, he needs to get over it and needs to know Arsenal want him to win things again for them. Yet, let me tell you, that is not an easy thing to get over psychologically. It can take a few weeks, even a few months.'

Lehmann believes Cech can offer Arsenal another 'five fantastic years.'

Mourinho, though, isn't afraid to back his judgement.

And there cannot be much more of a gamble than the season-long loan for
striker Radamel Falcao, with young midfielder Mario Pasalic joining Monaco on loan as part of the deal. Pasalic joined Chelsea the previous summer. The Croatia international spent

last season with La Liga outfit Elche, scoring three times in thirty-one top-flight appearances.

Mourinho is out to prove Louis Van Gaal wrong, after the United coach dispatched the Colombian striker back to Monaco after just the one-year loan spell at Old Trafford, which didn't exactly go according to plan. The former Atlético Madrid striker managed four goals before LVG opted not to sign him in a permanent £43.2 million deal.

Mourinho hopes to help the striker hit the heights he managed with Porto and Atlético, where he was rated one of the world's top goalscorers. Mourinho says, 'It hurts me that people in England think that the real Falcao is the one we saw at Manchester United. If I can help Falcao reach his level again, I will do it. He's a player I know, one that I've followed since Atlético Madrid.'

Talks with Falcao's representative, Jorge Mendes, were helped as Mourinho shared the same agent. A compromise was reached over the player's £265,000-a-week pay package and loan fee, with Chelsea paying £180,000 a week with a loan fee at £4 million.

Mourinho explained, 'We lost a striker [Drogba] who scored four goals in the Premier League, but three of these goals meant important points for us. A striker that was very experienced, who every minute was fantastic for us, even in the last 10 minutes to hold the ball, cool down emotionally the game. So we have to buy a striker because we want to have three strikers of a good level. We do not want to have just one. Then you lose a good position on the negotiation table.'

While there are many memorable Mourinho quips, quotes, and press-conference confrontations, behind the bravado hides a dedicated, meticulous and thorough planner. Mourinho arrives each day around 7.30am, goes into his office and locks the door, and remains there for the next two hours. As he told the *Telegraph*:, 'I need my time to be lonely. You know, in football, I'm not so old. At 52 maybe I have 20 years in front of me to coach. But I feel myself as ... you might say an "old fox". Nothing scares me, nothing worries me too much; it looks like nothing new can happen for me. I am very, very stable in the control of these emotions but I need my time to think. Not wake up in the middle of the night worrying about somebody's injury, or the tactic for this match. I need to reflect, I need to try to anticipate problems. I need my time.'

THE
VOTE

Jose Mourinho is, head and shoulders, the greatest of the current managers, and is marginally behind Sir Alex Ferguson for the title of the Greatest of All-Time Managers.

Mourinho has to win the Champions League again to overtake Sir Alex and, having built a new Chelsea team capable of challenging for the Champions League over the next few years, that is definitely within his grasp.

In our exclusive poll for this book, Sir Alex came out on top, with Mourinho a close second, and some distance ahead of Brian Clough.

We polled the fans, the coaches, the legends, the celebrity fans for as wide a cross-section of opinion as possible.

Here are the results:

THE FANS

1. Sir Alex Ferguson (%)   5pts
2. Jose Mourinho (%)   4pts
3. Arsène Wenger (%)   3pts
4. Bill Shankly (%)   2pts
5. Pep Guardiola (%)   1pt

From a poll of the 1 million-plus users of zapsportz.com, the football-dedicated website.

COACHES

1. Brian Clough   5pts
2. Jose Mourinho   4pts
3. Sir Alex Ferguson   3pts
4. Bill Shankly   2pts
5. Vicente Del Bosque   1pt

Brian Clough edges Mourinho because of the sources and squad at his disposal, yet to still win two European Cups was quite phenomenal. A lot of people in Europe wouldn't understand the constraints in which he worked, not only challenging the might of Liverpool who were so dominant at that time, but overtaking them. Mourinho has won three Champions Leagues in three different countries; Fergie hasn't managed that. Mourinho has challenged himself in new countries and, like never before, has proved himself in every country he has managed, whatever the conditions, with different types of clubs and different types of players. And it's not taken him ten years at each club to do it; he comes in and does it straight away. That takes some doing so, whatever managerial methods he uses, it works wherever he goes. I'd go next with Fergie, purely on the amount of trophies over such a long period of time with the one club. This sort of thing wouldn't happen in the modern era, as clubs just don't give managers that length of time. United could have sacked him if he didn't win anything in his first four years, and in this era they certainly would have sacked him. You have to admire the way he kept turning out new teams and reinventing his squads – that is fantastic, particularly have such hunger to keep on doing it over and over again. He was the sort that, after one day or two days of winning a major trophy, was planning the next one. It was the kind of attitude that had Liverpool dominating football in the 1970s. That brings me to Shankly, who built up a team from virtually nothing but then set about creating a dynasty to allow the likes of Paisley to prosper. Shanks set the template but he was also a true, true character, with so much charisma. Del Bosque deserves recognition for winning a World Cup and a Euro – that will make some beating. (Glenn Hoddle: managed England, Chelsea, Spurs, Swindon, Southampton, Wolves; coached QPR.)

1. Arrigo Sacchi   5pts
2. Jose Mourinho   4pts
3. Sir Alex Ferguson   3pts
4. Carlo Ancelotti   2pts
5. Pep Guardiola   1pt

Mourinho: He is a great coach, communicator and motivator. One of the best in our generation. (Roberto Di Matteo: Italian international player legend, and Chelsea manager who won the Champions League.)

1. Menotti   5pts
2. Fergie   4pts
3. Pep Guardiola   3pts
4. Rinus Michels   2pts
5. Mario Zagallo   1pt

(Ossie Ardiles: World Cup winner, manager of Spurs, Newcastle, West Brom and Swindon. Managed sixteen clubs all over the world.)

1. Sir Alex Ferguson   5pts
2. Jose Mourinho   4pts
3. Sir Matt Busby   3pts
4. Brian Clough   2pts
5. Bill Shankly   1pt

Sir Alex Ferguson rebuilt the club from the bottom up and created a dynasty. Also, [based on] the period of time he was at the club and the success he had. Jose Mourinho makes the difference and has been successful in a number of different leagues/countries. Sir Matt Busby took a club through a terrible tragedy and on to rebuild a team to achieve European glory. Brian Clough, is a big character , had great partnership with Peter Taylor, was very successful with Derby County and Nottingham Forest, and went on to win back-to-back European Cups with Forest. Bill Shankly, very successful in his own right, but put the foundations in for years of success at home and in Europe. All great mangers. (Gary Waddock, former professional and international footballer and manager)

1. Jose Mourinho   5pts
2. Sir Alex Ferguson   4pts

3. Bielsa   3pts
4. Sampaoli   2pts
5. Brian Clough   1pt
(Anthony Hudson, former player and coach, now manager of the New Zealand football team)

1. Alex Ferguson   5pts
2. Jose Mourinho   4pts
3. Bill Shankly   3pts
4. Arsène Wenger   2pts
5. Bob Paisley   1pt
(Paul Davis. PFA Coach Educator and Equalities Executive; formerly played for Arsenal.)

LEGENDS

1. Sir Alex Ferguson   5pts
2. Jose Mourinho   4pts
3. Bill Shankly   3pts
4. Brian Clough   2pts
5. Graham Taylor   1pt

Because they all created a winning team from scratch. Paisley and Kenny Dalglish took over great teams. Mourinho is slightly different; he had the money to be successful, but Porto winning the European Cup was incredible and, having not played, had to fight for respect from the start. Graham for taking Watford from Division 4 to second to Liverpool without spending money was unbelievable! (John Barnes: Liverpool, Watford, England.)

1. Sir Alex Ferguson   5pts
2. Jose Mourinho   4pts
3. Bill Shankly   3pts
4. Matt Busby   2pts
5. Jock Stein   1pt

(Bryan Robson: Manchester United/England legend and captain.)

1. Rinus Michels   5pts
2. Marcelo Lippi   4pts
3. Arrigo Sacchi   3pts
4. Fabio Capello   2pts

Rinus Michels was the first to start the total football. Marcelo Lippi was the master of defence. Arroyo Sacchi started 4-4-2. Fabio Capello is Mr Organiser and disciplinarian. (Jimmy Floyd Hassilbaink: Chelsea, Leeds, Holland, now a manager.)

1. Fergie   5pts
2. Jose Mourinho   4pts
3. Bob Paisley   3pts
4. Pep Guardiola   2pts
5. Arsène Wenger   1pt

(Darren Anderton: Spurs, England.)

1. Alex Ferguson   5pts
2. Brian Clough   4pts
3. Giovanni Trapattoni   3pts
4. Bill Shankly   2pts
5. Jose Mourinho   1pt

Chapman/Graham/Wenger would be next. (Perry Groves: Arsenal.)

1. Keith Burkinshaw	5pts
2. Graham Souness	4pts
3. Sir Bobby Robson	3pts
4. Bobby Campbell	2pts
5. Bill Nicholson	1pt

Keith Burkinshaw was the best – he was honest with you. Graham Souness was great. He was a winner and wouldn't accept anything less. Sir Bobby Robson was good; he knew how to beat teams when I was with England.

Bobby Campbell was a good motivator and I enjoyed being his captain at Chelsea. Those four were who I played under, but I think the great Bill Nicholson would have been great to play under, as he liked to play total football. (Graham Roberts: Spurs, Chelsea, Glasgow Rangers.)

1. Sir Alex Ferguson	5pts
2. Jose Mourinho	4pts
3. Bob Paisley	3pts
4. Bill Shankly	2pts
5. Brian Clough	1pt

If it's people who have managed in the English leagues! (Nigel Spackman: Chelsea, Glasgow Rangers.)

1. Sir Alex Ferguson	5pts
2. Brian Clough	4pts
3. Don Revie	3pts
4. Bill Shankly	2pts

5. Jose Mourinho   1pt
(Paul Miller: Spurs legend.)

1. Brian Clough   5pts
2. Bill Shankly   4pts
3. Sir Alf Ramsey   3pts
4. Sir Alex Ferguson   2pts
5. Jose Mourinho   1pt
(Stewart Robson: Arsenal.)

1. Sir Alex Ferguson   5pts
2. Rinus Michels   4pts
3. Marcelo Lippi   3pts
4. Jose Mourinho   2pts
5. Helenio Herrera   1pt

Sir Alex Ferguson: greatest number of trophies, spanned the longest during a time where the game changed in many ways yet still reinvented five or six winning sides. Domestic and European success. Rinus Michels: plenty of domestic and European titles but 'Total football', and that 1974 World Cup winning side was a joy to watch. Marcelo Lippi: won Serie A five times when it was strong as well as European Cup success. Biggest success was Italy winning the World Cup in 2006 in Germany – semi-final win over Germany was one of the best tactical displays and performances I've ever seen. Jose Mourinho: League winner in five different countries, plenty of silverware in Europe as well with big teams but, most impressively, got Porto the Europa League title and then the Champions League title in consecutive years. Helenio Herrera: winner domestically in Spain and

Italy as well as in Europe. First to really use psychology motivation and 'phrases'. Huge disciplinarian, 'catenaccio' was born and he was way ahead of his time. (Tony Dorigo: Chelsea, Leeds, England.)

1. Sir Alex Ferguson   5pts
2. Jose Mourinho   4pts
3. Pep Guardiola   3pts
4. Rinus Michels   2pts
5. Arsène Wenger   1pt

<(whose list is this? Author?)>

1. Jose Mourinho   5pts
2. Sir Alex   4pts
3. Pep Guardiola   3pts
4. Carlo Ancelotti   2pts
5. Del Bosque   1pt

Tough question – between Sir Alex and The Special One. I will go for Jose Mourinho.

Arrogance (He knows he's the best)

Motivational skills (A great influencer)

A winner (Drive and determination)

Charismatic (Charm)

Leadership (He doesn't just lead people but creates leaders)

(Marcus Gayle: Wimbledon, Brentford, Watford, Staines manager.)

1. Sir Alex Ferguson   5pts
2. Brian Clough   4pts
3. Jose Mourinho   3pts

4, Bob Paisley   2pts
5. Jock Stein   1pt

A hugely subjective discussion, as different generations /eras of managers /resources/but my reasons are:

Sir Alex, twenty-five years at one club, never will be surpassed, broke stronghold with auld firm with youth at Aberdeen and same template in building three generations at Manchester United.

Brian Clough has a very similar template with Derby and Nottingham Forest, but winning the European Cup twice is a phenomenal achievement.

Mourinho, in my view, is currently the best modern manager in the world; modern-day coaching/tactical methodology. Brilliant man manager, delivered championships in Portugal, UK, Spain, and an unprecedented treble in the unlikeliest of environments in Italy with Inter Milan, similar to amazing achievement with Porto winning Champions League. Only fifty-two with hunger and desire to achieve much more.

Bob Paisley: Three European Cups in 1980s in nine years when English clubs and great managers made a huge impact in European football. A gentleman manager.

Arsène Wenger: A huge contribution to the game, and the first real foreign manager that brought professionalism, a style of play, tactical and physiology, and education to the country. One only has to look at the way he improved players – for example, prolonged careers of Arsenal's ageing back line at that time with diet and training methods. His style of play, business in transfer market – for example, Anelka, Vieira, Pires, Henry, the economic transition of relocation while staying in the top four, thus qualifying for the Champions

League, as he has done for last sixteen years or so. More than a football manager, he's an economist.

(Paul Elliott: former professional footballer; appointed CBE for services to equality and diversity in football.)

1. Alex Ferguson   5pts
2. Bob Paisley   4pts
3. Jose Mourinho   3pts
4. Brian Clough/Bill Shankly   2pts

It's really difficult to pick, as the eras meant expectations and finances were very different. Should the categories have been narrowed down to biggest impact at the club, that would be Shankly or Clough for me. If we are talking about winning trophies, which is how managers are judged today, all of the above have done that, but should that mean the best manager has won the most trophies? The debate will rumble on. (Clive Wilson: defender; Manchester City, Chelsea, Spurs, QPR.)

1. Jose Mourinho   5pts
2. Carlo Ancelotti   4pts
3 Vicente del Bosque   3pts
4. Pep Guardiola   2pts
5. Marcello Lippi   1pt

There are so many arguments for Fergie and Paisley etc. over a long period at one club which can be harder in some ways to keep winning titles in domestic and Europe. Mourinho is my top but Ancelotti would my second or Vicente del Bosque. (Gerry Armstrong: La Liga Sky TV expert, Spurs and Northern Ireland legend.)

1. Sir Alex Ferguson   5pts
2. Brian Clough   4pts
3. Sir Alf Ramsay   3pts
4. Bob Paisley   2pts
5. Jose Mourinho   1pt

(Tony Cottee: West Ham legend)

AWARD-WINNING SPORTS WRITERS/EDITORS

1. Jose Mourinho   5pts
2. Sir Alex Ferguson   4pts
3. Rinus Michels   3pts
4. Ernst Happel   2pts
5. Brian Clough   1pt

Top five very tough. Mourinho always wins, all the time, everywhere he goes. If Ferguson had done it overseas as well as in the UK, he'd be top. (Ben Rumsby: *Daily Telegraph* sports writer.)

1. Brian Clough   5pts
2. Sir Alex Ferguson   4pts
3. Bob Paisley   3pts
4. Jose Mourinho   2pts
5. Herbert Chapman   1pt

If managing is about just that – managing what you have at your disposal – Clough has no peer. Two distinctly average provincial clubs were turned into superb trophy-winning sides by Clough. League titles and, incredibly, two European Cup wins with Forest beggars belief, even after thirty-five years. (Bill Bradshaw, award-winning journalists and sports editor.)

1. Sir Matt Busby   5pts
2. Jock Stein   4pts
3. Sir Alex Ferguson   3pts
4. Jose Mourinho   2pts
5. Brian Clough   1pt

Bill makes a very good case for Old Bighead. I've gone for Busby because he created a set of values that took football into a different dimension in this country – and we will never know where they might have taken us but for Munich. In Edwards, Byrne, Taylor and the young Bobby Charlton, he had surely shaped the nucleus of a potential World Cup winning team – and then ten years later he emerged from the despair to win the European Cup with the team of Best and Charlton and one deprived through injury of Law. That set the template for the very best of English football.

It is easy to despise Mourinho for his vanities and his cynical tactics but so much harder to deny that he is a one-off football genius. His Champions League win with Inter was a triumph of football's black arts. He did more than park the bus. He out-thought Guardiola and disabled the team that was supposed to be the best in the history of club football. For what it is worth, Stein was the master of man management and motivation, getting eleven Glaswegians to pick off the cream of the European game and destroy the mystique of the legendary Inter coach Helenio Herrera. Fergie had the nerve to build on Busby's legacy – and an astonishing drive to win – and Clough was a forerunner of Mourinho; a man who had a rage and an instinct to finish on top. (Jim Lawton, multi-award-winning sports writer.)

1. Chapman
2. Busby
3. Ferguson
4. George Ramsay (Aston Villa)
5. Shankly

If you include foreigners...

1. Chapman	5pts
2. Lippi	4pts
3. Michels	3pts
4. Pozzo	2pts
5 Mourinho	1pt

Chapman went where no one had ever gone before – and was a visionary – and left a massive legacy at two clubs. Busby built great team after great team – even after being nearly killed along with most of his very greatest team. Ferguson had incredible longevity at the top. Ramsey likewise. And Shankly almost redefined the arts of management, such as motivation and player selection, while creating a fortress. (Patrick Barclay, sportswriter, author and broadcaster.)

Brian Clough	5pts
Sir Alex Ferguson	4pts
Jock Stein	3pts
Sir Matt Busby	2pts
Bill Shankly	1pt

(Bob Cass, formerly of the *Mail on Sunday*.)

1. Sir Matt Busby	5pts
2. Rinus Michels	4pts
3. Helenio Herrera	3pts

4. Sir Alex Ferguson   2pts

5. Bob Paisley   1pt

Busby joined Manchester United in 1945 and steered the club from a homeless shell into one of the biggest in the world. Michels was the man who invented 'Total Football', the swapping of players from position to position. Won titles in Spain and Holland, won the World Cup and European Championships with Holland. Herrera – the man who forged AC Milan into a great team, with three titles and two European Cups, also hugely successful with Atlético Madrid, Barcelona and Roma. Ferguson – another Scot who picked up a rudderless United after the Busby era, and took them into the new age with thirty-eight trophies, including thirteen Premier League titles and two European Cups. Paisley – picked up Bill Shankly's mantle and in just nine years won nineteen trophies, including three European Cups.

Why not Mourinho? Hard to say. I would like to see him stay for a lengthier spell at Chelsea this time round and win the Champions League with them. The only thing that keeps him out of the five is maybe that he has not yet created a legacy at a club – though the Chelsea side he left went on to be successful for some time. I think in his second spell at the club he can really lay down roots. But it was a close-run thing – I can't have a top six.

Wanted to put Bill Nick in... (Tony Banks, football writer, *Daily Express*.)

CELEBRITY FANS

1. Sir Matt Busby   5pts

2. Brian Clough   4pts

3. Bill Shankly   3pts
4. Arsène Wenger   2pts
5. Bobby Robson   1pt

They were the ones who believed in style and had a way with words. They were the ones you could love as well as admire. (Sir Michael Parkinson.)

1. Sir Alex   5pts
2. Mourinho   4pts
3. Wenger   3pts
4. Trapattoni   2pts
5. Paisley   1pt
(Piers Morgan.)

1. Mourinho   5pts
2. Mario Zagallo   4pts
3. Alex Ferguson   3pts
4. Brian Clough   2pts
5. Bill Shankly   1pt

... and if there was a sixth, I'd give it to Roberto Di Matteo, as he's the only Chelsea manager to actually win the Champions League. Jose Mourinho is a manager who actually manages as well as coaches. In a game that is now dominated by massive egos, here is a man with possibly the biggest of them all, and one that he uses to deflect attention away from his players, allowing them to get on with their job. It's a master stroke, beautifully simple, yet effective.

He's a man who is obsessively thorough and regimented. If you play for him, you know exactly what is expected of you and you're prepared to do it to the best of your ability.

Once again, there's a brilliant simplicity to this. In any walk of life, clarity is vital. If you give someone absolutely clear instructions, they will know what is required of them. They can be focused; a vital part of the game.

Ultimately, though, Jose Mourinho is a man who knows how to win. He doesn't bottle; he sees the job through, no matter how hard that might. He knows that tough decisions are part of it, but he doesn't shirk and will do what is necessary to succeed. (Ivor Baddiel: known for his work on *X Factor* (2004), *Bus Life* (2004) and *We Know Where You Live* (2001). Brother of David. Chelsea fan and occasional sports writer.)

1. Brian Clough   5pts
2. Arsène Wenger   4pts
3. Alex Ferguson   3pts
4. Matt Busby   2pts
5. Bill Shankly   1pt

I will list my managers (presumably you with thinking about those who have managed in England or Scotland?). Once you move into world football, it becomes so much more difficult, for we are not fully conversant with the achievements of those managers, or how difficult it was for them. So let us concentrate of the Football League or Premiership. Mourinho's a far richer and more designer-stubbled George Graham. His emphasis on defence, as with Graham, doesn't appeal him to me. I have yet to see any evidence that he can produce a team that offers the spectator exciting and varied football. That said, why would he change his dull and winning system? (Porto? A side from nothing to win European Cup? I asked.) Yes, maybe, but I am not sure that it was all down to Jose. There were mechanics at work in the background. I won't deny he is an effective manager, but not inspired, as were Clough Hartlepool to twice winner of the European Cup. Busby, who built a shattered club into the best in England and then in Europe. Wenger, who came unknown to England and changed the way all English football is played (just watch most Premier League football before 1997). Shankly ... well, that almost goes without saying... and so on and so on. He certainly couldn't match Clough and Busby in producing sides from nowhere to becoming European Champions. Jose has done so with unimaginable (to most ordinary managers) amounts of money and, when his demands aren't met, he realises life is going to get tough.

I hope this testimony suits your book, although Mr Mourinho won't enjoy reading my opinion. (Laurence Marks: sitcom writer, half of writing duo Marks and Gran or 'Lo and Mo'.)

1. Arsène Wenger   5pts
2. Herbert Chapman   4pts
3. George Graham   3pts
4. Tom Whittaker   2pts
5. George Allison   1pt

You'll deduce the common factor, I imagine. I think what you need is a more partisan approach, so here are my top five managers. (Maurice Gran: Lo and Mo.)

1. Arsène Wenger   5pts
2. Herbert Chapman   4pts

3. George Allison   3pts
4. George Graham   2pts
5. Bertie Mee   1pt

I couldn't possibly comment on anybody else's, but for us in North London. (Tom Watt.)

1. Jose Mourinho   5pts
2. Sir Alex Ferguson   4pts
3. Sir Matt Busby   3pts
4. Brian Clough   2pts
5. Bill Shankly   1pt

(Lord [Herman] Ouseley.)

THE VOTE RESULTS

1. SIR ALEX FERGUSON   117pts
2. JOSE MOURINHO   89pts
3. BRIAN CLOUGH   64pts
4. BILL SHANKLY   33pts
5. SIR MATT BUSBY   27pts
6. ARSENE WENGER   26pts
7. BOB PAISLEY   20pts
8. RINUS MICHELS   19pts
9. HERBERT CHAPMAN   14pts
10. JOCK STEIN/LIPPI   9pts
11/12. SACCHI/ANCELOTTI   8pts
13/14/15/16. MENOTTI/   5pts
    TRAPATTONI/ZAGALLO/BURKINSHAW
17/18 /19. HERRERA/   4pts
    ROBSON/SOUNESS

WHAT DOES THE WORLD THINK OF THE SELF-ACCLAIMED SPECIAL ONE?

Such is the importance of a manager as astute and tactically aware as Jose Mourinno that Arsenal would have won the Premier League last season if they were managed by Jose Mourinho, according to former Chelsea striker Tony Cascarino, who is now a highly provocative media pundit.

Cascarino's view that Arsenal or Manchester City would win the League if they had Mourinho is guaranteed to ignite a debate among the clubs' supporters about the value of Arsène Wenger and Manuel Pellegrini. And with Mourinho in charge, he tips the West London club to retain their title this season as well.

Mourinho led Chelsea to their first title in five years last season and, as Cascarino says, Mourinho gives the West London side the edge.

Since returning to Stamford Bridge two years ago, Mourinho

hasn't lost a game against City, Arsenal or Manchester United. Cascarino argues that the head-to-head record among the elite group of clubs is the key to landing the championship title. He told Sky Sports, 'The difference between Chelsea and their rivals is the manager. I believe that, if Mourinho was manager of Arsenal, he'd have won the league. Likewise with Man City. That's the quality he brings. John Terry said Petr Cech is worth fifteen points. Maybe so. Mourinho is worth more than that to Chelsea. We saw two Chelseas in the season. We saw a very entertaining one and then, when it got tight, they became tight and didn't give too much away. That's to do with the manager. How did they win the league? By being tactically brilliant. It's no coincidence that in the last two years none of their major rivals have been able to beat them. That's a massive disadvantage for them; he's hurting every one of his rivals every time they play.'

Cascarino tips Chelsea to retain their crown as he is not convinced their rivals are catching up.

'Chelsea are the ones to beat. Arsenal and City have got to be better tactically. United is interesting because of the big kitty they have to spend but they'll still have to gel that group together if they bring in new players. All the things that other teams have to do – sort their tactics out, gel together – Chelsea have already done. All they're doing now is what United and, before that, Liverpool used to do: add one or two to a group that was being successful to refine it. If you want to win the league next season, you've got to beat Chelsea.'

Manuel Pellegrini has had a strained relationship with his Chelsea counterpart dating back to when Mourinho replaced him at Real Madrid in 2010. Speaking to Chilean newspaper

El Mercurio in his homeland, Pellegrini accused Mourinho of being a glory seeker.

'When he wins, Mourinho wants to take credit for everything,' he said. 'I never do that.'

Mourinho took City's Premier League crown last season, so Pellegrini does have an axe to grind.

'When I won the Premier League, I didn't say a word,' he added.

But the sixty-one-year-old, who in 2015 enters the final year of his contract at the Etihad Stadium, dismissed claims that the pair are enemies. 'I don't have any problem with Mourinho,' he said. 'He's not my enemy and there isn't any conflict – but I differ from him on all fronts. I have no interest in analysing him as a person.'

Chelsea could be even stronger than last season, with Damien Duff backing Mourinho to again win back-to-back Premier League titles.

Chelsea cantered to the Premier League crown, finishing eight points in front of Manchester City on eighty-seven points, while losing just three games. Duff was part of a Chelsea team that retained the Premier League under Mourinho in 2006, and the Irishman is convinced that, while the Portuguese boss is in charge at Stamford Bridge, the Blues will always be serious title contenders.

'Chelsea will be just as good, if not better, this time around. So long as Mourinho is there, Chelsea will be strong.'

The Irishman spent three years in West London between 2003 and 2006 before Mourinho sold him to Newcastle United, and also added that part of the Chelsea manager's secret in getting the best out of his team is getting every ounce of effort and commitment from his players. 'Under Mourinho, the reality is that no player can afford to take their foot off the gas or lose a bit of hunger, because they will be out of the door. You can't afford to take it easy. Jose is very good at recruiting and always makes sure he gets hungry players in his squad.'

Mourinho is following in the footsteps of Sir Alex Ferguson by building a dynasty that will bring success to Chelsea for many years to come, according to Chelsea legend Gianluca Vialli. He said, 'Jose has shown his ability as a skilful and accomplished manager in England, Italy, Spain and Portugal. When you have achieved so much then you look for something you are very passionate about, and his passion for Chelsea is second to none. He feels like he is at home here, he can run the football side of the club the way he wants, without any middlemen or anybody interfering with his work. He loves London so I can see him staying at Chelsea for a long time to come, maybe not 27 years like Sir Alex Ferguson, but he will stay for the long term.'

And just like Fergie, Mourinho will already be looking closely at his players to see if they are up for the fight to retain their title and add the Champions League. 'Basically it is all down to how motivated the players are. It doesn't matter how good you are, if you feel you have achieved everything you've wanted to, you are not the right player for a manager like Jose Mourinho,' added Vialli. 'He will be looking inside the players' minds to see who is motivated enough to carry on playing for Chelsea.'

Andy Murray, in an interview with the BBC Sport's Piers Newbery, talked about his friendship with Mourinho and his thoughts on the Chelsea manager. Murray says, 'Jose Mourinho has said one of the things he admires about tennis players is that, unlike footballers, they have nowhere to hide. That was certainly the case the last time he watched me play, at the ATP Finals in November when I lost pretty quickly to Roger Federer. Thankfully, I was in much better form against Gilles Muller at Queen's Club on Friday and afterwards I spent a few minutes with Jose, just chatting about what the two of us are up to and taking a few photos. Any chance to talk to someone who's been that successful over such a long time is worth taking and I'd love to spend a bit longer with him some time, to try to understand just what it is that makes him great.

'Jose is certainly a winner. I think he's very loyal to his players and he protects them well from criticism if they haven't had a great performance.

'I'm sure that behind closed doors he's very demanding and hard on the players if they're not doing what he wants, but in public he's very supportive of his players. He doesn't blame them for defeats.

'The first time I met Jose was in Los Angeles when he was Real Madrid manager and I was there for a tournament, so I went to watch them train at the UCLA campus. I then did a lot of rehab after my back surgery at Chelsea's training ground as it's near to my house. During the season the players do most of their work out on the pitch but I saw Fernando Torres in the gym, and chatted a little bit to Ashley Cole. He was around on one of the days I was using this underwater treadmill – it was the first running session I'd done back after my surgery.

'So is Jose right? Can footballers hide more than tennis players? Well, every sport has its own pressures and demands, but I think you probably can get away more with a bad performance in football. At the highest level of tennis, if you go out and play terribly, you lose the match. I guess in football you can get substituted or 10 other players might play great and that makes up for your bad performance, but you can also lose your place. You can be sitting on the bench for seven or eight weeks and that must be tough. In tennis, you get another chance the next week.'

Mourinho could not contain his emotions when Murray triumphed over long-time rival Novak Djokovic in the 2013 Wimbledon final, ending Britain's seventy-seven-year wait for a male singles champion. 'I have to say I had a couple of tears for Andy when he won Wimbledon,' Mourinho told the Aegon Championships Tennis Podcast in association with the *Telegraph*. 'It was something that obviously meant more than anything in his career. I could imagine it was something from another world. I don't think he would change the Wimbledon victory for another 10 victories in other Grand Slams. It's more than the game, it's more than a tournament. He has broken the psychological wall that was there for every British person that loves the game. I think that for sure it was the best day in his career and I shared that happiness from where I was.'

After claiming Chelsea's first Premier League title in five years, Mourinho relaxed with his daughter Matilda by watching the exploits of Murray and others at this year's Aegon Championships at The Queen's Club. Mourinho is full of respect for the mental-strength elite tennis players. 'In tennis they take penalty shoot-outs all day,' he added. 'Every point is a tough decision so they have to be really strong. I always say that in my sport sometimes we hide behind each other, we can always find excuses in success and in failure and in this way tennis is phenomenal because you have to be really strong.'

FOUR MORE YEARS, MANY MORE ROWS – AND HOPEFULLY TITLES

Jose Mourinho agreed a new four-year deal worth a massive £200,000 -a -week, and worth more than £45 million over the life of the deal, making him one of the world's highest-paid managers.

Mourinho's new contract underlined the stability at the club for the 52fifty-two-year-old, who has his sights set on even more records, and the accord between the Special One and Roman Abramovich.

The timing was fascinating, as it coincided with Manchester City extending the contract of their manager Manuel Pellegrini at almost the same time. But while Pellegrini, who won the Premier League title with City in 2014, remained under huge pressure to close the gap on current champions Chelsea, with Pep Guardiola being touted for his job virtually on a daily basis.

Chelsea announced their manager's new deal on the club website like this: 'Chelsea Football Club is delighted to announce Jose Mourinho has signed a new four-year contract. The new deal, announced on the eve of the new season, will keep the fifty-two-year-old at Stamford Bridge until at least 2019... ' Mourinho said: 'If the club is happy, I am happy. I think this is a normal thing for me to sign a new contract. It is important we have this continuity and I hope we can enjoy more success in the future – for the fans, the players and the club.

'I said when I returned here two years ago that I have a special feeling for this club and nothing changed. It is the club closest to my heart and I am very happy to know I will be staying here for a long time.' Club director Marina Granovskaia added,: 'We are very happy that Jose has committed four more years to the club. Since his arrival two years ago he has carefully developed the playing squad and brought trophies to Stamford Bridge. We look forward to the next four years and the continued success of the team.

'Mourinho led Chelsea to our first Premier League title in five years last season, while also securing the Capital One Cup by beating Tottenham at Wembley in March. During his first spell with the club between 2004 and 2007 he was twice a league champion, lifting both the FA Cup and League Cup (twice), before enjoying success at both Inter Milan and Real Madrid. Mourinho's 70 per cent win rate is better than any other manager in Premier League history, while our 95-point haul in 2004/05 remains unmatched. Last season we were the only club in all four divisions to be unbeaten at home, winning the title with three matches to spare.'

No sooner was the ink dry on the contract and the opening game of the new seasons under way, however, then that stability and scenery disappeared, with the first of the new season rows. Not any old row. It rarely is with Jose involved.

Mourinho was furious about Eva Carneiro's actions during a match against Swansea. He claimed that she and the physio were 'impulsive and naive' and didn't understand the game in attending swiftly to the needs of Hazard following an injury, because it meant Chelsea went down to nine men against Swansea, following a previous incident by Thibaut Courtois, which had already led to him being sent off and Chelsea being reduced the team to ten men, and with Hazard having to leave the field, Chelsea were reduced to nine men while trying to hang onto to their point. Mourinho felt Hazard didn't need to be treated so urgently and that he was just tired, and he let Eva have both barrels when she returned to the dug-out.

Carneiro was hurt by that and Chelsea fans rushed to send her messages of support. She posted on Facebook,: 'I would like to thank the general public for their overwhelming support. Really very much appreciated.' Eva received massive support.

The support wasn't universal, however, as Eva was accused of being a 'celebrity doctor' by her predecessor because she posted a 'thank you' message on Facebook after receiving nationwide supportfollowing her post. Ralph Rogers chose to side with Mourinho, whilst although many have condemned his actions. 'You're not supposed to take centre stage if you are a physician to a team,' Rogers told the *Daily Mail*. 'You have to understand your dynamic in the club. You are not a player. Her putting that "'thanks for the support'" on Facebook was extremely naive. That would upset anyone. What was she trying to achieve there? Are you bigger than the manager? You're never going to win, nor should you. You're the backroom staff, you're there to do a job. You're not there as a cheerleader. You're not supposed to be a celebrity. You can't be a celebrity doctor.'

There was universal outcry for Eva to be restored to her former duties after being told she wouldn't be needed on match days.

Australian cricket- team doctor Peter Brukner, Liverpool's former head of medicine, says said Mourinho should apologise for 'publicly humiliating' the Chelsea medic. Speaking to BBC Radio 5 live, Brukner, said Mourinho's criticism was '100 a hundred per cent wrong' and that Carneiro should not have her role changed. He added, 'He should apologise and the club should ensure that the doctor and physio are not demoted as a result of this.'

The backlash was intense. Anyone and just about everyone had their say.

Former Chelsea player Paul Cannoville was one of many who couldn't believe that Eva was relieved of her match day duties, as he tweeted,: 'Just heard of the decision made that Eva Carneiro will no longer be "'Chelsea match day physio'". What a shame!'

Former Charlton and West Ham manager Alan Curbishley was shocked, as he told Sky Sports,: 'Is there previous history; something we don't know about? It's a bit extreme.' Canoville added on kicca.com, added: 'What she did on Saturday I can only think was natural instinct for her – that she was looking to attend to a member of the squad with urgency, not realising the situation it would put us in that short time.' Another former Chelsea player, Graeme Le Saux, criticised Mourinho for his reaction, when he said on Twitter,: 'It was poor from Jose Mourinho. Medical staff have to be allowed to do their jobs in games (treat players) nothing else.'

Wenger backed Eva, as Premier League rules state clearly that only the referee can decide when the medics enter the pitch. 'It can be a problem inside a club,' said Wenger. 'It's difficult enough and if you're not united it's more difficult. Trust and unity inside a club is a strength. That story at Chelsea, I have not followed that and I do not have great interest in what's going on. After that, in this situation, I don't know. But the rules are quite clear. The referee makes the decision. Secondly, the rules are clear, when the ref give indication for the medics to come on they can come on.'

Pellegrini, when talking about insisted that Manchester City's clash with Chelsea at the Etihad, will be decided by 'football things and not other things' as he refused to be drawn on Mourinho's fallout with Eva.Pellegrini said,: 'I cannot give you an opinion about what happens at another club. The players will be more interested in the game. They will be trying to win. As I just said, it is a team that can win the title. To try and add points here at the Etihad is very important also. I think it will be just a game involving football things and not other things.'

Pellegrini refused to shake hands with Mourinho after his rival reacted jubilantly to Fernando Torres's late winner at Stamford Bridge in October 2013. He added,: 'As always. I said the first date I arrived here, I have my differences with him but to have difference is not the same as just another way to think what is this. I always shake hands with him.'

Pressure was stepped up another notch with the release of a video by Sky, which supposedly caught him Mourinho delivering an explosive, foul-mouthed tirade during the incident. Mourinho screamed 'son of a bitch' during his heated touchline row. The video footage released by Sky Sports showed a visibly angry Mourinho shouting the Portuguese term 'filho da puta' (which translates as 'son of a bitch').

Naturally, Mourinho's next appearance in front of the media would guarantee a full house. He wasn't to be disappointed. With both sides consulting lawyers, this was always going to be tense, interesting, and headline grabbing. Mourinho read a carefully prepared statement, leaving the door open for Eva and Jon Fearn to return to Chelsea's bench in the future. But with legal implications in the air, no one knew how much of it was said on legal advice. After reading a statement on the issue at the start of his press conference on the Friday in Cobham ahead of the clash with Manchester City, he refused to take questions.

When Mourinho addressed the room packed with the media at Cobham, the list of journalists and other media for the press conference at the clubs' training base filled two A4 sheets of paper – there was standing room only. Mourinho said, 'Look, I hope this room is full because the champions will be playing against the former champion, because of the transfer window is on fire because we have hopefully a big match on Sunday, but I knew it already. It is not a surprise. No question. Probably there are some here who don't like football and come for other reasons.

'I don't want to run away from it. I accept the question, and understand. First of all, I want to say I have a fantastic medical department, with a top doctor in Dr Paco Biosca, more than a dozen professionals, very good relation with them and, as they tell me all the time, they were never praised so much as in the last few years. I praise them lots of times. They don't forget that. I don't. We have disagreements during this period;, we need disagreements to improve. We work together.'

Mourinho doesn't didn't believe the players needed an explanation as to why Dr Carneiro and Dr Fearn won't wouldn't be on the bench on Sunday. 'The most important thing for the players is the medical care they have during the week. I have a fantastic relationship with everyone that works with me. I am open to mistakes, I am open to dialogue, I am open to critics. As some of the people in the medical staff said yesterday, we improve together.'

Asked to discuss concerns raised by medical professionals, Mourinho reacted,: 'I am not going to discuss it. You can make the questions and we don't stop you making the questions, but you cannot make me answer. I don't answer.'

Still the questions came. 'You shouldn't ask,' he then replied. 'It is my opinion and your opinion.'

He did then admit that the wellbeing of the athlete is paramount. 'The player is more important than the result,' he said. 'He is more important than the manager, he is even more important than the referee.'

Asked whether he had a message for worried supporters: 'Chelsea supporters are worried about the transfer window. Since Mr Abramovich bought the club, Chelsea supporters cannot speak in a negative way about the transfer market.

They can only praise the owner and praise the board. What he has done is absolutely amazing, it is a fantastic contribution. The club won titles.'

Asked if he regretted the incident, Mourinho continued: 'The game is emotional space for every one of us... football is football. The match is the match. And everything in the match can be different.' He continued, 'In the meeting I had with my medical staff yesterday, the feedback I got is that the relationships we had going back two years we good relations. If somebody thinks that a disagreement between two members of the medical staff and the manager can affect the week, that is don't have a clue about what football is and what the preparations for matches is. Your question about the bench. For some people it's important. For others, it's not... It's my decision. I have seven assistants, only four can go on bench. Seven kitmen, only two. Medical, only two on [the] bench... Dr Fearne and Dr Carneiro will not be on the bench, but [that] doesn't mean Sunday is the rest of the season or the rest of their careers. My decision does not mean they won't be on the bench in the future. If you want to speak about football, I'm here. If you want to talk about other issues, I'm not here.'

Mourinho is arguably one of the most influential men in football and, it was suggested, with that comes enormous power, it was suggested.

'Power? Oh my word. Jesus Christ! Power of what?' he said. 'The only power I have is to choose the team, to choose who is on the bench, to choose which exercises we do, which direction we try to take our game plan. That is not power. It is part of my job to advise my board to do something related to the transfer market, to do something in other departments in relation to my needs. But I have power for nothing.'

Mourinho's mood was dark and unforgiving. 'Don't make me another question or I go,' said a smouldering Jose Mourinho. 'I go. Think twice before you ask the question. Think twice.'

The question came anyway, asking if Eva and Jon Fearn had attended what he insisted was a cordial meeting with his medical staff on Thursday. Mourinho sprang to his feet. 'Now I go. Have a good weekend,' he said. Steve Atkins, Chelsea's communications director, asked Mourinho to sit back down again. He did, but he would talk only about football.

Acid-tongued Sky TV pundit Graeme Souness rounded on Mourinho, who in the past has clashed with TV pundits. Souness He said that Mourinho 'c**ked up big style' when he confronted Dr Carneiro. 'I think doctors have never been in a more difficult situation than they are now,' Souness said on Sky Sports. 'We watch games with the benefit of replays and don't know if players are feigning injury or not –, not suggesting that Hazard did this time –, but players go to ground so readily today. You're sitting there at ground level as a doctor or physio; you've not got a great view of that. Players have a lot to answer for today. They have to help their physio and help their doctor and not go down for an injury that doesn't exist. It's a really difficult thing for a physio or a doctor to get right ten times out of ten and the manager has cocked it up big style... a confrontation with a lady doctor as she walks off the pitch, do me a favour... How's that help them prepare for this game?'

Mourinho wasn't a happy chappie as he was more worried

about Costa's hamstrings, Falcao's level of performances and failing to sign John Stones. No doubt raw emotion would continue to be part of his character.

Glenn Hoddle felt the row with his medical team was a symptom of bigger issues revolving around his squad. In his *Mail on Sunday* column, Hoddle observed: 'Mourinho doesn't look happy. My guess is that he was hoping that he had the squad to retain the Premier League. And that what he's seen in the last few weeks has left him with major doubts. You can see he is man on edge and that is why he reacted so emotionally last weekend in blaming club doctor Eva Carneiro and physio Jon Fearn for running on to treat Eden Hazard, meaning the player had to go off. It was an over-reaction which has given them a political problem off the pitch in the first week of the season. That is exactly what you wouldn't want in the week running up to such a difficult game as Manchester City away, the team I believe will be their biggest challengers. Chelsea came back a week later than most clubs for pre-season training. They flew straight off to Canada, and played three games in the US, none of which was particularly impressive. They got back only a few days before the Community Shield and Arsène Wenger managed to win against Mourinho for the first time in that match. They looked some way short against Fiorentina in their last pre-season game and again against Swansea on Saturday. They haven't managed to sign John Stones yet, though they may get Abdul Rahman Baba from Wolfsburg. Then Diego Costa's hamstrings started to become a worry when he came off against Barcelona in Washington DC and missed the Community Shield. And if you're going into the season worrying about Costa, you would also have to have doubts about Radamel Falcao as your No. 2 striker. I suspect all these factors are contributing to Mourinho's unease and explain why he snapped at what seemed a relatively small issue with the medical team. It looks as though he has pounced on it as an issue, perhaps because he wanted to change things anyway. But if he had a problem with the medical team, why not change it in the summer? It's not as if he doesn't get rid of players he's not happy with quick enough. Think of Kevin de Bruyne and Andre Schurrle. This is an issue which should have been dealt with internally.'

Hoddle pinpointed Mourinho's main error – which he has failed to make two or three big name signings to freshen up his squad. Writing in his *Mail on Sunday* column, Hoddle, the former Chelsea and Spurs manager, said: 'It's hard not to make unfavourable comparisons with last season when Chelsea strengthened in all departments, started the season with an added zest and led the Premier League almost from start to finish. Now they face the possibility of being five points behind Manchester City after two games. This summer they simply haven't strengthened. Asmir Begovic for Petr Cech and Falcao for Didier Drogba are like-for-like replacements and though Rahman will be an interesting addition, he won't immediately be replacing Cesar Azpilicueta at left-back. The team are not functioning as Mourinho would expect them to. He knows what he's seeing on the pitch, and that his squad need an injection of something. And he will be hoping that the powers-that-be back him. But Chelsea are not the club they once were where an indifferent start to the season might prompt a £50 million spending spree. Books have to be balanced these days so this may be, by and large, the squad he has to work with. And he's probably already worrying that it isn't good enough.'

Hoddle, though, stuck by to his guns, and continued to tip Chelsea to retain their title as he did before a ball was kicked this season. 'Chelsea will of course be title contenders. I predicted them to win it and I still think they can do. But ideally I would like them to sign another striker before the transfer window closes to add that degree of energy which is required to freshen up a title-winning side. Then they would have cover for Costa and it would provide an impetus for the whole squad, as would adding Stones. Winning successive titles is an enormous challenge. Manchester City have shown over the past four seasons that sides tend to ease back after they win a title. City did that in the seasons following their title triumphs of 2011–12 and 2013–14. Mourinho will be determined that his players do not to fall into the same trap. They will be contenders and there is every chance they will win the League if Costa stays fit. But no team ever improved resting on their laurels, and Mourinho knows it. If it's not going to come from outside in the form of new players, then somehow Mourinho will have to provide it with his motivational skills. And it's going to be tough to do so against improved City, Arsenal, Manchester United and Liverpool squads. If he can't manage it, expect more confrontations. He's not a manager who copes very well when the team isn't performing or the board aren't delivering the squad he feels he needs.'

Carneiro and Fearn were replaced on the Chelsea team bench by Chris Hughes and Steven Hughes for the Premier League champions' match against Manchester City on the Sunday, and clearly the glamour had disappeared. In the place of the glamorous doctor were one bald-headed guy and another rather tubby one.

Thierry Henry believes there is more for Mourinho to worry about than his medical staff, saying Chelsea has looked 'lethargic' since pre-season. 'There's something wrong there... since the pre-season there's something missing,' the Sky Sports pundit said, 'They almost look lethargic in some games, especially in pre-season. The other day against Swansea, instead of talking about [how] they didn't play well, they talk about the incident. They look lethargic, there's no pace into it, not into the game, not the way the champions should look at the start of the season. There's something wrong, there's something behind it.'

And that was borne out as Chelsea crashed at the Etihad by 3–0 in a devastating defeat at the end of a long week of non-stop debate about the issues revolving around his Mourinho's medical team.

This wasn't the only spat involving a female. The first occurred in pre-season, when Montserrat Seara, new Real Madrid manager Rafa Benitez's wife, joked that her husband was 'tidying up' another Mourinho 'mess' at Real.

Rafa has now succeeded Mourinho at three different clubs, having previously taken charge at Inter and Chelsea. And Montserrat Seara believes it is fated that Benitez should continue to join clubs in the Portuguese coach's wake. 'We tidy up his messes,' she joked, speaking to *La Region*. 'If you think about it, of course you end up crossing paths. There are only a few world-class clubs out there.' Seara is a law professor from the northern region of Galicia.

Benitez did not directly replace Mourinho at either club.

'The lady is a bit confused,' Mourinho said. 'Her husband went to Chelsea to replace Roberto Di Matteo and he went to Real Madrid and replaced Carlo Ancelotti. The only club where her husband replaced me was at Inter Milan, where in six months he destroyed the best team in Europe at the time.'

Mourinho then made a jibe about Benitez. He said that if Montserrat Seara focused on taking care 'of her husband's diet' then 'she will not have any time to talk about me.'

Mourinho guided Inter to a European and domestic treble in 2010 before leaving for Real Madrid. Benitez replaced Mourinho at the San Siro but, despite leading Inter to wins in the Italian Supercoppa and the World Club Cup, was sacked after six months, with the team seventh in Serie A. Five years and seven managers separated Mourinho and Benitez at Chelsea. At Real Madrid, Ancelotti succeeded Mourinho in 2013 before being replaced by Benitez last month.

There was also a pre-season row over clubs' spending power. Mourinho had a dig at his rivals for spending big to become title contenders. Yet, according between 2004 and 2014 no manager in the world has spent more money than Mourinho during his spells with Chelsea, Inter Milan and Real Madrid. The report adds that Mourinho has spent £636 million – more than twice as much as Arsène Wenger, whose spending weighs in at £300 million.

Harry Redknapp on kicca.com commented on kicca. com: 'There's obviously not a lot of love lost between Jose Mourinho and Arsène Wenger, so they do tend to have a pop at each other. But I think Jose gets on very well with 98 per cent of the managers. I wouldn't think there are too many in all the divisions that he doesn't get on with. If you speak to lads in lower leagues he's very friendly towards them and returns their calls if they need advice. I certainly never had a problem with Jose, he's a fantastic manager. He's a different character to Arsène. Jose's very flamboyant whereas Arsène's very studious and very quiet in his own way. They're both top managers, both excellent and their teams win titles and play great football.'

On the subject of Mourinho's frequent comments about certain others in the game, Redknapp commented, 'As for why Jose called Rafa Benitez fat, I don't know. He and Arsène are the two people Jose doesn't get along with. You'd have to ask him why he said that. Rafa can stand up for himself, though, and am sure there'll be a bit of verbal coming back from him. All these mind games and jibes in the press didn't really happen in the past. I never had any problems with anybody really. I get on very well with Jose, get on very well with Fergie, I get on well enough with Arsène, I don't know him very well but I've never had any problems with him. I just let the team do the talking, if we were good enough we'd win. I wasn't one for getting involved with other managers with mind games I just let the players go out and play.

'Some people say it's part and parcel of the modern game. But I don't see anyone else indulging in it. I don't see Gary Monk doing it at Swansea, you wouldn't see Tony Pulis doing it, I don't see Mark Hughes doing it. Most of the British managers just get on with their job and, like me, let their teams do the talking. But sometimes when managers don't get on, as with Jose and Arsène, they have a little dig at each other.'

Mourinho sat down with English media during the pre-season tour in the United States, and suggested he would tinker with the team's style of play: 'Being more unpredictable is to have different ways to play. With the strikers we have, we can play with two strikers together more than we did before. We have three very good strikers, and all of them with special motivations. Rémy wants to go back to the national team and has a Euro to play in a year in his own country. Diego is very frustrated because the last three months of the season were full of frustration and injuries for him. Falcao had a very bad season and is frustrated because people in England don't know the real Falcao. All of them are very enthusiastic. And my wingers can play all play very well defensively. Hazard couldn't, but now he can. Willian can; Moses, Ramires when they play in the side. We have options to be different and to be more unpredictable. We can create problems for the opposition when they play against us. We can play with two strikers or one, so we have more options.'

Of Falcao, he commented: 'I don't have a secret. I just feel it's a new opportunity for him. He comes after a bad season, but it's not up to me to speak about it or find the answers for it. I can just say that the analysis we did, and we did a lot of it, showed he is in good condition. We believe he can be very useful for us. He's the kind of player who's proved people wrong all of his career – at Porto, at Atletico and even at Monaco before his injury. It's easy to feel he's a very good professional. Even two weeks ago Mr Van Gaal said he has nothing negative to say about him as a person or a professional. He's a guy who always tries to be ready for the team and ready to work. We believe he can be very important for us.'

Mourinho was concerned that Hazard was targeted by the hitmen and would eventually be injured: 'The Premier League is a competition where last year he was lucky, clearly. He's getting stronger and stronger, not just in his body, but in his attitude. He's getting physical, very strong. He's not the kind of guy who overreacts. After a bad tackle he never rolls and rolls like many players do as a protection to themselves to push referees to make certain decisions. Eden is not this guy. He's loyal and honest, and gets lots of respect from opponents because of that. But the reality is that last season he was lucky – let's see what happens next season. He could have been injured many, many times. He suffered more than a couple of very nasty tackles and that could have been in trouble. I saw lots of players breaking legs and ankles with less than that. I don't want to say names because it's not nice. Last season is finished and let's have a fresh start. I don't want to say Mr A, Mr B or Mr C, but he had some very nasty tackles last year.'

Mourinho wanted more protection for Hazard: 'I want but it's not in my hands. The only I can do is what we are doing and what Eden is doing, which is to work and work and work to be stronger and stronger. I don't want to change his mentality or personality. I don't want him crying or overreacting. I don't want someone touching his shoulder and he reacts by throwing his hands in his face like lots of people is doing now. I want Eden to be what he is – and he's fantastic.'

He then lavished praise on his player: 'Eden is coming with big status now and was voted one of the top 10 players in Europe last year. In my opinion he should be in the top three, not in the top 10... On the pitch he leads. He is not afraid to take responsibility. He is not afraid to get the team from a dark situation and bring blue sky again for the team. He is not afraid of this. He is a guy with great discipline. He is not the kind of guy you see setting bad examples and so on. So I think he can. His ambition is coming, he is also the vice-captain of the Belgian national team. He has four seasons at Chelsea, so he didn't arrive yesterday. I think he is in this group. Eden, Fabregas, Cahill are in this group behind the captains. I believe he has go to better, because the normal tendency is for people to find another star; to find somebody new to get these individual trophies. But he has all the conditions to improve. With his age he can improve. I think he is the best player in our country. The best player in England. You [the Football Writers Association] voted him too, the best player in the English Premier League. The Premier League is the top competition in the countries, I think he is in the top players. Two years ago we reached the Champions League semi-final but he didn't play. He didn't play in [(Atletico]) Madrid, he played injured at home. So he arrived in that crucial moment not in condition. Last year we did bad in the Champions League and we were out immediately so he also needs a good Champions League. I'm not saying winning but I say a proper Champions League. But he is fantastic.

'Messi won the treble. He won three competitions last year, he reached the Copa America Final. he had a fantastic season for him and for his team. In spite of the fact that Ronaldo was fantastic. He scored an incredible number of goals. I am not saying he is not fantastic. I am not saying he was not fantastic. I am just saying that, in my personal view, every football player in the world should understand that a team has to be in front and no titles.'

Curiously, Mourinho seems to call the Manchester City manager 'Pellegrino'. Maybe it's because he just likes the mineral water! But here is the reason from the man himself: 'Because I had a player called Pellegrino and because there were two in football at the same time, one was Mauricio Pellegrino and Mr Manuel Pellegrini. I always made a mistake by calling one the other. But the last thing would be a lack of respect.'

They have a rivalry that dates back to when Mourinho succeeded Pellegrini as Real Madrid boss in 2010 and made unflattering comments about his Chilean predecessor. They did not shake hands after their first meeting in England in October 2013. Pellegrini says: 'I said the first day I arrived here I have my differences with him but I always shake hands with him.'

Mourinho was more concerned about the threat City posed with their lavish signings, while he opted out of big money purchases. He commented: 'I think everyone is buying well, there is no reason to buy bad. When you have big money to spend there is no reason to buy bad, you buy good players and you always buy well. After that there is the unpredictability of the game. Sometimes you buy a fantastic player and for some reason he doesn't play so good as you would have expected. But no big player [club] with a lot of money buys bad players. Everybody is buying very well.'

Pellegrini signed a new contract after finishing second in the league in the previous season, despite the fact that Pep Guardiola seemed destined to succeed him at City. When asked if he was surprised by the deal, Mourinho couldn't resist a sideways snipe at Wenger, as he said,: 'Why? Some other clubs, they have disappointed for 15 years and the manager is the same.'

Sky TV pundit Jamie Carragher tipped Chelsea to win the league last year, and, before the new season kicked off, he was convinced that the title would remain in West London. Why? Because of Jose Mourinho.

Carragher explained in the *Mail* why it had to be Chelsea again: 'One answer. Jose Mourinho. Just as Sir Alex Ferguson used to be, he is now the best manager. Having the best manager is worth points on the board. Jose is worth 10 points a season to Chelsea. They haven't really strengthened at all, but they don't need to have the best team – they have the best manager. They can have the equal best team, but Jose is the difference.'

There was an introspective start to the new season, having dropped vital points at home in the opening game against Swansea, the 2–2 draw distracted by the highly contentious 'Eva-gate'. Courtois had been red carded in that opening game and Mourinho moaned that Chelsea's appeals, he noted, always fail, as, indeed, did the appeal on behalf of their banned keeper.

Mourinho used fewer players in the league last during the previous season than any other manager, as the team started so well and hardly needed changing. Overused, they were shattered towards its end. Mourinho gave them one month off but the pre-season, he said, was too short and the club were forced to go 'in another direction'. Key signings last summer, Costa, Fàbregas and Courtois, arrived early, whereas this time, the club had not made major signings. 'You can say "Why didn't we do our business before the start of the pre-season?" like we did last year but it's not because we don't want to, it's because it's not possible,' Mourinho said. 'So, in this moment, we are a bit limited but I have no doubt that the club will give the squad a couple more players. We were tired towards the end of last season and the team had problems. We went for a slower start – a short pre-season, with only three matches before the Community Shield – and we knew that the start is not going to be the same kind of start that we had last year. Clearly we know what we are doing. Clearly some bodies didn't react as well as we expected. We are not at the top of our game. The normal tendency is, week after week, to improve.'

There would be no greater test of Mourinho's management then the new season after the opening- day draw with Swansea, the row with Eva, followed by a 3–0 defeat at Manchester City when he had to defend his decision to substitute captain John Terry at half-time. The thirty-four-year-old was replaced by Kurt Zouma with City leading 1–0 – the first time he has been taken off by Mourinho in the Premier League, as tactics were behind his decision. 'It was clear to me Zouma has to play,' said Mourinho.

The manager said in May that Terry would have left Chelsea without him. 'I don't know if you asked questions to Rafa Benitez, Andre Villas-Boas, Roberto Di Matteo, to the ones that never played him. I'm the one you shouldn't ask because I'm the one that plays with John in every game. I made John captain. I recovered John from a difficult situation with other managers. I brought my captain off and he was on the bench and still captain on the bench because the armband is just an armband. I can tell you he was not dancing in the dressing room and I can also tell you he was not having a bad reaction.'

Mourinho's response to the mini-crisis was to act immediately by bringing in a new star to freshen up his team, but he insisted that he did not intend to 'beat' Manchester United to the signing of £22.1 million Pedro.

United executive vice-chairman Ed Woodward had flown to the Catalan capital to finalise a deal, but Mourinho intervened personally, which was one of the factors that persuaded Pedro to choose Chelsea. 'I only want to beat Man United on the pitch,' explained Mourinho. 'I don't want to go in that direction. Our job is not to get a player another club wants.' Another new signing joined Pedro: Augsburg left-back Baba Rahman. Mourinho said that the 'opportunity window' allowed him to strengthen the squad. 'While the transfer window is open, it's the opportunity window,' he said. 'We have a very good young left-back with potential, and have one of the best attacking players in the world.'

Mourinho suggested that a one-minute telephone conversation with Pedro was all it took to secure him for the team. '[I asked,] "Is it true that you want to leave Barcelona?" [Pedro:] "Yes, it's true. I love it here. It's my home, but it's time for me to move." [Mourinho:] "Did you sign already for another club?" [Pedro:] "Almost, but not yet." [Mourinho:] "Do you want to come here?" [Pedro:] "Yes, I want [to]."

Asked whether Chelsea were now a bigger draw for leading players than United, Mourinho stressed that players decide for themselves. He did not rule out the arrival of John Stones from Everton, or another major deal. 'It depends on the opportunities, whether you can do something you really believe you cannot pass up. Let's see what can happen.'

Mourinho was not happy with his personal form, he said.

'Because I used to get better results than I'm getting now. This is the start of everything. I'm not happy with Ivanovic's form, I'm not happy with Cahill's form, I'm not happy with John's form, I'm not happy with Azpi's form, I'm not happy with Eden's form, I'm not happy with Fabregas's form, I'm not happy with Matic's form. But, for me, the start of everything is, I'm not happy with my form. What we are trying to do this week? Work better; spend more time thinking about it; watching more videos; trying to find better training exercise[s]; being more active in training; looking for the feedback. Even myself, I go to the gym every day now to get fitter. Maybe I need more action on the touchline, so I need to be fitter. I promise you! No one is happy. We have one point from two matches. I'm not happy at all. I'm not happy with anyone. I'm either happy with everybody or I'm not happy with anyone, and at this moment I'm not happy.'

Mourinho came out on top to avert the poor start with his team's first Premier League win of the season. Chelsea failed to win either of their first two Premier League games for the first time in seventeen years. In typical mood, he suggested that would disappoint those who 'love' to see the champions lose. John Terry sent off in a 3–2 win at West Brom as Pedro scored on his Chelsea debut. 'I prefer to have no views and try to keep quiet,' Mourinho said of Terry's red card. 'Many people are disappointed with this result. They love Chelsea to lose a game.'

On his side's first win, he added, 'I am so happy that the players got what they deserved. [But] if we are happy with the start to the season, we are ready to go home. The performance was not dramatic and not bad but, obviously, four points in three matches is not enough. There is a feeling we are fighting against a lot but today we won.'

Chelsea held a 3–1 half-time lead after Pedro scored the opener and set up a second for Costa but they were fortunate not to go behind early on when Courtois saved James Morrison's fourteenth-minute penalty with the score still goalless. 'Pedro played well,' said Mourinho. 'There are lots of top players who come to the Premier League and it takes time to adapt but it looks like he has been with us for a long time because straight away he was in the game and he was important.

'A hard worker? This is Pedro. I played in the same league [in Spain] as him for three years so I know him well. This is why for so many years he wins cups and plays for one of the top teams in the world. Everyone who has shared a dressing room with him speaks well of him.'

Mourinho's future began to dominate the media agenda as he suffered meltdown on the touchline and an uncharacteristic sequence of poor results.

Mourinho felt it necessary to have discussions with the board following a shock 3–1 defeat at home to Southampton, as there was something fundamentally wrong within a few months of being crowned champions with four losses in eight games. Also worrying was the state of their Champions League position: third after two matches in Group G.

Some newspapers reports suggested Mourinho's prospects at Chelsea were in serious doubt but it was premature and there was a deep resolve within the club to end the damaging headlines, which were beginning to have a negative impact within the dressing room; the club released a surprise statement on the Monday afternoon after the defeat by Southampton in an unprecedented attempt to quash any speculation.

This was an unusual step, and clearly had the ultimate approval of Roman Abramovich, who would have sanctioned it in consultation with his inner sanctum of friends and advisors. Normally, Abramovich prefers to ignore media speculation, leaving it to his in-house communications department to deal with such situations – sometimes with briefings, sometimes to play a straight bat and refuse to rise to any speculation.

To have issued the dreaded 'vote of confidence' in a manager was something I had never experienced since Abramovich bought the club from Ken Bates and I had set about writing a series of books, including a detailed account of the takeover from former chairman/owner Bates, and of the inner workings of the Abramovich regime.

In my opinion, there were two main reasons for this: the manager's insecurity and the club's determination to end the speculation, as Mourinho felt it was undermining the dressing room and his ability to hold it together. The club's board agreed – even though Abramovich actually doesn't sit on the board, he authorises all major decisions.

For those two key reasons, it was imperative to act and a statement was duly released. Because it was extremely out of character for Abramovich, it had the desired effect in quelling the speculation, if only temporarily, as it turned out.

It read, 'The club wants to make it clear that Jose continues to have our full support. As Jose has said himself, results have not been good enough and the team's performances must improve. However, we believe that we have the right manager to turn this season around and that he has the squad with which to do it.'

When asked by Sky Sports reporter Greg Whelan for his thoughts on the Southampton defeat, Mourinho spoke for seven minutes, which involved a number of accusations and a declaration that the club would have to 'sack the best manager in their history' to get him to leave.

'People can say what they want. I think you should go straight to the players,' said Mourinho, who had already received public backing from club captain John Terry. 'Get a table at Cobham next week – John Terry doesn't go to the national team, Diego Costa doesn't go, Ramires doesn't go. Ask them. If they tell you they don't trust me, that is the only thing that can make me resign. The only thing. But not fake sources. The players at the table.'

Mourinho had already confessed a week earlier that he was experiencing the 'worst period and results' in his managerial career, while Terry was happy enough to the defend his under-siege boss over the weekend, despite being phased out by him. Terry said, 'I have been here a long time and I have seen managers come and go and, if anyone is going to get us out of this hole, it is going to be Jose Mourinho.'

Gary Cahill believed it too – well, at least publicly, as he commented while away with the England squad.

'[The statement] is important,' he said. 'I think everybody knows the situation we're in at the moment. It has been a very, very difficult start. The Southampton game, for me personally, was a real low and I've come away here totally determined to make that right when I come back. That's the kind of attitude I've got towards it all and I am sure my other teammates are probably feeling the same – pure determination to turn it around and make sure that, when we have the good times again, they're even sweeter because of what we've been through. I think that's important. I think, in terms of backing the manager, of course we all back him; of course we are all around him... When you've done so much in the game, got the CV and been through everything that he has been [through] – not just in this league or what he has done for Chelsea but in other leagues –I don't even think he needs backing but, obviously, it is nice to have that and he has certainly got that from the players and the club.'

Mourinho had a hugely significant result at the beginning of November, which created a renewed credibility rush as he put the clubs Champions League campaign back on track.

While Chelsea continued to survive in the Champions League, their season was being held together by the glue that this most elite of competitions can provide. The knock-on effect was a compelling reason to shelve discussions on the managers' future.

It seemed to me, at least, inconceivable, that Chelsea could contemplate sacking their manager while they remained in this competition and, funnily enough, while working on my football website, zapsportz.com, with Glenn Hoddle, the former Chelsea manager, I was confidently predicting that, provided they could get through the group, they might just come good in March and be the Premier League's main hope in the Champions League. The impetus that would provide could yet propel them on a run of results in the Premier league that would make it possible to make it into the top four.

An emotional Mourinho praised the show of support by Chelsea's fans, claiming, 'This is my moment,' as his team beat Dynamo Kiev for a second win in nine matches. Willian curled in a stunning winning goal – his fifth free-kick this season – seven minutes from time and Chelsea moved above Kiev into second place in Group G.

The temperamental and tempestuous Mourinho drew huge encouragement as his name was chanted regularly by the majority inside Stamford Bridge. After less than co-operative post-match appearances in recent weeks, Mourinho was effusive in his post-match conference of his deep and sincere gratitude for the fans for sticking with him.

'What the fans did for me is not normal, or they don't read papers, listen to television, pundits and commentators – or they have a big heart, or they recognise that I am good professional that gives everything to the club,' Mourinho told BT Sport. 'I brought great moments for the club and they have a great memory. But it's not normal for such support – with not just such a bad run of results but, fundamentally, due to what people read in newspapers, listen to on television – and I don't know how to thank them. The only thing I can say is that, until my last day with this club – be it four years, ten years, fifteen years: it doesn't matter how long – I will give everything for them.'

The significance of the tie was that Mourinho was watched by his family from just behind the dugout. It was a demonstration of family unity, of those closest to him, acknowledging the strain, and his determination to put it right and to survive.

In football, you are only as good as your last result and the Porto tie bought him valuable time.

The manner of the win was also grounds for encouragement, to silence the hawks within the Abramovich inner circle who would have wanted Mourinho out.

Mourinho had seen his side collapse in similar situations as when Aleksandar Dragovic conjured a late equaliser. Chelsea wilted against Southampton and Liverpool but not this time and that gave Mourinho enormous grounds to convince Abramovich that a revival was in sight, something Mourinho was cocksure he could engineer given time, but this is an industry where time and patience are always in short supply.

'I was impressed when I saw Liverpool at Anfield, when we beat them 4–1 [in October 2005] and, in the last ten minutes, Anfield was singing for that team,' said Mourinho. 'In good moments, you see the streets full of people celebrating in a buzz and it's easy for kids to go to school in a Chelsea shirt when Chelsea win every match. But it's not easy for ten- or twelve-year-old kids to go to school with a Chelsea shirt when Chelsea are losing matches; when probably they are bullied by other kids whose teams are winning. The win is a big relief. To qualify, we didn't need a win. So at 1–1, it was not a drama. But, from a mental point of view, it was important to provide a reaction to a negative moment. In other matches we've played well but, when a negative moment arrived, the team felt it too much and it was difficult to emerge again in the game; to have control in the game. The team was strong mentally and kept trying and I'm happy with that.'

On the back of the result against Kiev, the manager thought much the same as Glenn Hoddle, that his position was secure while he continued to make headway in the Champions

League and that a string of results in the league to propel the team back into the top four was not out of the question.

There was 'no chance' of him leaving, according to his agent Jorge Mendes, even though still fifteenth in the Premier League, as Mourinho's side leaped to second in Group G with a feeling that, with six domestic league losses in eleven games and a stadium ban coming up for their next outing at Stoke, there could be a turning point in sight.

The omnipotent manager's representative, Mendes, was confident his high-profile managerial client could turn it around. 'He doesn't need to prove anything to anybody,' Mendes told BBC Sport. 'He knows what to do. Many people are saying these things but there is no chance [he will leave]. He will solve the problem. He is the best.'

Again, that statement smacked of being approved by Mourinho, or at least Mourinho knew that Mendes intended to speak out on his behalf. This was another indicator that Mourinho knew he was under intense pressure and that the slightest thing might tip the balance against him.

But the feel-good factor wasn't to last very long.

The shock home defeat to promoted Bournemouth, who were deep in a relegation fight themselves, was Chelsea's eighth in the season's Premier League, to bring an abrupt end to a recent improvement in results, and reports in the media were again gathering pace that Mourinho's job was under threat if they failed to progress in the Champions League, despite a vote of confidence from the board back in October. The media have never been fooled by such votes of confidence. Abramovich will not be pleased at how badly wrong that vote of confidence had gone.

Around this time Bobby Campbell had been taken seriously ill and soon afterwards died of cancer. Bobby was a dear friend of mine and, to give him his due, never leaked a single piece of information to me, staying rock solid loyal to Abramvoich. Bobby was a former Chelsea manager who craved a foothold back in the game and we worked together on a football-legends project along with Glenn Hoddle. He had met Abramvoich by chance in the Chelsea gym and forged what seemed an unlikely friendship. The abrasive Liverpudlian became a trusted member of the Abramovich elite inner circle.

'If I told you what I know, I'd have to kill you,' he often told me and anyone else with one of his huge deep throat chuckles.

However, knowing his football philosophy inside out and knowing the man from a personal level, I know for sure that he would have advised Abramovich against sacking Mourinho for a second time and given him more time, at least till the team had run their course in the Champions League and with the FA Cup still to come.

Bobby was old school ,very much in the mould of Sir Alex Ferguson, whom he knew very well.

Sir Alex commented that Chelsea would be sacking 'one of the best coaches of all time' if they got rid of Mourinho, and I am convinced Bobby Campebll would have shared that view.

Sir Alex said, '[Roman Abramovich] has sacked so many coaches in the last ten years that I am sure he has learned by it. He has to trust and have confidence [that] Jose can turn [things] around. There is no point in sacking one of the best coaches of all time. He's won the European Cup twice, he's won the league in each country he's managed in, he's won the big trophies.'

Mourinho suffered a stadium ban in November but wily old fox Fergie believed his old rival had recovered his cool and was close to reviving Chelsea's season. Speaking at the TechCrunch Disrupt London event, he said, 'I have been watching Jose recently and spoken to him a couple of times and this is the first time he has been confronted with non-success. If you look at his whole career, there has been nothing but a rise all of the time so, for the first time in his life, he has had to deal with bad publicity, adversity, and that is a challenge for him but there are signs he is getting back to a balanced level, although they lost on Saturday. I watched the match on Saturday and they could have won by a few goals but they lost and then he has still has to face that sort of negative publicity and it is never easy for a manager in present-day football because the media attention is huge.... I think he will find a solution and will get back to normal [but it] is not looking great at the moment. But I know the guy and I know the work he has done in football and I can't see it lasting long, I can't see it.'

Despite wise words from Sir Alex, there were forces within the camp that wanted Mourinho out.

Once again the whispering campaign from those who were getting it in the neck from Mourinho behind the scenes were happy to put the knife in, while there were those closer to Mourinho who never wanted him rehired in the first place.

Mourinho could emulate Roberto di Matteo and win the Champions League while failing to make the top four but there was now a feeling that it was time to bring down the curtain on the Chelsea career of their greatest ever manager.

Mourinho misjudged the mood when he publicly declared in a press conference that Abramovich would not 'change with the wind' and would stick by him, despite being fourteenth and having lost eight of their fifteen Premier League matches, not to mention having yet to clinch Champions League last-sixteen qualification and being out of the League Cup.

Asked why he would be retained, Mourinho said, 'Because I think I did lots of good things for this club. I don't think the owner is a person to change with the wind. Abramovich believed in me twice: one, when he brought me back to the club, and the second time when he gave me a new four-year contract in the summer. I know the wind of results is an important wind and I know this wind is really strong because the results in the Premier League are really bad.'

Mourinho was speaking at the news conference previewing the Champions League match against Porto. The club had to avoid defeat to confirm their place in the last sixteen. It was crunch time, with no more margin for error, as they went into the match on the back of a surprise home defeat by Bournemouth before meeting league leaders Leicester on the Monday.

It was confidently reported that Mourinho could be sacked if Chelsea lost their next two games.

Yet Chelsea forgot their domestic woes by easing into the Champions League knockout stage with a victory over Porto, enjoying some luck for a change for the opener as Diego Costa's low shot was saved by Porto keeper Iker Casillas and rebounded in off Ivan Marcano.

Porto, needing to win to join Chelsea in the last sixteen, but Mourinho's defence looked far more solid.

Willian ensured Chelsea advanced as Group G winners by thumping in a rising shot from twenty yards after the break.

Eden Hazard struck the post from a tight angle, while recalled striker Costa wasted two clear opportunities as Chelsea threatened a third.

Mourinho insisted before the match that he retained the unwavering support of Abramovich and winning their group meant Chelsea avoided Barcelona, Real Madrid and Bayern Munich, giving the club every chance to progress towards the Final.

Mourinho was able to restore Terry following injury but, more significantly, summoned Costa back after leaving him on the bench against Tottenham and Bournemouth. Costa drew the save from Casillas that led to Chelsea's opener and linked up neatly with Hazard for Chelsea's second, holding up the ball to bring in the Belgian, who played in Willian for his seventh goal of the season. Costa failed to score himself and was bundled over by defender Danilo when clean through in the final fifteen minutes. He received a standing ovation when he was replaced in the final few minutes and a warm embrace from Mourinho.

Porto, who were second in the league, arrived with ten wins in their previous twelve matches. Julen Lopetegui's side had only lost once in nineteen matches that season and beat Chelsea 2–1 in September's reverse fixture.

Chelsea travelled to Leicester seventeen points behind. Claudio Ranieri had previously been sacked because Abramovich had wanted the new kid on the block, Mourinho, to replace him, when the new owner's attention was drawn to the young Jose's incredible Champions League exploits at Porto. Ranieri went into the semi-final clash with Monaco knowing he was already a dead man walking and his tactical tinkering was, in part, responsible for Chelsea's shock defeat.

Now Mourinho's very survival depended on getting a descent result at high-flying Leicester, the surprise team of the season but no bigger a surprise than the fact that, with Ranieri chasing top spot, Chelsea were in an embarrassing position, just above relegation. It was a lively build-up, with the media refusing to give up their belief that the manager would be fired if they lost to Ranieri's team. Mourinho exchange with one journalist went as follows:

Journalist: 'If you lose your next game at Leicester, do you expect to lose your job?'

Mourinho: 'There are no ifs. I win, or draw, or lose.'

Journalist: 'But what about—'

Mourinho: 'You are a pessimist guy, I am an optimist guy.'

Journalist: 'Let's say you lose: if that happens, do you expect to lose your job?'

Mourinho: 'There are no ifs.'

When Leicester returned to the top of the Premier League with a victory over Chelsea at King Power Stadium, Abramovich's patience snapped.

Jamie Vardy's fifteenth goal of the season put Leicester ahead before half-time and Riyad Mahrez's brilliant curling strike just after the break sealed the win. Substitute Loic Remy pulled one back but Leicester survived in relative comfort to move back ahead of Manchester City at the top of the table.

The reigning Premier League champions, in contrast, were just a point off the relegation zone in sixteenth place.

The pace and movement of Vardy and Mahrez exposed Terry in the style that has troubled so many teams on Leicester's remarkable rise to the top but this was the champions playing like chumps.

Terry being replaced by Cesc Fàbregas after only fifty-three minutes was a sign of the times. Terry had been a magnificent servant for Chelsea but the ageing captain, who turned thirty-five on 7 December, looked like he had run his race. Mourinho recognised as much when Chelsea bid £40 million for Everton's John Stones, only to be met with resistance at Goodison Park. One of the key reasons for the current position can be traced back to the fialure to sign Stones and secure the back line, plus the sale of Petr Cech and the early injury to Courtois. Terry making his way to the bench so early on in the second half emphasised Chelsea's defensive plight.

Ranieri's side were buzzing, high on confidence and adrenalin, the reigning champions fearful and tentative. Seven months earlier Chelsea were crowned champions and Leicester were pulling off a remarkable escape from relegation. Leicester's best start to a top-flight season in their 131-year history, compared to Chelsea's worst ever as a defending champion with a 9th loss in 16 games. This was Mourinho's ninth defeat in the Premier League this season – the same number as in 2013–14 (six) and 2014–15 (three) combined. Chelsea lost nine of their opening sixteen top-flight games for the first time since 1978–79, a season in which they were relegated. Ninety-six teams have gained fifteen points or fewer from their opening sixteen games, fifty were relegated and the average finishing position of those ninety-six teams was seventeenth.

The stats were powerful ammunition to fire the bullet at Mourinho's head.

SACKED AT
CHRISTMAS

The timing and method of sacking a manager is almost never good, irrespective of how it's done; by email, text, or just letting the manager hang out to dry on the touchline when all the fans know he's already history.

It happened to Martin Jol at Spurs as he stood on the touchline as Twitter began to alert the fans to his imminent demise and managers have suffered all sort of indignities come the fateful moment of truth when their time is up. Way back, I can recall Kenny Dalglish driving to the training ground at Newcastle, only to be stopped in his tracks by a *Daily Mirror* headline proclaiming he was about to be replaced by the former Chelsea manager Ruud Gullit

Jose Mourinho was fired after enjoying a Christmas roast dinner during a seasonal bonding session with his players and coaching staff at the club's lavish lunch. After all the trials and tribulations of a season that no one could possibly have anticipated would be so bad, it was time to unwind, pull some crackers, and tell some jokes.

The joke, though, was on the Chelsea fans who adored their manager and who had not lost faith in him, even if the Roman Abramovich inner circle had done.

The 'Emperor' sat among his disciples with his thumb pointing downwards as Mourinho and his expensively gathered legions had their last supper together.

Mourinho was called to Chelsea's training ground and sacked at 2pm on the Thursday of the club's Xmas party by club chairman Bruce Buck and director Eugene Tenenbaum, two of Roman's trusted aides, with a third ready to put his head above the parapet and explain why the manager had 'lost the dressing room' – the knife with which the club's technical director plunged into his back.

Mourinho's contract was terminated at the training ground after a meeting between Abramovich and senior board members that took less than five minutes. It was their third meeting of the week to discuss what to do to arrest the slide, with the fear of relegation uppermost in their minds.

For me, there was zero chance of relegation with one of the strongest squads assembled in the Premier League, so this was a fear bred by panic and a few whispers from players about 'discord' in the dressing room.

Guus Hiddink had a successful spell as interim boss at Stamford Bridge in 2009, winning the FA Cup, and was liked by players and owner alike. He'd been sounded out and was now willing to move in again; his wife loved it in London and was itching to return, so this was sounded out before the axe fell on Mourinho.

The meeting between Abramovich, chairman Bruce Buck and director Eugene Tenenbaum concluded weeks of talks between Chelsea's lawyers, the manager's agent Jorge Mendes and the manager's legal team over his £250,000-a-week contract.

TV pictures showed Mourinho covering his face as he was driven away from the club's base in Cobham, Surrey, two hours later.

Chelsea released a statement in which they insisted that the departure was mutual and that they remained on good terms. No one would have believed either sentiment.

'Chelsea Football Club and Jose Mourinho have today parted company by mutual consent,' it read. 'All at Chelsea thank Jose for his immense contribution since he returned as manager in the summer of 2013. His three league titles, FA Cup, Community Shield and three League Cup wins over two spells make him the most successful manager in our 110-year history. But both Jose and the board agreed results have not been good enough this season and believe it is in the best interests of both parties to go our separate ways. The club wishes to make clear Jose leaves us on good terms and will always remain a much-loved, respected and significant figure at Chelsea. His legacy at Stamford Bridge and in England has long been guaranteed and he will always be warmly welcomed back to Stamford Bridge. The club's focus is now on ensuring our talented squad reaches its potential. There will be no further comment until a new appointment is made.'

The club then confirmed that the press conference scheduled for the following day was off. A statement read, 'To advise there will be no media conference Friday 18th December 2015.'

As the reactions flooded in, mainly through social media, Mendes insisted his client was still the best manager in the world. 'Jose Mourinho does not stop being who he is and he is still the best coach in the world despite leaving Chelsea,' Mendes told Portuguese newspaper *A Bola*. 'When Mourinho left Chelsea the first time, he accepted a tremendous challenge and did what no one in the football world believed he could do and that was to take on Inter and lead them to win the Champions League, Serie A and Coppa Italia – a truly remarkable achievement. Then he went to Real Madrid and inspired a historic achievement in the Spanish league by beating all possible records against a great Barcelona and also winning the Copa del Rey.'

Technical director Michael Emenalo revealed on Chelsea TV, that Chelsea sacked Mourinho because of the breakdown of his relationship with the players, saying that dressing-room problems played a part in the decision to let him go.

'While there is huge sentiment for the individual who has done so much for the club, the fact of the matter is that Chelsea Football Club is in trouble,' said Emenalo. 'The results are not good. There obviously seems to be a palpable discord between the manager and the players and we felt it was time to act. The owner is forced to make what is a very tough decision for the good of the club. Chelsea is one point above relegation and that's not good enough. Anybody who has any kind of affiliation to the club can understand that the club is in trouble and something had to be done.'

Chelsea faced Sunderland at Stamford Bridge two days later, before hosting Watford on Boxing Day, both games that Chelsea would have been expected to win. With the right result, they could have yielded six points to make a significant difference in the league, which might have saved Mourinho. Why was he not given this opportunity?

The fans were already pointing accusing fingers at key under-performing players but Emenalo disagreed with their accusations. 'I think that some people need to remember that this is essentially the same group of players who won the league last season,' Emenalo said. 'They did it in style and by showing commitment, by sweating tears and blood when needed. They played to instruction; they did everything that the manager asked them to do. We know now that the players have a responsibility to go out and prove everybody wrong and show a certain level of commitment to the decision that has been made tonight.'

Emenalo had never been a manager and had never experienced the dynamics of being a manager, and was providing reasoning for sacking one of the world's best managers. This is not the way to run a football club, surely.

That a senior figure so close to Abramovich publicly put his head above the parapet to suggest that the manager had lost the dressing room will rankle with Mourinho, as this went as far as possible to confirm all the deluge of media rumours about dressing-room unrest being the defining factor that sealed Mourinho's fate.

Yet club captain John Terry used his Instagram account to pay tribute to the 'very best I have ever worked with.' Terry wrote, 'Thank You doesn't seem enough Sad sad day Gonna miss you Boss The Very Best I have EVER worked with, unbelievable memories together.'

According to former Chelsea striker Mateja Kezman,

Hiddink already had the job. 'I don't know if it's been officially confirmed yet, but Hiddink just told me he was the new coach,' Kezman told Croatia's Index HR news website. Football Federation Australia, which employed Hiddink as the nation's coach for the 2006 World Cup, even announced him as the new manager on their website and Twitter pages.

David Cameron also had his say in the social media frenzy that greeted the sacking, in tune with the current trend, with a tweet from his spokesman on #JoseMourinho sacking, which read, 'PM is always sad to see anyone lose their job but he would point to the 740k vacancies in UK economy.'

Twitter went into meltdown after the sacking and the clubs' website crashed following the stunning news.

'Thank you for all you have done for me. I owe you a lot and we will all miss you. Good luck in the future and I know you will be back soon,' Chelsea midfielder Cesc Fàbregas (@cesc4official), who posted a picture of himself with Mourinho's arm around him as they celebrated the previous season's Premier League title success.

'Jose gone... Pep in next...???' Former England and Manchester United defender Rio Ferdinand (@rioferdy5) suggests Bayern Munich coach Pep Guardiola could be the man to fill Mourinho's boots.

'I know there's been plenty of rumours but still shocked to hear of Mourinho's sacking. Who is out there that's better! Could be a huge fight looming for Guardiola's services between Chelsea and the Manchester clubs.' Ex-England striker Michael Owen (@themichaelowen).

'Eva Carneiro!' Former England striker and television

pundit Gary Lineker (@GaryLineker) mischievously adds the name of Chelsea's former team doctor to the mix.

'Sad to see Jose leave @chelseafc but sadly inevitable with the results the way they have been. He won't be out of work for long though.' Former Chelsea and England manager Glenn Hoddle (@Glennhoddle) expects Mourinho to bounce back quickly.

'I'm hearing Jose has gone, shame he has been immense for @ChelseaFC #Legend as a fan I wish him well in the future.' Former Chelsea defender Frank Sinclair (@FrankMSinclair).

'Prior to the beginning of this season, Mourinho had lost 5 of his 249 league home matches. Chelsea have lost 4 of their 8 at home in 2015/16.' Infostrada Sports (@InfostradaLive) puts Chelsea's slump into perspective.

'The Special One will always be Special and he'll be back of that i'm sure...' West Ham United vice-chairman Karren Brady (@karren_brady) tips Mourinho to bounce back.

'Terrible news to wake up to here in Aus! You gave us more pleasure than most, Jose! Guus Hiddink better than Jose?!?! Filthy sacking? Just absolute filth!' Outspoken former England batsman Kevin Pietersen (@KP24) not sitting on the fence, as ever.

'Jose, I take it all back.... We'd welcome you with open arms at Man Utd!!!' World number three golfer and Manchester United fan Rory McIlroy (@McIlroyRory) backtracks on previous mockery of Mourinho's travails.

'Mourinho won Premier League 6 months ago – SACKED. Wenger hasn't won Premier League for 11yrs – UNSACKABLE.' Piers Morgan (@piersmorgan) suggests Arsenal manager Arsène Wenger should suffer the same fate as Mourinho.

FAN
FALLOUT

The love-affair with the Special One was there for all to see in all its glory.

Chelsea fans showed support for their sacked boss by wearing T-shirts, badges and leaving messages of good luck for him in the home match with Sunderland, the first game since he had been axed.

The trauma of the worst title defence in Premier League history failed to deter their enthusiam to show their loyalty and affection for Mourinho, in what must be the most amazing show of support for a sacked manager ever at any club.

Fans displayed banners and masks showing the Special One's face as they arrived at The Bridge, as Mourinho spent his Saturday watching his former assistant Aitor Karanka's side Middlesbrough at Brighton.

The show of support for Mourinho took on many guises,

including a banner draped from the Matthew Harding Stand – which was still fluttering after the final whistle – that read, 'Jose Mourinho: Simply The Best'.

Fans took what might be their last chance to be pictured alongside Mourinho in the giant squad picture that adorns the back wall of the Britannia Gate.

John Terry and chairman Bruce Buck both addressed Mourinho's departure in their columns – the only references to the club's most successful ever manager in Chelsea's seventy-four-page match-day programme.

Guus Hiddink's appointment as caretaker boss was announced less than ninety minutes before kick-off and the Dutchman was joined in owner Roman Abramovich's private box by club legend Didier Drogba, who was expected to return to the club in some coaching/playing capacity sooner rather than later. The desire to draw a line under Mourinho was clear by the appearance of Drogba, the club's most popular player of recent times and one who epitomised work rate, effort and a winning mentality.

For a few days, the Cheslea faithful had been bombarded by opinions from all quarters and it boiled down to the Manager v. Rebel Players.

The strength of pro-Mourinho feeling manifested itself before kick-off, when the names of Cesc Fàbregas and Diego Costa were read out and loud jeers swept around Stamford Bridge – repeated when the pair were substituted in the second half.

Even more remarkably, each Chelsea goal was greeted with chants for Mourinho as much as a celebration, with the second, from Pedro, met with a wicked chant demanding to know why these same players had suddenly lifted their standards now the manager had been sacrificed.

Mourinho was supported with chants and banners, many making further accusations against the players.

In Eden Hazard's absence, through injury, the names of Costa and Fàbregas were booed twice when the Chelsea team was announced prior to kick-off and there was a mixed reception when they were substituted. One banner read, 'The 3 rats. Hazard, Cesc and Costa'. Another was emblazoned with the words '30 Pieces Of Silver Judas. The Players v Jose, One Of Us' and yet another read 'Our Jose'.

The better Chelsea looked, with Oscar seemingly rejuvenated and Branislav Ivanovic looking more like his old self, the more the discontent grew in a surreal first half.

When the chant 'Stand Up For The Special One' started up, virtually the entire stadium rose to their feet. Except those in the Abramovich box!

Michael Emenalo was seated, inconspicuously, three rows behind Steve Holland – in charge for this match – at the start but ended up joining the 'Roman Empire' in the Abramovich box. Spotting Emenalo, who had not referred to Mourinho by name during his infamous Chelsea TV interview, which described the 'palpable discord' that had existed between the manager and his players, one fan unveiled a banner that urged the board to reinstate the Special One and sack the technical director – described as 'the one who does nothing' – instead. He wisely retreated to the back of the stand when approached by a steward.

Chelsea scoring two goals inside the first thirteen minutes – first when Ivanovic headed home from a corner to be greeted by an extravagant pump of the fist by Emenalo, and then Pedro's smart finish after a mistake from Sebastián Coates – remarkably heightened frustration in the stands, rather than easing them. 'Where were you when we were shit?' asked the fans.

Oscar's penalty three minutes into the second half, after Willian was felled by Costel Pantilimon, was enough to secure a win for Chelsea, although the old jitters did return when Fabio Borini soon pulled a goal back for Sunderland.

When the substitutions of Fàbregas and Costa were greeted by boos, Emanalo made a point of rising to his feet to applaud the players, perhaps wanting to show unity with the Abramovich hierarchy that the players were right and the manager wrong. If that was the case, it was a clear sign of player power having too much influence at the Bridge.

Chelsea's captain had to admit he had never seen anything like it before. 'The fans showed the loyalty they have for José Mourinho,' reflected John Terry. 'The memories he has brought to this club from 2004 and 2005 and last year, the fans will never forget that. There is obviously disappointment from a lot of them and rightly so because of what he has achieved at the club. We had to stand up and be counted.'

When Abramovich and the newly installed interim manager, Guus Hiddink, strode across the pitch to speak to the players in the dressing room after the match, Costa was already long gone.

'It's been a tough few days for sure,' admitted Terry. 'We spoke on Friday about staying together; all of us sticking together – not just today or tomorrow but over the next five or six months and getting ourselves back up the league table.

Unfortunately, the manager's head is on the block, he loses his job and, collectively, we have to take responsibility for that, which we have done.'

Holland admitted it had been a difficult week for everyone at the club, not least Abramovich. Holland said, 'Obviously the supporters have a right to express their opinion but, clearly, the fans had a view on certain things and it is their right to do that. I'm sure, if the players play and compete like they did on Saturday, then I don't see any reason why the supporters won't be happy with that. He will be back in football quickly because there will be big clubs that want him and secondly because he needs football. In my opinion, he's not the sort of guy who's going to spend six or seven months at home doing nothing in particular.'

Pedro acknowledged that the performance against Leicester, which eventually cost Mourinho his job, had been 'shit'.

Terry commented, 'We've got strong characters. Honestly it all comes down to results. When you are losing games, it is difficult to dig people out and pick each other up. After this result, the dressing room is buzzing. It's amazing what one win can do and how it can turn.'

The sudden upturn was described as 'disgraceful' by BBC Sport pundits Mark Lawrenson and Chris Sutton.

Former Chelsea player and now well-established pundit Jason Cundy, with good contacts still at the Bridge, claimed the players struggled in pre-season and that it carried on during the season. 'I think the players stopped listening to him,' he told Sky Sports. 'They didn't win a game in pre-season; didn't keep a clean sheet in pre-season. It is hard to turn it around. They got into bad habits and that is hard to get out of. Mourinho demands a lot from his players and a lot from himself.'

It wasn't long before the fans were getting a greater understanding why Mourinho was pushed out. Hiddink said Mourinho got the sack because the club were 'frightened' at being just a point above the relegation zone.

At his first media conference, Hiddink said Abramovich decided to axe Mourinho because he feared relegation. 'Sometimes, after a title, you might relax as a team and get a wake-up call in September but the situation is one point above zone, which was frightening for the club. But it is too easy to say, "I am here and the problem is solved."'

The veteran Dutchman had not given up on a top-four spot but, having seen his team beat Sunderland, Hiddink said he was seeking to take the club back to where they believe they belong. 'I shouldn't be here halfway through the season. It means things are not going well. I'm glad to be back. It was a few years ago when I came here in a similar situation. I'm here and it is the reality of the situation. To work with the players is always a pleasure. If you look at his [Mourinho's] record, I don't know by heart what he won but I have a lot of respect for that. People take decisions, which they have taken, and I have to go on when asked but, theoretically, I should not be here, it's true. I can fix the problems. If you look back to last season, where there was this huge success in winning the title: you have your targets and aims, getting the Premier League again, even though it is not easy. That's a main target. The other are the Champions League and FA Cup.'

Mourinho departed amid suggestions of fallouts with players but that was something Hiddink wanted no part of as he discussed what he had said to the squad when he met up with them. 'I told them things happen in football and I want them to look in the mirror – not just two seconds but longer – and see how they can contribute on the way up. I told them, as professionals, to look in the mirror and be ultra-critical. Now is more relevant [than the past]. That's what I said inside. I didn't want much of any information as it can sometimes be corrupt. I want my own judgement.'

Carlo Ancelotti believes Mourinho paid the price for his players' lack of motivation after winning the title. Ancelotti, who was sacked by Chelsea in 2011, despite guiding them to a Premier League and FA Cup Double, and who replaced Mourinho at Real Madrid in 2013, believes the problem was a failure to keep the players motivated. 'When things are going well, there is a risk of relaxation; when things are going badly, obviously there is a loss of confidence. The coach must always keep a good balance in that sense, lifting the confidence levels, particularly when things don't seem to be working. It's a little of this that Mourinho paid for: the fact the team had not started like last year, when they had a tremendous desire to do well after a bad year. This year it was exactly the opposite: he paid for the lack of motivation among the players.'

When asked about his thoughts on Mourinho's departure, Arsène Wenger insisted he wished his bitter rival had stayed. 'There's no need to add anything,' Wenger said. 'I don't want anyone to lose their job. I think it's always sad when people lose their job.'

Demba Ba joined Chelsea from Newcastle United after scoring twenty-nine goals in fifty-eight games, signing for the London club in January 2013. The Senegalese striker made twenty-two appearances in the second half of that season, scoring six times.

Mourinho arrived that summer and Samuel Eto'o followed in the same window, moving Ba down behind the Cameroonian striker, as well as Fernando Torres and André Schürrle. Ba left for Besiktas in 2014, having made just nineteen appearances in Mourinho's first season back at Stamford Bridge. Now playing in China, he believes he knows why Mourinho 'lost the dressing room' at Chelsea. 'When he loses, you feel as if the sky as fallen on his head,' Ba told French radio station RMC. 'It's rare for him to do three years in a row. For a player, it's so tiring, exhausting. He pushes his players to the limit to see what they've got in them. It's up to you alone to gain confidence again if you lose it.' So this is not 'losing the dressing room'; it is the effect simply of losing. Players left out of the team have 'left the dressing room' first, and those who have lost form are eager to deflect focus from themselves.

Barcelona legend Xavi doesn't agree with Mourinho's style of football and says that he is not true to his philosophy. He says he respects Mourinho's approach to football but would not use the same methods if he were a manager. 'He always wanted to win at any price and that shows in the way he goes about things,' Xavi told media outlet *Record*. 'I respect that philosophy but winning at any cost means you can't stay true to a playing style. For me, the means don't always justify the ends. I have a lot of respect for him, he has achieved great things, but I see football in a different way to Mourinho.'

Mourinho's agent denied that a deal had been struck for his client to replace Louis van Gaal as Manchester United manager. Mourinho was instantly linked with the position at

Old Trafford after United dropped out of the top four and crashed out of the Champions League at the group stage. Mourinho's agent Jorge Mendes, speaking to Globoesporte, insisted there had been no approach from United for his client's services. 'There is nothing,' Mendes said when asked about reports that the former Chelsea manager had agreed to take over at Old Trafford. 'We don't know what will happen in the future, but now there is no agreement. There isn't an official proposal either, that's not true.'

Mourinho watched a game at Brighton then spent the week in Portugal with his family but was looking for a quick return to management and, with van Gaal's United floundering, the inevitable media chatter centred on Old Trafford.

Van Gaal walked out of his weekly press conference in protest at speculation that he was on the brink of losing his job to Mourinho. With United preparing for the Boxing Day trip to Stoke City, having lost three successive games and suffering Champions League elimination during the process, van Gaal insisted he was addressing the media at the club's Carrington training ground only in order to avoid breaking Premier League regulations by failing to attend his pre-match press briefing. Mourinho was van Gaal's former assistant at Barcelona and Mourinho had already made it clear he would not consider any discussions with United while his former mentor was still in the hot seat.

The Dutchman hit out at suggestions that his job was on the line over the Christmas period, claiming that the reports had affected his family. He answered just two questions in the space of four minutes and fifty-eight seconds before walking out. When asked whether he agreed with Arsenal manager

Arsène Wenger that reports of his imminent demise had been disrespectful, van Gaal replied, 'Has anybody in this room not a feeling to apologise to me? That's what I'm wondering. I think I was already sacked. I read I have been sacked. My colleague [Mourinho] was here already. What do you think happens with my wife or my kids? Or with my grandchildren? Or with the fans of Manchester United? Or my friends? What do you think? They have called me a lot of times and also Arsène Wenger is saying something about that. So you think that I want to talk with the media now? I am here only because of the Premier League rules. I have to talk with you. But I can only see, when I say something, that you use my words in your context. I want to say only I have tried to lift the confidence of my players. I have done everything this week. I held meetings with the players, with my members of staff, I hold a Christmas lunch, I did a speech and I feel the warmth and support of everybody in Carrington, this Aon training complex. But I didn't feel that in the media and, of course, I can imagine that you can write about that subject. We are not in a good position but four weeks ago we were first in the Premier League and in four weeks' time we can be back in that position again.'

When it was put to van Gaal that he should expect speculation over his position following a run of three wins in thirteen games in all competitions, he insisted that was not the case and that he had received the backing of the club's hierarchy, including former manager Sir Alex Ferguson. 'No, I don't think that you can do that because you have to stick by the facts,' van Gaal said. 'And when I get calls off Alex Ferguson and [director] David Gill and [executive vice-chairman] Ed Woodward because you are creating something that is not good – what is not being the facts – now I have to answer questions. I don't think I want to do it. I only say now I am focused on Stoke City and I help my players. I wish you a merry Christmas and also maybe a happy New Year when I see you. Enjoy the wine and a mince pie.' Van Gaal then walked out, refusing to answer further questions.

Mourinho was also heavily linked with a return to Real Madrid, irrespective of the problems whilst he was there, but yet another 'return' seemed hugely remote, despite Rafa Benitez facing troubled times during his management tenure at this very point and Real believing he would, at least, bring back success to a team falling further behind Barcelona.

In one of the incredible knock-on effects of the bizarre events at the Bridge and the rumour mill going into overdrive about the fallout with the players, former Chelsea winger Pat Nevin was forced to apologise for suggesting that Cesc Fàbregas would 'rather lose than win' for Mourinho. In November it was alleged by BBC presenter Garry Richardson on his *Sportsweek* radio show that an unnamed senior Chelsea player had made the remark in relation to Mourinho. Asked about the allegation days before Mourinho's sacking, Nevin told Radio 4's *Today* programme, 'Yeah, that was Cesc Fàbregas, wasn't it?'

Nevin was forced to backtrack furiously, with the player threatening legal action. 'During an interview with BBC Radio 4's *Today* programme, I asked in passing, while talking about some other recent happenings at the club, if the player who said the phrase six weeks ago, "I would rather lose than play for Jose," had been outed in the press as Cesc? I absolutely wasn't having a go at Cesc but asking the question, as the reporter I was talking to was the one who originally broke that story. Basically, I thought this had been the press line in the following days back then. Cesc denied it all at the time, of course (honestly, as it turns out!), and, odd though it may sound, I couldn't have cared less anyway. The reason I wasn't that bothered was because the BBC reporter (a man I like and admire, I may add) had made it perfectly clear that it was something said in the heat of the moment, in a fit of anger and it certainly did not mean that player wasn't going to try for the team really. When a story appeared in one of the newspapers this Saturday, it was reported as if I was deliberately outing Cesc. Now, whether it was mischievous on the newspaper's part for deliberately misunderstanding me or whether I was not clear enough in what I was saying and the fault was, thus, partially mine, it doesn't matter (I accept my accent, diction and even clarity of meaning aren't always picked up perfectly, especially by some southern ears). In short, I did not mean to have a go at Cesc in any way at all; I was merely asking a question. At this point, I then decided to get all CSI about it and called the original Radio 4 reporter and he obligingly told me that, whatever was said or intimated in the press six weeks ago after his story was first aired, it definitively was NOT Cesc Fàbregas who was the culprit! So, deep breath, when Cesc got a negative reaction as he was substituted on Saturday, if any of that was anything to do with what I was reported to have said, first I am sorry to Cesc, I absolutely didn't mean that at all, it was misconstrued, but none the less I apologise. Secondly, I plead with the fans they adapt that reaction for the upcoming games. Cesc has released a number of statements of late that have been brave, honest and self-deprecating. He has been badly wronged and he didn't deserve that on Saturday, full stop. I hope that is crystal clear.'

Fàbregas later welcomed Nevin's apology in a post on his Instagram account. 'I'm pleased that Pat Nevin and the BBC have now apologised and corrected their comments. I can reiterate that I had an exceptionally good relationship with Jose Mourinho as I will aim to have with any coach that I play for. The football club is more important than any one player. We have all let the manager and club down this year as a collective unit. We will get this right, of that I am sure. With all your help we can put this period behind us and make @ chelseafc great again.'

Mourinho's camp issued a statement saying he will continue to live in England, while insisting his batteries are fully charged and that he has no intention of taking a sabbatical. One line of the statement his representatives released carried a further sting: 'During his career Jose has sometimes chosen to leave a club, but only at Chelsea has the club decided that he should leave.'

Oscar's botched penalty, when he slipped with a chance of a winner at home to Watford, was symptomatic of Chelsea's lack of confidence and indicative of the teams luck throughout the season. But Hiddink focused on the positives in his post-match interview with Sky Sports following a 2–2 draw against Watford. 'What I liked very much was the reaction of the team after two unfortunately conceded goals,' he said. 'The team reacted well.' Asked if the fightback might not have occurred under Mourinho, Hiddink was diplomatic. 'I don't know,' he said. 'I was not here earlier in the season so I cannot judge about that but, nevertheless, I think we have to learn a lesson and show ambition now to go forward.'

Hiddink was grateful to Chelsea supporters, who got behind the team after showing their disgust at Mourinho's sacking during the 3–1 win over Sunderland in the previous week. 'This crowd is a very loyal crowd but also we must not deny that they had the right to express themselves in a previous period, but now we have to go forward and the crowd was supporting the team very well.'

Chelsea were held to a disappointing draw in Hiddink's first game in charge, the second game since Mourinho's sacking and The Mourinho banner that usually hung proudly in the Matthew Harding Stand was no longer there.

The Roman Abramovich regime may have started the process of eliminating the Jose Mourinho legacy. However, the fans will never forget.